SILK ROADS · CHINA SHIPS

An Exhibition of East-West Trade

An Exhibition of East-West Trade

Silk Roads ◆ *China Ships* will be on view at the
Royal Ontario Museum, Toronto, from
10 September 1983 to 8 January 1984.
The exhibition will then travel to a number of
museums and art galleries in the United States
and Canada in a tour that will last through 1986.

SILK ROADS · CHINA SHIPS

Silk Roads ◆ *China Ships*
has been organized and circulated by the
Royal Ontario Museum, Toronto, Canada.
This exhibition was made possible by generous grants
from the American Express Foundation.

SILK ROADS · CHINA SHIPS

John E. Vollmer   E. J. Keall   E. Nagai-Berthrong

ROM
Royal Ontario Museum
Toronto, Ontario

©The Royal Ontario Museum, 1983
100 Queen's Park, Toronto, Canada M5S 2C6
ISBN 0-88854-301-8

Cover photograph: Length of silk velvet furnishing fabric, Iran (see page 141).

Title page photograph: Vase, porcelain, overglaze polychrome enamel, China, early 19th century. Height 30.8 cm, diameter 17.8 cm. Royal Ontario Museum, 911.8.162. Gift of Mrs H. D. Warren.

Mary Terziano, editor
Jean Lightfoot, designer
Hugh C. Porter, production coordinator

Photographs

We acknowledge with thanks the following photographs and permission to reproduce them in this volume:

Art Gallery of Ontario, Toronto: pages 64, 160, 234 (2), 235 (3), 239.

Berry-Hill Galleries, Inc., New York: pages 156, 158 (right).

Elie Borowski, Toronto, page 25 (left).

China Trade Museum, Milton, Massachusetts: pages 154, 159 (right).

Cleveland Museum of Art, Cleveland, Ohio: pages 31 (top), 136.

Richard Edwards, Ann Arbor, Michigan: page 54 (right).

E. J. Keall, Royal Ontario Museum: pages 35, 36 (3), 37 (3, bottom), 38 (2, top), 39 (4), 44 (bottom left), 77, 78, 87.

Louise Mackie, Royal Ontario Museum: page 7 (bottom).

Members' Volunteer Committee, Royal Ontario Museum: page 10.

Metropolitan Museum of Art, New York: page 18.

Musée des Beaux-Arts de Montréal, Montréal, Québec: page 190.

Mystic Seaport Museum, Mystic, Connecticut: pages 159 (left), 240.

E. Nagai-Berthrong, Royal Ontario Museum: pages 28, 51, 54 (left), 55 (3), 56 (2), 57 (2), 174.

Jeannie Parker, Royal Ontario Museum: 58 (bottom), 139 (top).

Elsie Holmes Peck, Detroit, Michigan: 31 (bottom).

William C. Pratt, Royal Ontario Museum: pages 40 (2), 41 (2), 42 (top left), 43 (3).

Staatliche Museen Preussischer Kulturbesitz, Museum für Indische Kunst, West Berlin: page 33.

Canadian Cataloguing in Publication Data
Vollmer, John, 1945 –
    Silk roads, china ships

1. Asia – Commerce – Foreign influences – History – Exhibitions. 2. Europe – Commerce – Foreign influences – History – Exhibitions. 3. Asia – Manufactures – Foreign influences – History – Exhibitions. 4. Europe – Manufactures – Foreign influences – History – Exhibitions. I, Keall, E. J. (Edward John), 1939 – II. Nagai-Berthrong, E. (Evelyn), 1946-   III. Royal Ontario Museum. IV. Title.

Handbook to accompany an exhibition held at the Royal Ontario Museum, Sept. 10, 1983–Jan. 8, 1984, and travelling to other institutions.
ISBN 0-88854-301-8

HF3753.E8V64   382'.09   C83-098659-6

Typesetting by Canadian Composition Limited
Printed in Canada by McLaren Morris and Todd Limited
Bound in Canada by John Deyell Company

CONTENTS

WITH PLEASURE AND PRIDE the Royal Ontario Museum marks a venture that is unprecedented in the seventy-year history of the institution. *Silk Roads • China Ships* is the first major ROM exhibition to be circulated internationally after its Toronto opening. The exhibition, which draws primarily from the ROM's extensive holdings, ranges from rare Chinese tomb figures to a stuffed crocodile. In fact, all art and archaeology and life sciences departments that form part of the ROM are represented. To the ROM objects and specimens we have been able to add forty pieces lent by other institutions and by private collectors. To these lenders we offer sincere thanks.

Since a project of this magnitude requires generous support, we are delighted that the American Express Foundation is joining us in sponsoring the exhibition. The Royal Ontario Museum welcomes the American Express Foundation, whose substantial contribution has helped to make *Silk Roads • China Ships* possible.

We hope that this travelling exhibition will be only the first of many that will permit the Museum to take the message carved in its façade to people throughout the continent: "The record of nature through countless ages; the arts of man through all the years."

James E. Cruise
Director, Royal Ontario Museum

THROUGHOUT HISTORY people have been captivated by the exploration of civilizations foreign to their own familiar sights and sounds. Nowhere is this more evident than in the exhibition *Silk Roads • China Ships*, which unveils objects that chronicle the cultural, economic, political, and social effects of trade between the Orient and the West through nineteen centuries.

As an international corporation, dedicated to the encouragement of world trade, American Express is pleased to join the Royal Ontario Museum in presenting this special exhibition. Over the past several years we have been supporters of many major cultural events in Canada and around the world. The global nature of these underwritings reflects our continuing commitment to strengthening the understanding of one people for another.

The poet Pablo Neruda has said that "all paths lead to the same goal: to convey to others what we are." The objects in this exhibition certainly convey to us today a great deal of what occurred on the Silk Roads so many years ago. We hope that our visitors will achieve their own sense of excitement and discovery as they view this exhibition and the treasures it includes.

American Express wishes to acknowledge all those who have been involved in this exhibition, giving special thanks to Dr James E. Cruise, Director of the Royal Ontario Museum, Mr Charles S. Tomsik, Exhibitions Manager, and curators Dr E. J. Keall, Dr E. Nagai-Berthrong, and Mr John Vollmer, and the entire staff of the Royal Ontario Museum.

James D. Robinson III
Chairman, American Express Company

FOREWORD

It is a great pleasure for me to be asked to contribute a foreword to the handbook for the exhibition *Silk Roads • China Ships*. For more than forty years past I have been occupied with the problems of the history of science, technology, and medicine in Chinese culture, and the volumes of *Science and Civilisation in China* have been the result. From the outset it was palpably evident that the study would have to be done in a comparative way. It is no good explaining what the Chinese did without some parallel description, even if short, of contemporaneous happenings in India, Persia, the Arab world, and the West. And so it came about necessarily that we found ourselves fascinated by the relations between the civilisations, and the passage of ideas and techniques from one to the other. I believe our attraction to East-West relations is shared by many others, both scholars and laymen.

Many of the gifts of China to Europe were of immense importance. One might instance the invention of the escapement, so essential for all mechanical clockwork, or again the standard method of interconversion of rotary and longitudinal motion. We know now, for example, that the Chinese made clockwork for six hundred years before the Europeans; and that the combination of eccentric, connecting-rod and piston-rod goes back in China as far as the 6th century A.D.

Cannon, bronze barrel, iron core, China, early 15th century. Length 22 cm. Royal Ontario Museum, 921.1.15.

It is surely evident that all the civilisations have been intimately connected, handing on one thing after another to each other, whether by the roads along which came the silk or in the ships that carried porcelain to Africa, to Turkey, and to Europe. While it is clear that both objects and ideas were exchanged, it is often difficult to trace their intermediate way stations.

One question, for example, that is often asked is "Who invented gunpowder?" It so happens that I have just completed relating the gunpowder epic for the appropriate military technology volume of *Science and Civilisation in China*. There is no doubt whatever that gunpowder was an invention of the Chinese in the 9th century A.D., and the first appearance of the mixture is in a Daoist book which advises alchemists not to make it, because those who did sometimes had their houses burnt down and their beards singed. Its first appearance in warfare occurred as a slow-match in a Greek Fire flame-thrower in 919, and by 950 it was packed into tubes and wielded on the ends of spears, hence the name "fire-lances". The formula for the mixture itself first appears in print in the year 1044. After that, bombs and grenades, first of all in weak casings and then in strong ones, became widespread. Rockets originated and developed between 1150 and 1250. In the following century they acquired wings, like the fins of present-day rockets, and by 1350 multi-stage rockets were actually designed and used. All these prefigured the giant rockets of the present day which can take man out into space. Finally, the true metal-barrel hand-gun and bombard were developed in China by 1280, distinctly earlier than the first mention or illustration of such a thing in Europe, which belongs to the third decade of the 14th century.

• Flintlock sporting gun, steel barrel, lock, and mounts (barrel blued, decorated with scrollwork), gold inlay. Spain, Madrid, Gabriel Algora maker, dated 1744. Length 138 cm. Royal Ontario Museum, 910.42.47.

Now as for the passage to Europe, we have been impressed by the fact that it seems to have taken place in three stages. First of all, Chinese fire-crackers had to come by 1267, in time to be described by Roger Bacon; and here we think that the friars who travelled in Mongolia and China were almost certainly responsible. Other devices had to come by about 1280, to be in time for the book of Marcus Graecus and that of Hasan al-Rammah; here we have in mind bombs and grenades, fire-lances and rockets. It looks as if the intermediaries here were rather different, notably the merchants (of whom Marco Polo was simply the most famous), but also the Arabian military experts who took service under the Mongols for their Chinese warfare, and would naturally have kept in touch with their Arabian friends. Actually, we do have the name of one gunner from East Asia who came to the Western world just at this time prepared to disclose much "restricted" information—it was Qi-Wu-Wen. This looks like a Mongolian name, but he may well have been Chinese. Finally, the hand-gun and the bombard had to arrive in Europe by about 1310 or so. If this was not through the Arabs, then there is the possibility that the knowledge travelled directly across Russia. Such were the ways in which Europeans got to know about gunpowder, and the fire-arms in which it was used.

By the 15th century capitalism was developing in Europe and great advances in gunpowder technology quickly followed. There was a return journey of European inventions to China, so that, for example, the Portuguese *culverin* or *fa-lang-ji*

• Musket, steel barrel and lock, brass mounts, wooden stock. England, early 19th century. Length 140 cm. Royal Ontario Museum, 948.78.17. Bequest of Dr N. C. Wallace.

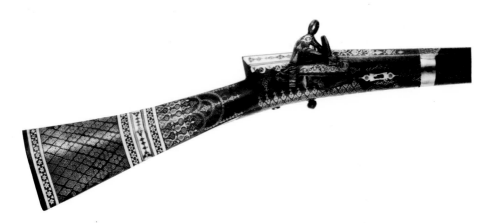

Flintlock gun, steel barrel and lock with silver bands and inlay, wooden stock with ivory and brass inlay, Turkey, 18th century. Length 75 cm. Royal Ontario Museum, 908.20.6.

breech-loader reached China by about 1510. Similarly, the serpentine may have been a Chinese invention, but it was quickly developed into the matchlock musket or arquebus, either by the Turks or by the Europeans, and again travelled eastwards. There is much to be said for the view that the Chinese got it through the Turkish people of Central Asia by about 1520, and not through Portuguese-Japanese contacts, as is usually thought, about 1550.

All this goes to show how intricately intertwined the civilisations of the Old World have been throughout medieval and later history. This asseveration hardly needs further emphasis, but there is one important note which must be struck before we open the exhibition, as it were, to public view.

This final statement which must be made is that although the reader, from what has been said, has no doubt been assuming that the main significance of gunpowder in history has been for warfare — this is quite wrong. Gunpowder, the first chemical explosive known to mankind, the invention of Daoist alchemists in the 9th century, has been at least as important for the arts of peace. John Mayow put it extremely well when he wrote in 1674 that "saltpetre, that admirable salt, has made as much noise in philosophy as it has in war, filling the world with its thunder." We all know about meteorological rockets, and life-saving rockets, and we can readily recognize that our modern world could never have come into being without the rock-blasting of civil engineers, essential both for modern mining and for the making of the myriad lines of communication of our modern age. But all these uses almost fade into insignificance before the extraordinary fact, quite insufficiently known, that before the steam engine came into its heyday from 1700 onwards, the first attempt was to make gunpowder engines. It was only when this explosive, even in the hands of Christiaan Huygens, proved too awkward for such use, that Denis Papin had the idea of using steam instead. Gunpowder would produce a partial vacuum under the piston, but always one-fifth of the air and gases remained. So Papin bethought himself that if he used water, and condensed the steam by a jet of cold water, he would get an almost perfect vacuum, and the piston would come right down to the bottom of the cylinder. This was the essential step which led to the first effective steam engine — the vacuum, or atmospheric, engine — set up by Thomas Newcomen in 1712. But there is more.

The cannon, after all, constituted the simplest of internal-combustion engines, though the cannon-ball was not tethered like the piston. If one asks who first thought of making a projectile to fit the bore, the answer can only be the military engineers of China, like Jiao Yu and Mao Yuan-yi. It was they who first succeeded in getting the djinn into the bottle. And even after the steam engine attained its great successes, men's minds were still haunted by the idea of the internal-combustion engine. At first gas and air were exploded in the cylinder, but gas engines could never go far from abundant supplies of gas; so when, in 1841, Luigi di Cristoforis made an internal-combustion engine with naphtha, the way was open towards the internal-combustion engine as we know it. And what was the fuel that made its great success? Nothing else than Greek Fire, a flammable compound, essentially the same as that distilled by Callinicus in 7th-century Byzantium, which had spread to China by the 10th century, inviting the appearance of gunpowder in the flame-thrower of 919. Thus all the wheels came full circle.

Once again it is deeply impressive that the same discoveries and inventions which can be used for hurtful purposes can also be used for beneficent ones. This is the nature of mankind's relations with the world around him. As in the case of fire itself, everything depends on what you do with it, cooking food and warming people, or killing and torturing people. This is the eternal choice.

In the meantime let me wish every success to this admirable exhibition organized by the Royal Ontario Museum.

Joseph Needham, F.R.S., F.B.A.
East Asian History of Science Library
Cambridge, England, 1983

PREFACE

While much of this account of international trade was gleaned from historical records, documents, and archaeological evidence, the core of the story lies in the surviving examples of the trade goods that were transported from East to West and from West to East and in the cultural influences that travelled with them. The problems of "stepping back into history", however, are compounded by the nature of the evidence. Seldom were the affairs of merchants and traders recorded with the interest and precision devoted to documentation of political events and the lives of leading statesmen. Even the records that exist are frustratingly incomplete.

What is more, evidence is prejudiced not only in the types of records that survive but also in the variety of cultural distortions that are intrinsic to ancient documents. Confucian policy in late imperial China, for example, placed merchants at the lowest end of the social scale. In effect, China did not officially recognize commerce, and yet the state obviously maintained a far-reaching trade in manufactured goods, which were often produced specifically for foreign markets. Another example of such distortions exists in accounts of trade among illiterate nations, which were largely viewed through the filter of Western vision. Moreover, cross-cultural comparisons, particularly in the areas of equivalent values and contemporaneous names for products, are exceedingly difficult to make, and the results are problematical.

This particular story of international trade reflects the interests, the expertise, and perhaps regrettably the biases of its originators—a textile historian with a strong bent towards Asian textiles, an archaeologist whose interests lie in the Middle East, and an art historian specializing in Indian and Buddhist art. Our concern has been to document the nature of trade, our aim to explore the role of commerce in the dissemination of widely divergent arts, technologies, beliefs, and customs that accompanied the trade goods along the Silk Roads and in the China Ships.

For the most part the collections and research of the Royal Ontario Museum were used in our exploration. The ROM collections, like those of museums everywhere, are less than complete records of the past, but they encompass a broad range of art, archaeological evidence, and natural specimens related to the East-West trade. Several institutions and private collectors kindly lent pieces to complement the ROM objects (they are listed in the acknowledgements section).

We are indebted to many scholars, some of them colleagues, whose work in various aspects of international commerce has inspired and assisted us. In particular we wish to thank Joseph Needham of Cambridge University, both for the fund of knowledge in his monumental series *Science and Civilisation in China* and for his foreword to this volume. H. A. Crosby Forbes was very helpful in searching out materials from the China Trade Museum, and from other sources as well. Professor John Munro of the University of Toronto provided advice on economic history and helped to develop the chart on page 162. Professor S. K.

Sim, also of the University of Toronto, verified information on ancient pharmacology. Special thanks are due to all our colleagues at the Royal Ontario Museum who gathered materials from their collections and helped to organize them for the exhibition.

The exhibition was developed by a design team headed by Charles Tomsik, Exhibitions Manager. The team included designer Keith Wagland, who was assisted by Douglas Cinnamon and Gene Sanzo; programmers Gwen Smith, Leslie Patten, and Terry Burborough; graphic designer Lawrence Finn; Lorne Render, Head of Exhibit Design Services; Ron Miles, Head of Education Services; and the three curators who are the authors of this handbook. Linda Ritchie designed and fabricated the reproductions of architectural ornaments and the site model of Qaleh-i Yazdigird. John Thompson constructed the Japanese tea setting. The Metropolitan Museum of Art, New York, very kindly granted Elena Phipps, Conservator of Textiles, American Wing, leave of absence to mount the textiles for display in this exhibition.

With the exception of those credited individually, the photographs for this volume were undertaken by Bill Robertson and Brian Boyle of the Photography Department of the ROM. The diagrams of ships and navigational instruments and the maps—with the exception of those reproduced from rare volumes—are the work of Jim Loates. We are particularly indebted to Publication Services: to Mary Terziano, whose Herculean task involved editing our manuscripts into the unified text of this volume; to Andrea Gallagher Ellis for editorial assistance; to Jean Lightfoot, whose sensitive design so ably supports the message of the text; and to Hugh Porter for his contribution to the production.

Acknowledgements

Our sincere thanks are due to the institutions and private collectors who graciously lent pieces for this exhibition.

Art Gallery of Ontario, Toronto: *Port of Venice* (page 181); *Moses striking the rock* (page 234); *Noah's ark on Mount Ararat, a camel train outside a city in foreground* (page 234); *Les baigneuses* (page 235); *Printemps* (page 235); *Rue le soir, sous la pluie* (page 235); *The reception of the diplomatique and his suite at the court in Pekin* (page 239).

Berry-Hill Galleries, Inc., New York: *Portrait of the hong merchant* Puan Ke-qua III (page 181).

China Trade Museum, Milton, Massachusetts: *Robert Bennet Forbes*, courtesy the heirs of Allan Forbes, on permanent loan to the China Trade Museum (page 181); *Foreign warehouses outside Guangzhou* (page 213).

Cleveland Museum of Art, Cleveland, Ohio: Six-fold screen, left of a pair, with Portuguese ships and traders (page 181).

Collection of Dawn B. van Graft-Blackstock, A.O.C.A.: String of myrrh beads (page 184).

Collection of Dr and Mrs George Ignatieff: Tea glass and holder, tea caddy, teaspoon (page 191).

Collection of Dr Vladimir Ignatieff: Samovar (page 191).

Collection of Hillel Kaslove: Coin (page 184).

Elinor Merrell Collection: Valance (page 233).

Musée des Beaux-Arts de Montréal, Montréal, Québec: *Futaoki* (page 190).

Museum of the History of Medicine, Academy of Medicine, Toronto: Four apothecary jars (pages 211-212); Opium scales, spirit lamp for opium, and three vials (page 213).

Mystic Seaport Museum, Mystic, Connecticut: Model of American clipper ship *Houqua* (page 179); Model of a junk (page 240).

Teruko Shin Collection: Hanging scroll (page 188); and accoutrements for tea ceremony.

Margaret Woodbury Strong Museum, Rochester, New York: Cabinet, corner chair, desk and chair (pages 223-224).

University of Toronto, East Asian Library: *Er-ya yin-tu* (page 238); *Er-ya tu yin ju* (page 238); *Wakan Sansai Zui* (page 238).

University of Toronto, Malcove Collection: Tombstone with family of weavers (page 180).

University of Toronto, Thomas Fisher Rare Book Library: *Medical Botany containing systematic and general descriptions, with plates of all the medicinal plants, indigenous and exotic, comprehended in the catalogues of the Materia Medica, as published by the Royal College of Physicians of London and Edinburgh*, William Woodville, 3 volumes (page 211); *Voyages faits principalement en Asie dans les XII, XIII, XIV et XV siecles, par Benjamin de Tudele, Jean du Plan-Carpin, N. Ascelin, Guillaume de Rubruquis, Marc Paul Venitien, Haiton, Jean de Mandeville, et Ambroise Contarini: Accompagnés de l'histoire des Sarasins et des Tartares, et précédez d'une introduction concernant les voyages et les nouvelles découvertes des principaux voyageurs*, Pierre de Bergeron (page 238); *A Description of the Empire of China and Chinese Tartary together with the kingdoms of Korea, and Tibet: containing the geography and history (natural as well as civil) of those countries*, Jean Baptiste Du Halde (page 238); *Histoire des grands chemins de l'empire romain*, Nicolas Bergier (page 239).

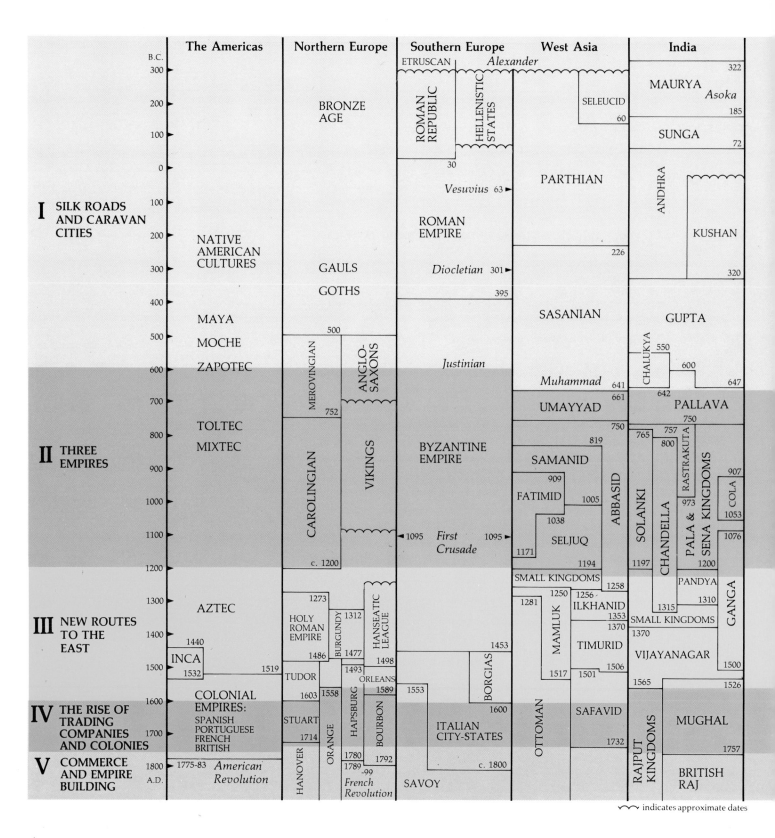

		The Americas	Northern Europe	Southern Europe	West Asia	India

I SILK ROADS AND CARAVAN CITIES

II THREE EMPIRES

III NEW ROUTES TO THE EAST

IV THE RISE OF TRADING COMPANIES AND COLONIES

V COMMERCE AND EMPIRE BUILDING

∼∼∼ indicates approximate dates

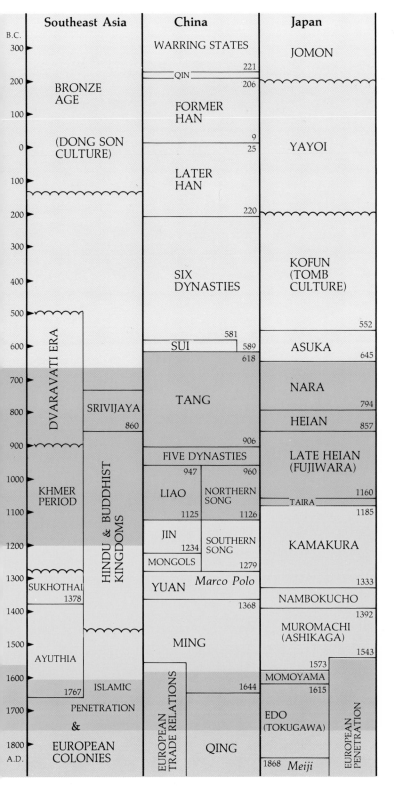

Chronological chart and dates of important persons in the story of trade

Abbas I, shah of Safavid Iran (r. 1587–1628)

Akbar, Mughal emperor (r. 1556–1605)

Albuquerque, Afonso d', Portuguese admiral in the East (1453–1515)

Alexander the Great, king of Macedon, conqueror of Asia (r. 336–323 B.C.)

Alexius IV Angelus, Byzantine emperor (r. 1203–1204)

Augustus, first Roman emperor (r. 29 B.C.–A.D. 14)

Babur, Mughal emperor (r. 1526–1530)

Balboa, Vasco Núñez de, Spanish conquistador (1475?–1519)

Buddha, founder of Buddhism (563?–483? B.C.)

Cabot, John, Italian explorer for England (fl. 1461–1498)

Cabral, Pedro Alvares, Portuguese explorer (1467?–1520?)

Cão, Diogo, Portuguese explorer (fl. 1480–1486)

Catherine of Braganza, queen consort of Charles II of England (1638–1705)

Charles II, king of England, Scotland, and Ireland (r. 1660–1685)

Charles V, emperor of Holy Roman Empire (1519–1558), king of Spain as Charles I (1516–1556)

Clive, Robert, Baron Clive of Plassey, British soldier and statesman in India (1725–1774)

Columbus, Christopher, Italian explorer for Spain (1451–1506)

Confucius, Chinese philosopher (551?–479? B.C.)

Constantine I, called the Great, Roman emperor (r. 306–337)

Cook, Captain James, English explorer (1728–1779)

Copernicus, Nicolaus, Polish astronomer (1473–1543)

Cortez, Hernando, Spanish conquistador (1485–1547)

Covilhã, Pero de, Portuguese explorer (1460?–after 1526)

Crassus, Marcus Licinius, Roman consul (r. 70 B.C. and 55 B.C.)

Darius III (Codomannus), shah of Achaemenid Iran (r. 336–330 B.C.)

Darwin, Charles Robert, English naturalist (1809–1882)

Dias, Bartolomeu, Portuguese explorer (d. 1500)

Drake, Sir Francis, English navigator and admiral (1540?–1596)

Dupleix, Marquis Joseph François, governor of French colonies in India (1697–1763)

Elizabeth I, queen of England (r. 1558–1603)

Eratosthenes, Greek scholar (276?–c. 195 B.C.)

Ferdinand V, king of Castile and Leon (r. 1474–1504), king of Aragon as Ferdinaind II (1479–1516), king of Sicily (1468–1516), king of Naples (1504–1516)

Francis of Assisi, saint, founder of Franciscans (1182?–1226)

Gama, Vasco da, Portuguese explorer (1469?–1524)
Genghis Khan, Mongol ruler (r. 1206–1227)
Gregory IX, pope (r. 1227–1241)
Grünwedel, Albert, German archaeologist (1856–1935)

Al-Hakim, Fatimid caliph (r. 996–1021)
Henry VII, king of England (r. 1485–1509)
Henry VIII, king of England (r. 1509–1547)
Henry, prince of Portugal, called the Navigator (1394–1460)
Hideyoshi (Toyotomi), ruler of Japan (r. 1590–1598)

Idrisi, Arab geographer (b. 1099?, d. after 1154)
Ieyasu (Tokugawa), shogun of Japan (r. 1603–1616)
Innocent III, pope (r. 1198–1216)
Innocent IV, pope (r. 1243–1254)
Isaac II Angelus, Byzantine emperor (r. 1185–1195, 1203–1204)
Ivan III, called the Great, grand duke of Moscow (r. 1462–1505)
Ivan IV, called the Terrible, tsar of Russia (r. 1547–1584)

James I, king of England (r. 1603–1625)
John II, king of Portugal (r. 1481–1495)
Justinian I, Byzantine emperor (r. 527–565)

Kublai Khan, Mongol emperor (r. 1260–1294)

Le Coq, Albert von, German archaeologist (1860–1930)
Linnaeus, Carolus, Swedish botanist (1707–1778)
Li Shih-min, emperor of Tang China (r. 626–649)
Li Yuan, emperor of Tang China (r. 618–626)
Louis IX, king of France (r. 1226–1270)
Louis XIV, king of France (r. 1643–1715)
Luther, Martin, German leader of the Protestant Reformation (1483–1546)

Magellan, Ferdinand, Portuguese navigator for Spain (1480?–1521)
Mani, prophet, founder of Manichaeism (216?–276?)
Marcus Aurelius, Roman emperor (r. 161–180)
Mercator, Gerhardus, Flemish geographer and cartographer (1512–1594)
Mithradates II, Parthian king (r. 124–87 B.C.)
Montcalm, General Louis Joseph de, French general (1712–1759)
Muhammad, prophet, founder of Islam (570?–632)

Münster, Sebastian, German geographer (1489–1552)
Mutsuhito, Meiji emperor of Japan (r. 1867–1912)

Nobunaga (Oda), Japanese commander (1534–1582)

Ogodai Khan, Mongol ruler (r. 1229–1241)
Ortelius, Abraham, Flemish geographer (1527–1598)

Perry, Matthew, American commodore (1794–1858)
Peter I, called the Great, tsar of Russia (1682–1725), emperor (1721–1725)
Philip II, king of Spain, Naples, and Sicily (1556–1598), king of Portugal as Philip I (1580–1598)
Polo, Marco, Venetian trader (1254?–1324?)
Ptolemy, Claudius, Graeco-Egyptian astronomer and geographer (fl. 127 to c. 150)

Qin Shih-huang-di, emperor of China (r. 246–210 B.C.)

Ricci, Matteo, Jesuit missionary (1552–1610)
Richard I, called Richard the Lionheart, king of England (r. 1189–1199)
Richthofen, Baron Ferdinand von, German geographer (1833–1905)
Roe, Sir Thomas, English ambassador (1581?–1644)
Roger I, ruler of southern Italy (r. 1085–1101)
Roger II, king of Sicily (r. 1130–1154)

Salah-al Din, called Saladin, sultan of Egypt (r. 1174–1193)
Seneca, Roman senator (4? B.C.–A.D. 65)
Stein, Sir Marc Aurel, British archaeologist (1862–1943)
Strabo, Greek geographer (63? B.C.–A.D. 19?)

Tamerlane, Mongol conqueror (1336?–1405)
Tiberius, Roman emperor (r. 14–37)

Urban II, pope (r. 1088–1099)

Verrazano, Giovanni da, Italian explorer for France (1485?–1528?)
Vespucci, Amerigo, Italian navigator (1454–1512)

Waldseemüller, Martin, German geographer (1470?–1522?)
Wolfe, James, British general (1727–1759)
Wu-di, Chinese emperor (r. 140–87 B.C.)

Yazdigird III, shah of Sasanian Iran (r. 632–642)

INTRODUCTION

In the history of trade, few words are more evocative of mystery and opulence than *Silk Roads* (*Seidenstrassen*), the name coined by Baron Ferdinand von Richthofen in the 19th century for the ancient routes that linked Asia and the West. Irresistibly romantic though the name may be, however, it is less than descriptive of the reality.

Silk, China's famed and for centuries exclusive export, was not the only cargo carried by the caravans of camels that steadily made their way over treacherously shifting desert sands and ice-bound mountain passes. Through the centuries the caravans transported a host of natural and man-made products, both from East to West and from West to East. Similarly, the Arabian dhows and Portuguese carracks that first left Chinese ports laden with translucent porcelain — whose formula

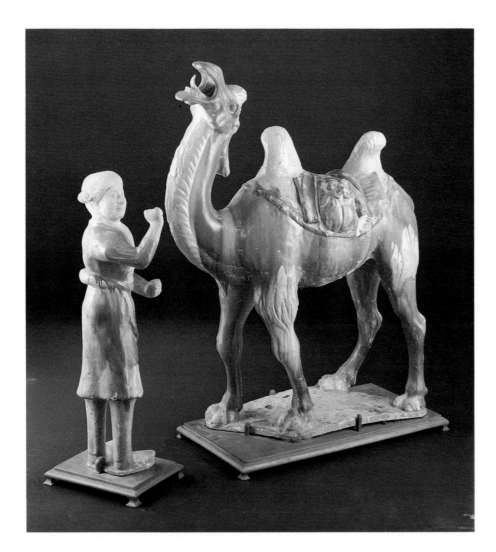

Tomb figures of Bactrian camel and West Asian groom, earthenware, China, late 7th to 8th century. Height of camel 80 cm, of groom 67 cm. Royal Ontario Museum, 918.22.11, 918.22.8. George Crofts Collection. Gift of Mrs H. D. Warren.

1

defied the talents and skills of Middle Eastern and European alchemists for centuries—had not arrived empty in China. They had come with cargoes of silver, gold, and foreign goods with an appeal for Eastern populations.

All too often the romantic image of the East-West trade in exotic goods obscures the very real hardships of the journeys and the tremendous risks to life and capital endured by merchants to maintain the sometimes tenuous links between widely separated markets. The modern English word *trade*, which denotes the buying, selling, or exchange of commodities, derives from an Old Saxon word *trada*, which meant *footstep*. In part, this volume—and the exhibition it celebrates—attempts to retrace the footsteps of commerce between East and West. The chapters that follow outline the historical context in which the trade was conducted from the 2nd century B.C.

A 20th-century perspective often makes it difficult for us to imagine the past, much less to understand it. The coming of the electronic age irrevocably altered old notions of time and space. For us rapid travel to any part of the globe is not only feasible but a fact of daily life. What is more significant, communications networks afford constant contact over vast distances; we have even come to take for granted reports from outer space. Little wonder then that we find it hard to assimilate the fact that in the 13th century Marco Polo waited sixteen years to learn of his father and uncle's journey to the court of the Kublai Khan. And what seems even more astonishing is that until the last century international traders regularly risked permanent loss of contact with their ventures.

The enormous increase in the population of the world has created market dynamics that were unimaginable even a century ago. At the height of Spain's missions of discovery and conquest in the New World, the country's population never exceeded five and a half million. And most of that population was desperately poor and unable to sustain Spain's ambitions for overseas possessions, large fleets of trading vessels, and even expansion in Europe. Although fabulous amounts of gold flowed into Spain from the New World, much of it soon found its way into the hands of Italian, German, and Dutch bankers, who helped to finance the European wars of the Hapsburg kings.

It is amusing to recall that Augustus the Strong, king of Poland and elector of Saxony, an avid collector of oriental ceramics, was reportedly willing to exchange a battalion of soldiers for a roomful of porcelain dishes. Yet the ban imposed by the French government in the late 17th century on the importation of Indian chintzes, because they threatened the market for locally woven silks and woollens, strikes a sympathetic chord in the light of recent experiences of negotiated quotas on Japanese automobiles.

Two factors dominate the history of international trade: the pursuit of profits and the allure of the exotic. The basis of any commercial transaction is the wish to own something that belongs to someone else; trade is the means of fulfilling that wish to the satisfaction of both parties. On the level of international trade, commodities are often associated with notions of status. Acquisition of objects that are rare and expensive seems to enhance the status of the owner. In an absolute sense, the motivation for such acquisitions is the inclination to own something that

Constellation *Navis*, ink and colour on paper, al-Sufi, Iran, Isfahan, late 17th century; in *Suwar al-Kawakib al-Thabitah* (Treatise on the Fixed Stars). Each leaf 15.5 cm × 23.6 cm. Royal Ontario Museum, 971.292.13.

no one else has. But the commodity cannot be unique. It must exist in sufficient quantity — at least as to type — to be available to members of the segment of society desirous of owning it and able to purchase it. Without supply no fashion can flourish; without fashion no market demand develops. Thus trade in any commodity survives only as long as the demand for it continues, the supply lasts, and transportation from place of origin to place of ultimate sale is assured. The other requirement, of course, is a continuing favourable return on capital investment.

In spite of problems posed by climate, terrain, politics, wars, famines, extortion, bribes, taxes, robbery, uncertainties of supply, changing fashions, and natural disasters, merchants were irrepressible in their search for commodities and markets, and for the means of linking the two. Risks were high, but rewards were phenomenal. Successful ventures repaid their backers a hundredfold, sometimes even a thousandfold, return on invested capital. The greatest profits were to be gained by concentrating the business of long-distance caravan trade or maritime commerce in as few hands as possible. Such monopolistic practices permitted merchants to inflate prices at will. The search for new trade routes, the development of faster means of conveyance, the maintenance of trade stations and colonies, and the imposition of blockades and embargoes were all aimed at preserving economic advantage.

This manipulation of the market by merchants has created insidious consequences for the historian. Trade goods for the European market were often designed and produced to meet established tastes in specific markets, and they were also copied and adapted in those markets. As a result, it is extremely difficult at times to identify actual trade goods and their sources of supply. We learn, for example, from Pliny the Younger that Chinese silk was imported by Imperial Rome either as skeins of thread to be woven into silk fabric on Syrian looms, or as silk yardage to be unravelled and rewoven into the sheer silks favoured by Roman women. Sometimes merchants tried to gain a monopoly on a particularly valuable product by changing the source of supply. Arab merchants introduced Asian sugar cane to the Middle East, where Western traders gained access to it. Western traders then took sugar cane, and Middle Eastern coffee as well, to the New World.

Thus over the centuries as empires expanded, declined, and changed hands, trade between East and West remained a constant—sometimes stronger, sometimes weaker, sometimes controlled by one group, sometimes by another, but always persisting through whatever vicissitudes befell. *Silk Roads • China Ships* is then a passage through time with the trade goods and cultural influences that moved from East to West and from West to East along the trade routes.

Notes and Conventions

The description of each object gives first the material of which it is made and then the decorative materials and techniques, followed by the provenance, the date, the measurements, and the details of the collection or institution to which the object belongs.

Materials: For the sake of consistency, ceramics have been categorized as earthenware, stoneware, or porcelain, depending on composition and resonance. Unless qualified by (soft paste), all porcelain is assumed to be of the characteristic hard-paste type.

Dating: All dates pertain to the Christian Era (A.D.), except where B.C. is specified.

Measurements: All measurements are metric, and standard conventions apply: for figures and vessels height only; for textiles, paintings, prints, and reliefs an equation of two dimensions, with height preceding width; for coins, plates, and globular vessels diameter only. When three measurements are given for an object, height indicates the vertical dimension, and length the greater horizontal dimension.

Place names and personal names: To avoid confusion, the modern place name is used in most instances. The historical cities of Peking and Canton are rendered by their modern Chinese names Beijing and Guangzhou. Modern *pinyin* Romanization has been employed for all Chinese names.

Illustrations: The symbol • accompanies captions for illustrations in the text of objects in the exhibition, which are described in detail in the catalogue at the end of the volume.

SILK ROADS AND CARAVAN CITIES

THE PRELUDE: EAST MEETS WEST

Alexander the Great

Western history was set on a new course when Alexander the Great invaded Asia in 334 B.C. Before Alexander died, a brief twelve years later, East and West had not only met but they had taken the first steps towards a regular exchange of ideas and trade goods.

In the two years following his accession to the throne of Macedonia in 336 B.C., Alexander had secured the submission of mainland Greece and the Balkan Peninsula. Now, with an army perhaps 35,000 strong, he was resolved to pursue his dream of world empire. The first three years of campaigning took Alexander from Turkey through northern Egypt to Syria and Iraq. In the autumn of 331 B.C. he entered Babylon. By late winter he had reached the Iranian heartland, and before the following spring Persepolis, the Persian capital, was in Greek hands. When the fugitive King of Kings Darius III was assassinated later that year, Alexander claimed title to the Persian Empire. During the next five years, through a series of remarkable marches and battles, he conquered the eastern provinces of Iran, journeying as far as the Syr Darya in Turkestan.

Later writers tended to exaggerate the hardships endured by Alexander's army in the marches through Asia, perhaps because of an ingrained suspicion of

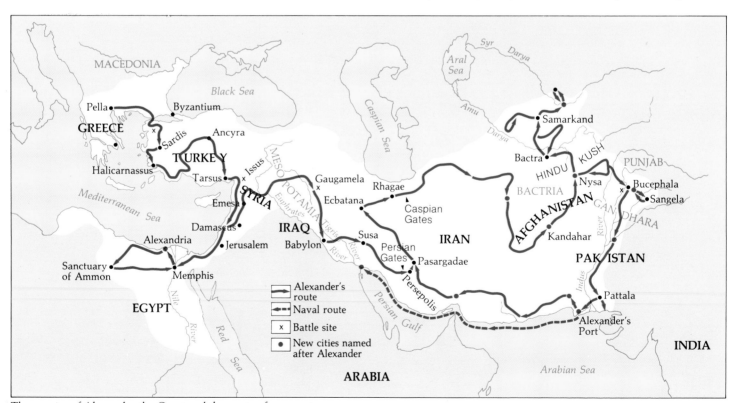

The empire of Alexander the Great and the route of conquest.

the "unknown East". While there is no question that the environment of Asia was different from that of mainland Greece, the inhabitants of the provinces of the Persian Empire—the administrators, the farmers, the artisans, the scribes—found their homelands neither uncivilized nor inhospitable. Regular lines of communication connected even the far reaches of the empire, and military contingents were stationed throughout it. The central government encouraged commerce through its network of roads, and international trade through its sponsorship of marketing and banking systems. Reports of peacocks and parrots in Greece in the 5th century B.C. reflect the role of India in this trade. After Alexander's time, spices, ivory, and Indian cotton were known in Athens.

It is true, nevertheless, that the progress of Alexander's army through Asia was often perilous. There were extensive deserts, salt wastes, impenetrable mountain ranges, sulphurous springs, and vast distances from one cultivated region to the next. Those were the things that distressed men born near the Mediterranean.

In his descriptions of Alexander's exploits, written three centuries after the hero's death, the Roman historian Quintus Curtius reflected the traditional view of Asia as harsh and forbidding.

Tetradrachm of Lysimachos of Thrace, silver, obverse with head of deified Alexander, c. 305–281 B.C. Diameter 3 cm. Royal Ontario Museum, 925.2.28.

> He [Alexander] had come to a pass blocked with perpetual snows, which the violence of the cold had bound with ice, and the desolation of the landscape and pathless solitude terrified the exhausted soldiers, who believed that they were beholding the end of the habitable world. In amazement they saw that everything was deserted and without trace of human cultivation, and they demanded that they should return before even the daylight and the sky should fail them.

With the constant exhortation of their indomitable leader, however, the Macedonians penetrated Central Asia, crossing the high ranges of the Hindu Kush before retracing their steps to conquer the fertile plains of the Punjab in the north of the Indian subcontinent. From there they journeyed to the mouth of the Indus River. Alexander contemplated an eastward march across the continent to the Ganges, but at last his soldiers resisted. The exhilaration generated by Alexander's stirring early victories had passed, and morale had begun to ebb. For the Macedonians the Indus was indeed the end of the habitable world.

Alexander's achievement was extraordinary. When he returned to Babylon in 323 B.C., he was master of all the lands from Greece, through Turkey and Egypt, to India. No European had ever been so far east; no single authority had ever controlled so much of Europe and the Middle East at the same time.

Alexander's premature death in Babylon later that year brought an end to the glorious dream of world empire. The general who won control of the eastern part of the Persian Empire founded the Seleucid dynasty, which was plagued by the very problem that the Persians themselves had faced: the sheer size of the territory made it difficult to control. In the more remote areas, particularly in Central Asia, native aristocrats took matters into their own hands. They appointed their own governors and refused to acknowledge the authority of the Seleucid king, who

Sam Desert in India, "the end of the habitable world".

ruled the eastern provinces from his capital in Mesopotamia. By the mid-3rd century B.C. the governor of Bactria had proclaimed independence and an Iranian chieftain had staged a successful revolt in Parthia. In India the Punjab had been wrested from Greek control.

Although his remarkable accomplishments were to be dissipated, Alexander the Great became a legend. A natural hero in the West, where there has always been a tendency to exalt the Greek ideal, Alexander came to be regarded as something more than a man—just as Solomon and Confucius over the centuries grew to represent more than the sum of their thoughts and actions. Centuries after Alexander's death, writers and artists, even in the Islamic world, presented him as a heroic figure, who had not only penetrated unexplored lands of the East, but who had communicated with sages living there.

Alexander's conquests extended the horizons of both the Greek and the Asian worlds. Western scholars, for example, gained access to Babylonian and Indian knowledge of mathematics and astronomy. Even the renowned philosopher and naturalist Aristotle benefited from the information brought back, or sent back, by scholars who accompanied Alexander on his campaigns. Unquestionably the knowledge contributed to the development of the theories on the reproductive structures and the habits of animals that Aristotle expressed in his *History of Animals*, a treatise that remained without peer in its field until the age of Darwin.

Conversely, Greek influence made an impact in Asia, particularly since Alexander encouraged his soldiers to marry local women. The many cities he founded for Greek-speaking settlers became centres of Greek culture, spread across the conquered territory from the Mediterranean to India. For at least two centuries these Hellenistic centres fostered Greek ideals, which became universal expressions that deeply affected the arts, the natural sciences, and the religious and political thought of local cultures.

Miniature painting, gouache on paper, from *Shahnameh* manuscript, Persian, 17th-century interpretation of Alexander conversing with the talking tree. 9.5 cm × 7.0 cm. Royal Ontario Museum, 970.268.2.

Head of Buddha, grey schist, Gandhara, 1st to 2nd century. Height 27.5 cm. Royal Ontario Museum, 939.17.18. Bequest of Reuben Wells Leonard. The head reflects the influence of Hellenistic style.

China

The West knew little about China during the lifetime of Alexander the Great, although garbled accounts of Seres, the land of silk, had begun to reach Greece in the 6th century B.C. But the reality was that northern China (the name had not yet been associated with the country) had been undergoing a distinctive cultural evolution since the second millennium B.C. A pattern of principalities had evolved; they were in effect city-states, each under the absolute rule of a small hereditary aristocracy. Political control was bolstered by large, well-equipped armies. An expanding urban culture was based on extensive agriculture, concentrated in the valleys of the Huang Ho and the Yangtze.

Towards the middle of the first millennium B.C., the stability of the system was increasingly undermined by the incursions of northern nomads, as well as by the rise of new families with wealth and power that accrued from land holdings and from commerce. Early dynastic rulers lost their political and military power, until they were little more than figureheads for religious and ceremonial functions in the capital of Loyang. The 5th century B.C. saw the beginning of a period of bitter struggles, as rival states vied for territory and power; this has been recorded as the Warring States period.

Although horseback riding was unknown in China before the middle of the 4th century B.C., the nomads of the northern steppes had been expert riders for some time. Their mobility and warlike attitude made them a constant threat to the settled agrarian states to the south. The Qin rulers of one of the Chinese states became the successful contenders in the power struggle; they adopted the

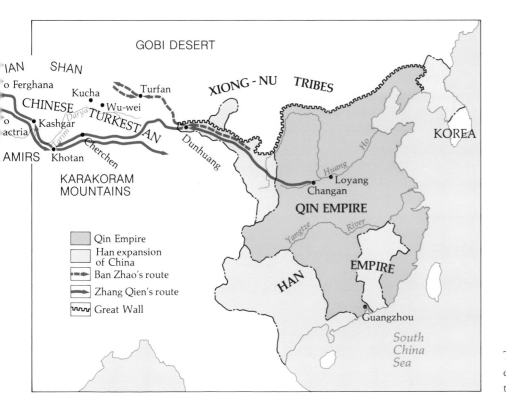

The Qin unification of China and the Han expansion set the stage for Zhang Qien's journey to the west of China.

9

The Great Wall of China.

nomads' battle tactics by replacing their horse-drawn chariots with cavalry. The change gave rise to the need in China for more and better horses. In fact, a continuing search for a stronger breed indirectly paved the way for regular trade between China and Central Asia.

The centuries of strife fostered many humanist movements—known as the Hundred Schools—as philosophers and rulers sought to reestablish social and political order. The most famous of them was that of Confucius, whose ethical philosophy was to have a lasting effect on Chinese culture. The Qin, however, adhered to the Legalist philosophy, which held that right consisted in what the ruler desired and dictated.

In a relentless pursuit of power, the Qin prince eliminated the last of his rivals in 221 B.C.; he established the Qin state as the supreme authority and took the title Qin Shih-huang-di (First Emperor of the Qin). The dynasty lasted less than two decades, but in that brief time the idea of Chinese empire was born, as was the name China (Qin is pronounced chin). The pattern of a strong central authority that imposed autocratic control through a bureaucracy became the model for future political organization in China. Imperial standards for weights and measures, coinage and taxes, language and education unified the kingdom. Imperial will was demonstrated in programmes for colossal new buildings.

To maintain security and restrain the northern tribesmen from encroaching on the empire, the Qin emperor ordered the consolidation of a series of earlier protective walls into a continuous system. The result was an unbroken line of defence extending fourteen hundred miles from Gansu to Manchuria. It came to be known as the Great Wall, a designation that is now synonymous with China.

Soon after the death of Qin Shih-huang-di in 210 B.C., the people rebelled against the autocratic rule of the Qin. The ensuing struggle for control of the empire culminated in the emergence of a new force, which was to found the Han dynasty in 202 B.C. Although early Han emperors were almost as Legalist in outlook as their predecessors, during the course of the dynasty Confucianism became the dominant philosophy.

In spite of the defensive Great Wall, the depredations of the northern tribesmen continued. Known by this time as the Xiong-nu, they had formed a federation of tribes, which were spread from western Manchuria through Mongolia and southern Siberia into Turkestan as far as the Pamirs. In the 2nd century B.C. the Han emperor Wu made attempts to enlist allies among the nomads. In 138 B.C. he sent one of his courtiers, Zhang Qien, on a diplomatic mission to the Yue-zhi, a tribe that had been driven from Gansu and was now in Afghanistan.

The plan was for Zhang Qien, accompanied by a hundred men, to follow a route through Turkestan by way of Kashgar to beyond the Tian Shan. Unfortunately he was captured by the Xiong-nu and detained for ten years. When he finally escaped, he managed to make his way to the Yue-zhi, only to find that they were content in their new domain and had no interest in becoming allies of the Han against the Xiong-nu. To avoid recapture, Zhang Qien returned to China by way of the Pamirs, with only two of his original one hundred men. Although he was unable to fulfil the prime objective of his mission, his travels yielded knowledge of the lands west of China that was to have a marked effect on Chinese trade. Zhang Qien's report, recorded by the historian Suma Qien, noted:

> When I was in Dasha [the Bactria of the Greeks] I saw bamboo canes from Qiong and cloth made in the province of Shu. When I asked the people how they had received such articles, they replied that their merchants went to buy them in the markets of Shen-du [India].

Zhang Qien also speculated that the safest route to the Central Asian markets might be through India, since the northern routes were controlled by the Xiong-nu.

Tomb figure of Han nobleman, grey earthenware, China, 1st century B.C. to 1st century A.D. Height 23.5 cm. Royal Ontario Museum, 918.17.71. Gift of Sir Edmund Walker.

Plaque with chariot and warrior, bronze, Ordos, c. 2nd century. 5.0 cm × 10.2 cm. Collection Elie Borowski.

11

The emperor Wu was especially gratified by the description in the report of the fabled "blood sweating" horses of Ferghana. He associated the Ferghana horse with an oracle predicting that "the heavenly horse" would come from the northwest. It was not, however, until 101 B.C. that the Chinese secured breeding stocks of the Ferghana horse, which was stronger than any they had ever seen and well able to carry a heavily armed man into battle. The Ferghana horse became a status symbol, eagerly sought by individuals as well as by the army.

Zhang Qien's remarkable journeys (he made a second one in 116 B.C. to the region north of the Tian Shan) made him a legend. To him was attributed the introduction into China of a whole range of plants, including the grape vine and alfalfa. To him went the credit for increasing Chinese awareness of India, Mesopotamia, and other lands to the west—an awareness that soon brought about regular communication with Parthian Iran. China's initial diplomacy was prompted by a desire to keep her borders secure, but soon trade became an instrument of foreign policy, with the aim of glorifying the imperial household and enriching its treasury.

Some states in North China had exported silks to peoples beyond the Huang Ho for at least five hundred years before the emperor Wu commissioned Zhang Qien's embassy. Although the history of these fabrics is undocumented, some of them changed hands many times and have survived in burials of nomadic chieftains from the High Altai, the Crimea, and central Europe. Now China instituted a regular state-controlled international commerce in silk yarn and silk fabrics that enriched the treasury to an extent undreamed of in preceding centuries. Trade in silk became a tool to enhance the political power of the imperial government, since by manipulating the supply of silk the Chinese state was able to create advantageous tensions beyond its borders. Silk continued to be turned to diplomatic advantage through gifts of fabrics and garments to China's neighbours.

♦ Horse, bronze, China, 2nd to 1st century B.C. Height 15.24 cm. Royal Ontario Museum, 930.21.24. Bishop White Collection.

♦ Tomb tile with horse, grey earthenware, China, Henan province, 2nd to 1st century B.C. Height 45.7 cm; length 117.0 cm; width 14.2 cm. Royal Ontario Museum, 931.13.261. Bishop White Collection.

Silken webs of imperial dreams . . .

The importance of silk in Chinese culture is attested by the attribution of its mythic discovery to the consort of the Yellow Emperor, the legendary founder of Chinese civilization.

Portrait of a sixth-rank civil official, China, late 16th century. 153.0 cm × 95.4 cm. Royal Ontario Museum, 923x56.7.

Sericulture, the rearing of silkworms for the production of silk filament, was an invention of Neolithic farmers living along the Huang Ho in north-central China more than four thousand years ago. Through the centuries the state encouraged sericulture by making taxes payable in silk. And it controlled production to ensure the prestige of silk— to make its use, in effect, an imperial prerogative demonstrating the special status of an aristocracy. Fine silk clothes and furnishings marked special occasions in life and were often interred with the dead.

Pendant in the form of a silkworm, white jade, China, probably 8th century B.C. Length 4 cm. Royal Ontario Museum, 932.16.19. Bishop White Collection.

Traditionally sericulture was a specialized activity of farmers. Each stage of the labour-intensive production demanded skill and coordination. At maturation the silkworm spins a cocoon of silk filament. The keepers had to be alert for the right moment to gather the cocoon and unwind the filament, which might be almost a kilometre long. If the chrysalis emerged from the cocoon, the continuous filament was broken.

The Chinese obtained silk from the *Bombyx mori* moth.

These illustrations were among twenty-three woodcuts illustrating silk production in an imperial encyclopedia describing the branches of knowledge. *Gengzhitu*, 1697 edition.
East Asian Library, University of Toronto.

Silkworms were fed only freshly gathered white mulberry leaves.

The keepers had to maintain a stable environment for the silkworms.

14

The cocoons had to be gathered and unwound at just the right moment.

Once the skeins of silk were ready, the production moved to centrally controlled workshops. There aesthetic and mechanical standards imposed by the state ensured silk fabric that reflected official styles, or that met the dictates of foreign markets.

Waste silk was carded to form floss for padding winter clothes, or it was spun to form threads for weaving so-called raw silk. The dead chrysalis was often roasted and eaten.

The silk thread was woven into fabric on a drawloom.

Special fabrics were made into fine clothes.

Detail of brocaded silk gauze fragment, China, 18th century. 35.0 cm × 12.2 cm. Royal Ontario Museum, 950.100.405. Krenz Collection.

Although very thin, silk filaments are extremely durable and possess tensile strength greater than that of steel. Their ability to withstand strain and manipulation probably accounted for the fact that certain loom-controlled techniques were favoured in the weaving of silk fabrics. In gauze weaves, for example, alternate sets of warp threads were displaced laterally within a shed to form a half-twist between each weft element and thus create a fabric with a series of voids. More intricate patterns evolved when areas of warp twists were coordinated with areas of plain weave.

Silk threads formed by reeling have lustre, since no irregularities interrupt the reflection of light along the length of the smooth silk filaments. This reflective property can be exploited in satin weaves, which throw long threads to the surface of finished fabrics; or in damasks, which contrast the shiny side of satin with a matt reverse face. Similarly, silk embroidery enlivens the surface of plain cloth.

The variety of surface stitches developed by Chinese embroiderers demanded refined sewing equipment, including needles with eyes, thimbles, and needle pushers. Since the instruments required for cutting fine silk fabrics and embroidery threads must be extremely sharp and precise, it is not surprising that one of the earliest forms of scissors with opposing blades was developed in China.

Scissors, iron, China, 3rd century. Length 34.6 cm. Royal Ontario Museum, 967x246.3.

Detail of embroidered silk satin coverlet, China, made for the Western market, early 18th century. 272 cm × 215 cm. Royal Ontario Museum, 914.7.17.

Detail of silk damask fragment, China, made for the Portuguese market, late 17th century. 92.5 cm × 22.3 cm. Royal Ontario Museum, 925.22.355.

During the 13th century the Mongol Empire extended from the Pacific to the frontiers of the Levant on the Mediterranean. Transcontinental trade flourished, and many new markets for Chinese goods were established. The willingness of Chinese artisans to cater for foreign styles contributed to the international commercial success of trade silks throughout history. In the 13th and 14th centuries many fabrics with Arabic motifs were regularly shipped to Egypt and other Islamic markets.

Detail of blue silk damask fragment, China, said to be from the necropolis of Al Azam in Egypt, late 13th to early 14th century. 28.0 cm × 21.5 cm. Metropolitan Museum of Art, Fletcher Fund, 46.156.20.

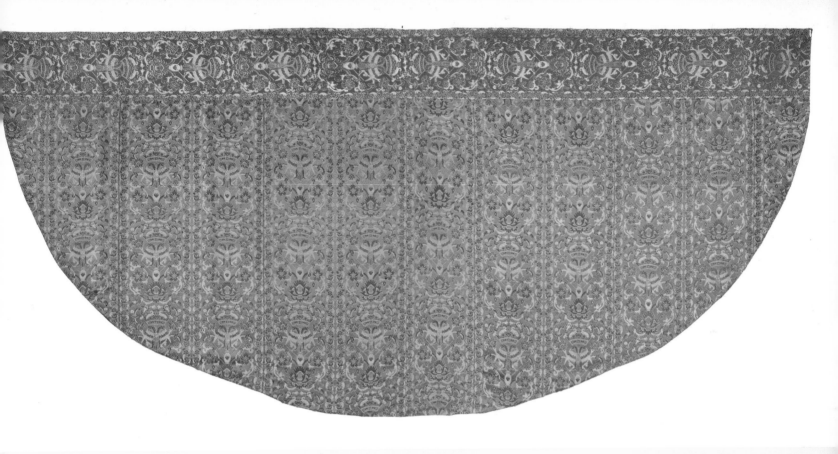

Brocaded silk compound satin furnishing fabric made into priest's cope, with detail, China, Macao, for the Spanish or Portuguese market, late 16th to early 17th century. Royal Ontario Museum, 973.422.

When European traders arrived in China in the early 16th century, silk manufacture was similarly adapted to suit Western market demands. At first only the motifs were foreign—for example, the double-headed eagles derived from the coat of arms of the Hapsburg monarchs who ruled Austria and Spain in the 16th and 17th centuries. Beginning in the 17th century, however, Chinese textiles were often manufactured specifically for European uses. Many of these exotic trade items were made to order from patterns supplied by Western merchants.

19

Details of embroidered silk satin bed curtain, China, made for the Portuguese market, late 17th to early 18th century. 337.7 cm × 108.6 cm. Royal Ontario Museum, 970.88.29a. Anonymous gift.

English formal dress of painted silk tabby, with detail, China, 1745–1750. Royal Onario Museum, 925.18. Gift of Royal Ontario Museum of Archaeology staff in memory of Ethlyn M. Greenaway.

Embroidered silk tabby shawl, with detail, China, made for the Western market, mid-19th century. 180 cm × 175 cm, plus fringes 34 cm. Royal Ontario Museum, 945.8.7. Gift of Mrs Eric Duke Scott.

When Mithradates II came to the throne of Parthia in 124/23 B.C., the Parthian Empire of Iran was in disarray: the state was under attack and Babylonia was in revolt. During his reign Mithradates secured the Parthian homeland, reconquered Babylonia, and extended the empire's sway northwestwards along the Euphrates River. He established and maintained contact with both China and Rome. Parthia was to grow rich from the rewards of its position as middleman in the trade between China and the West.

The first known contact between China and Parthia occurred towards the end of the 2nd century B.C., when the Han emperor Wu and the Parthian king Mithradates II exchanged ambassadors. The Chinese embassy bore gifts of silk. Parthia's tribute consisted of acrobats and what some scholars have interpreted as ostrich eggs.

This official exchange of gifts was frequent throughout the 1st century B.C., and in addition increasing volumes of manufactured goods and raw materials began to be traded. In both countries the new goods led to changes in consumer habits, so that products that at first were luxuries came to be regarded as essentials.

Parthian Iran

Stair-riser with Parthian men, grey schist, Gandhara, c. 2nd century. 23.6 cm × 50.8 cm. Royal Ontario Museum, 939.17.19. Bequest of Reuben Wells Leonard.

Rome

The dynasties founded by the three Macedonian generals who emerged as the successful contenders for the empire of Alexander the Great—the Seleucid in East, the Ptolemaic in Egypt, and the Antigonid in Macedonia—held the balance of power in the eastern Mediterranean through most of the 3rd century B.C. In the 2nd century B.C., however, Rome superseded Greece as arbiter, and after the middle of the century Rome began to annex Greek territories as provinces.

The need to secure her eastern frontiers kept Rome at war intermittently for many decades. In 53 B.C. legions of heavily armed foot-soldiers led by Crassus, the governor of the Roman province of Syria, confronted a mounted Parthian force on the open steppe near Carrhae. The Romans were outmanoeuvred in a battle that was disastrous for them. During the course of the battle, the Parthians unfurled gleaming banners of silk—a novel material to the Romans and one that obviously made a strong impression. Within seven years, silk canopies were reported at Julius Caesar's triumphal entry into Rome.

Soon silk was the predilection of Roman patricians from Syria to Gaul, although stoic Romans deplored the extravagant taste. In 14 B.C. the Senate issued bans against men's "disgracing themselves with the effeminate delicacy of silk apparel." The new fashions scandalized the moralist Seneca: "I see garments," he said, "in which there is nothing to cover either the wearer's body or her shame."

The reign of Augustus, which began in 27 B.C., ushered in a long period of peace, during which trade with the East flourished, both along the overland route through Parthia to China and on the sea route to India via the Red Sea and the port of Alexandria. The spoils of war and advances in agriculture, mining, and manufacturing had made Rome rich; the new money economy and the credit banking system of the empire supported an increasing trade in luxury goods.

By sea from India came household slaves, pets and arena animals, exotic furs, cashmere wool, raw and finished cotton, and some silks. Overland from China arrived silk, skins, iron, lacquer, rhubarb, and cinnamon—but especially silk. Silk thread, which was woven into fabrics of Roman specifications in Syria, made up more than ninety per cent of Rome's imports from China.

A host of other trade goods from the East appeared on the Roman markets: precious gems and jewellery, ivory, tortoise shell, pearls, ornamental woods, aromatics, and gum resins. New spices—pepper, ginger, cardamom, cinnamon, and cloves—added savour to Roman meals. New substances—cochineal and indigo— expanded the range of colours available to the fabric dyers. And new cosmetics pandered to the vanity of sophisticated Romans.

In return Rome sent to the East entertainers; wool and linen textiles, including carpets; amber and coral; asbestos; bronze vessels; lamps and glassware; wine; and papyrus. But notably she dispatched myriads of coins and large quantities of bullion.

Portrait bust of Lucius Verus, white marble, Roman, 165–170. Height 96 cm. Royal Ontario Museum, 933.27.3.

Fragment of wall painting with fashionable Roman lady in silk robe, Campania, early 1st century. 54.6 cm × 34.9 cm. Collection Elie Borowski.

Beaker, glass, light green, Syria, Roman period, second half of 1st century. Height 12.6 cm. Royal Ontario Museum, 950.157.40. Gift of Miss Helen Norton.

THE STRUGGLE TO MAINTAIN TRADE LINKS

From the 1st century B.C. trade goods moved regularly overland between the Chinese capital and the Mediterranean, a distance of more than seven thousand kilometres. The transfer of wares in slow-moving camel caravans, however, was less a continuous passage than a series of journeys from link to link in a network of trading centres, where buyers and sellers of goods converged. No individual caravan traversed the entire route. Merchants transported wares in stages from one marketplace to the next, where they traded or sold them to other merchants who carried the goods they had acquired farther along the route.

Rugged terrain and unpredictable weather took heavy tolls of the cargoes, and consequently of the profits. Bandits were no less inimical to the trade, although they could be restrained to some extent by the armies of political powers along the route. But that protection required payment in the form of taxes or fees, as did the safeguarding of the lives and cargoes of merchants in the trading centres. Although all the requisite charges ate into profits and increased the cost of trade goods, keeping the networks secure was vital to the success of international commerce.

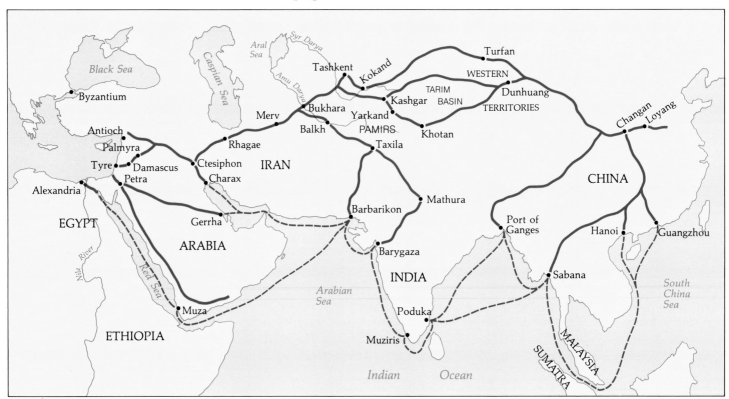

East-West trade routes by land and sea.

When certain routes became unsafe, trade shifted to less hostile environments; if the risk to life and capital became excessive, trade ceased until the problems were resolved.

States along the trade routes stood to gain in several ways. The network provided a means of shipping local goods to foreign markets, and at the same time an opportunity for increasing revenues through the imposition of customs duties and taxes on goods passing through their territories. Many of the earliest recorded embassies, both from the East and from the West, were charged with the opening up of new routes that would facilitate exploitation of untapped markets and circumvention of uncooperative powers.

Trans-Asian commerce relied on a delicate balance of control. Initially the balance was maintained by Rome, Parthia, and China. Soon after that pattern was established, however, the Parthian kings lost their dominion over the northern steppes, which the trade route crossed after leaving the Amu Darya. Even some of the outlying Parthian provinces in the central Iranian highlands declared their independence of the central government in the Mesopotamian capital of Ctesiphon, although independence did not deter them from continuing the royal privilege of collecting customs tolls. From time to time such tolls also enriched the treasuries of robber barons who flourished in the wake of the decline of the central government. Trade persisted, but as security diminished, fees for passage of goods beyond the Parthian borders soared, and the price of imports in the markets of Rome and China skyrocketed.

In Central Asia part of the power vacuum was filled by the Kushans, a semi-nomadic tribe descended from the Yue-zhi peoples visited by Zhang Qien two centuries earlier. The Kushans imposed stability west of the Tarim Basin and encouraged trade by protecting the routes through the Pamirs and the trading centres in the region of Samarkand, Bukhara, Balkh, and Merv.

Both China and Rome tried to profit from these shifts in power to expand their empires. In the 1st century China sought control of the oases of the Tarim Basin, designating them part of her new Western Territories. Ban Zhao, a Chinese general, eventually gained command of the Tarim Basin and cleared the way to the Pamirs. While he was protector general of the Western Territories, he dispatched an embassy to what he imagined was the Roman Empire.

Towards the end of the 1st century Ban Zhao's embassy reached the small principality of Characene at the head of the Persian Gulf. The city of Charax, which was independent of Parthia, acted as an entrepôt for the trans-shipment of goods from the sea routes of the gulf to the caravan routes across the desert to the Mediterranean. History relates that the Chinese inquired about the possibilities of travelling by sea to the Mediterranean. The Characenians—no doubt with the preservation of their trade monopoly in mind—thwarted direct contact between China and Rome with tales of pirates and other horrors of sea travel.

Rome, too, vigorously pursued control of the trade routes. In the 1st century B.C. Pompey succeeded in clearing the eastern Mediterranean of the pirates who had impeded the development of Roman maritime commerce. Coral reefs and sandbars in the Red Sea made sailing in its uncharted waters treacherous, and so

View of the Hindu Kush from the top of the colossal Buddha at Bamiyan in Afghanistan.

Roman merchants linked the port of Alexandria with the Indian Ocean by a less hazardous journey. Goods were taken by camel caravan across the desert from the Nile to a port in the southern half of the Red Sea. Merchants also learned to take advantage of the monsoon winds that blow steadily from the southwest across the Indian Ocean from March to September, and steadily from the northeast from November to January. This navigational technique, whose discovery in the West is traditionally ascribed to a Greek sailor named Hippalus, enabled ships to avoid the slow, coast-hugging voyages that characterized sea trade until the 1st century. The potential for greater speed and cargo capacity made sea trade extremely lucrative.

During the reign of Augustus as many as 120 Roman ships laden with trade goods, gold bullion, and coins set out from Red Sea ports each year. From March to September they sailed eastwards from the Horn of Africa to the ports of southern India. In November they began their return voyages, now carrying cargoes of exotic Eastern goods. Rome continued this direct contact with Asian markets well into the 2nd century. Roman embassies are reported to have called at the courts of Sumatra, Malaysia, and Tonkin. The history of the Later Han dynasty includes this record:

> In the beginning of the Yuan-jia period of the emperor Huan the king of Da-Qin, Antun [identified as Marcus Aurelius] sent envoys who offered ivory, rhinoceros horns, and tortoise shells from the boundary of Annam; this was the first time they communicated with us.

The event described may well have been a private mercantile undertaking, rather than an official embassy, since no mention of it appears in Western records. Whatever the purpose of the mission was, the end of the anecdote indicates that the Chinese were little impressed: "Their tribute contained no precious stones whatever, which makes us suspect that the messengers kept them back."

Secure routes and generous financial backing encouraged Roman merchants to foster a demand for an increasing range of exotic Asian products. The resultant costs to the Roman economy were alarming. Early in the 1st century the emperor Tiberius noted that gold was being used to pay for "articles that flatter the vanity of women; jewels and those little objects of luxury which drain away the riches of the empire. In exchange for trifles, our money is sent to foreign lands and even to our enemies."

A century later Pliny the Younger observed that the annual drain on the treasury was "55 million sesterces paid to India and 45 million to Seres and Arabia." By then the Ethiopian kingdom of Aksum was challenging Rome's monopoly of Asian trade by way of the Red Sea, while Parthian Iran continued to exact duties on Indian goods travelling overland from the Persian Gulf or from Central Asia. Despite Rome's exports of large quantities of manufactured glass-wares and metalwares produced in the empire, a major trade imbalance resulted in a severe deficit in the Roman economy, which was based on gold and silver. The Roman aristocracy refused to invest its wealth productively and continued to purchase ever-increasing quantities of exotic Eastern products at spiralling costs. To keep pace with the drain of payments, Rome had to find new sources of gold, or alternatively to effect drastic reductions in the prices of imported goods. Early in the 2nd century the emperor Trajan tried to redress the imbalance by invading Parthia.

The outcome of this imperial power play, however, was the very opposite of its aim. Rome's control was overextended, and as Parthia fought to reassert authority, caravans were unable to journey safely along the trade routes. Merchants became reluctant to risk capital in ventures that had little prospect of success. As imperial economies continued to deteriorate, internal power struggles increased. Dissatisfied groups attempted to rectify matters through revolution and internecine fighting. By the 3rd century the empires along the trans-Asian routes had disintegrated, and as a consequence, large-scale international trade collapsed.

Economic and political crises in the 3rd century made Rome vulnerable to invasion of her territories by the northern Vandals, Franks, Germans, and Goths in the 4th century. The centre of the Roman Empire shifted to the eastern Mediterranean when the emperor Constantine settled in Byzantium in 330. Although the desire for exotic Eastern goods remained undiminished among fashionable Romans, the West was in effect isolated from direct sources of supply. Access to overland routes through Central Asia was blocked by Sasanian Iran. Control of the Red Sea traffic was in the hands of Ethiopia, which barred Byzantine trade in the Indian Ocean. Barbarian tribes dominated the lands north of the Danube, preventing Byzantium's access to the routes across the Eurasian steppe north of the Caspian and Aral seas.

• Tetradrachm of Commodus, billon, reverse with
Roman merchantman alongside the lighthouse at
Alexandria, Roman, dated 189. Diameter 2.5 cm.
Royal Ontario Museum, 910.159.644(1).

In China, too, trade with the West was at an impasse. With the collapse of the
Han dynasty in 220, the country regressed into many separate states. The
economic focus shifted to the east and the south. Almost four centuries would pass
before China was reunified under a single ruler.

In Iran, however, the Sasanian revolution in the 3rd century had brought
dynamic new leadership to power and reestablished the notion of empire. Trade
flourished once again, but in a much changed form. The Sasanians absorbed the
Kushan territory in the 4th century and thus linked trade networks across crucial
areas of Central Asia. They also dominated the sea lanes in the Indian Ocean and
the Persian Gulf. With control of both overland and sea routes in her hands,
Sasanian Iran gained a monopoly on Asian trade with the West. The situation,
however, was volatile; while trade agreements and treaties, particularly for the sale
of silk, smoothed relations between rivals, issues of territorial control frequently led
to war.

Iran dispatched embassies to various states in northern China, but by the
middle of the 6th century new disturbances had erupted on the steppes of Central
Asia, and once again central authority was lacking. Trade continued, however,
partly as a result of the activities of religious minorities, whose communities
provided settings for the exchange of trade goods. Followers of the persecuted
prophet Mani had fled from Iran in the 3rd century and settled in Central Asia,
where they established communities that found it profitable to provide protection
for travellers. Farther east, in Turfan and elsewhere, Buddhist communities
provided the same kind of sanctuary. In the more remote stretches of the silk
routes, this pattern was to remain in effect for several centuries.

The next major bid for power came in the 8th century, when the Chinese and
the Arabs fought for control of Turkestan. The victories of Ziyad ben Salih, the
commander of the Arab armies, took the Muslims beyond the Amu Darya, and
without question established Islam as the power to be reckoned with west of China
for the next thousand years.

SOME CONCOMITANTS OF THE TRANS-ASIAN TRADE

As international trade increased and expanded, written descriptions and eye-witness accounts of distant places were circulated. The factual reportage helped to dispel many of the myths that informed early views of the world. Augustus, the first Roman emperor, is generally believed to have commissioned what was essentially the original travel guide, *The Parthian Stations*, written by Isidore of Charax. It listed places and distances along the route from Mesopotamia to Central Asia. A comparable guide to the sea lanes, *The Periplus of the Erythraean Sea*, had appeared in the 1st century B.C. Although as travel guides the two works fall short of modern expectations, they transmitted information that promoted an appreciation of the global context in which individual states existed.

In China, too, awareness of the outside world was growing. Suma Qien's history of the Han dynasty, begun in the 2nd century B.C., carefully recorded knowledge acquired by Chinese travellers about peoples and places beyond the Han borders. The work served as a model for subsequent dynastic histories, which chronicled most of the embassies dispatched by and received at the Chinese imperial court.

While the prospective profits of international trade frequently provoked aggression between neighbouring states, trans-Asian trade also facilitated productive exchanges, often generated by missionaries and pilgrims who attached themselves to caravans so that they might travel in greater safety. Buddhist pilgrims established a series of religious communities that paralleled the trading centres of the oases along the overland route from India through Afghanistan and Central Asia to China. From there Buddhism spread to Korea and Japan. The Buddhist sites played an integral part in the dissemination of diverse cultural ideas and artistic styles over vast distances.

Because both rulers and merchants congregated at the temples and monasteries, Buddhist monks helped to smooth the path of commerce between transient and local populations. The vitality of Buddhist centres, like that of the neighbouring oasis cities, depended on commerce. With the collapse of international trade in the 10th century and the rising persecution of Buddhists as Islam spread, the monasteries were abandoned and fell into ruin. Many of the Buddhist sites in Eastern Turkestan were covered by desert sands and remained hidden until Sir Marc Aurel Stein made the first staggering discoveries at Khotan and Miran in the first two decades of the 20th century. His finds spurred a great rush of treasure hunters after World War I. While some excavators were scholars in search of knowledge, others were motivated simply by greed.

Another concomitant of the expansion of trade was the spread of sericulture. Silk, after all, had provided the strong impetus for early international trade. After the collapse of the Han dynasty, the demand for silk continued. The lack of imperial control over what had been a state industry and the consequent

Fragment of a textile with bird motif in roundel, typical of Sasanian art, silk, compound twill weave, Iran, 6th to 7th century. Width 11.4 cm. Cleveland Museum of Art, 51.88.

Element of a relief with detail of king's robe, showing roundels and *senmurv* motif, Iran, Taq-i Bustan, 6th century.

Buddha, grey schist, Gandhara, 1st to 2nd century. Height 1.12 m.
Royal Ontario Museum, 939.17.13. Bequest of Reuben Wells Leonard.

Figure of a Buddhist monk, marble, China, 10th to 11th century.
Height 1.7 m. Royal Ontario Museum, 922.20.95. George Crofts
Collection.

32

Albert von Le Coq, Albert Grünwedel, and other archaeologists discovered many cities buried in Central Asian sands. Museum für Indische Kunst, West Berlin, MIK B 956a.

uncertainty regarding supplies probably contributed to the illicit traffic that resulted in the dissemination, both eastwards and westwards, of the closely guarded secret of sericulture and the production of silk. By the 3rd century Korea and Japan were producing silk. In the 4th century the oasis cities of China's former Western Territories had the secret. In the 6th century, when Byzantium was desperate about the astronomical costs of Asian silks moving through the Sasanian trade monopoly, certain "monks from Serindia" arrived at the court of the emperor Justinian with silkworm eggs concealed in hollow staffs and the necessary knowledge that led to the founding of a silk industry in the West.

Although overland trade routes continued to play an important role throughout the Middle Ages, after the 4th century much greater use was made of the seas. The Sasanians enjoyed wide-ranging control over the sea routes, and the greater speed and tonnage possible with ships made sea trade more economical than overland travel routes.

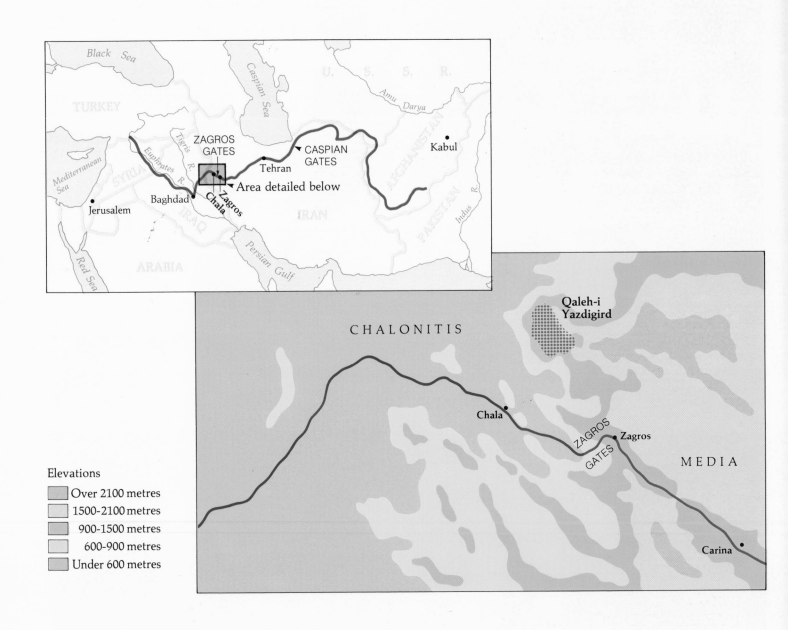

Elevations

- Over 2100 metres
- 1500-2100 metres
- 900-1500 metres
- 600-900 metres
- Under 600 metres

A Persian castle on the Silk Roads...

In the unremitting search for the past, each new discovery adds to the store of accumulated knowledge. Fresh ground was broken in the continuing study of ancient trade routes when archaeologist E. J. Keall led an exploratory expedition to the site of Qaleh-i Yazdigird in the mid-1960s.

Qaleh-i Yazdigird means "the castle of Yazdigird", and according to legend the castle was built in the 7th century as a stronghold for Yazdigird, the last king of kings of the Sasanian Empire of Iran. The legend, handed down from generation to generation by the villagers who over the years cultivated the land nearby, accounted for the ruins that dotted the fields.

Qaleh-i Yazdigird, situated on a tableland at the edge of the Zagros Mountains in western Iran, overlooks the main East-West trade route. The tableland looms up as the traveller crosses from the west towards the principal pass through the mountains; ancient writers called the pass the Zagros Gates.

Great archaeological finds are often accidental. A Chinese farmer, in the process of digging a well in the 20th century, came upon the first of the army of life-sized clay figures in the tomb complex of Qin Shih-huang-di, China's first emperor. And chance was instrumental in the first discoveries at Qaleh-i Yazdigird. Success in unearthing clues to the history of the ruins was proving elusive — until local villagers suggested a search in a particular ploughed field. Within ten days the expedition had opened up several trenches in the field. A deep sounding revealed that walls of a building stood to a height of more than four metres just below the surface of the ground.

The villagers were in the habit of digging up old gypsum plaster in the field.

One of the trenches defined a decorated wall.

They periodically reclaimed the plaster for repairs to a local holy man's shrine.

Without knowing it, the villagers had been destroying a storehouse of artwork. Remnants of decorated walls, preserved by the debris of the collapsed super-structure, lay only centimetres below the surface. Hidden in the debris were dozens of fragments of plaster wall decorations, encrusted with salts from the damp earth.

In the decorative scheme, motifs were frequently repeated. The drawing represents an artist's reconstruction of the original intact figure of a winged Cupid, based on several incomplete pieces. The motif may owe its inspiration to a Western personification of Sleep.

Artist's reconstruction of winged Cupid. Height of figure 46 cm.

In this fragment of a repetitive figure the wings of a Cupid are discernible.

In this view of the same composition, the column against which the Cupid leans is apparent.

Here the pose of the Cupid is clearly defined: the head is inclined to the left and the right hand clasps the left shoulder.

Between 1975 and 1979 the Royal Ontario Museum mounted three full-scale expeditions to explore the entire stronghold of Qaleh-i Yazdigird, which covered an area of twenty-five square kilometres.

The cliffs at the edge provided natural protection for the residence nestled in the hollow of the tableland.

A man-made defensive system designed to reinforce security included a long wall that snaked across the countryside.

• The model of the Qaleh-i Yazdigird complex shows (1) the defensive walls, (2) the lookout posts, (3) the upper fort, (4) the inner stronghold, and (5) the garden of paradise with its ornate palace.

Massively buttressed walls represent a stronghold within the fortress.

Walls with arrow slots dominate the cliffs that overlook the route.

Traces of guard chambers can still be found along the defensive wall.

According to legend, the upper fort was the ultimate retreat of King Yazdigird against the advancing armies of Islam.

The rather unexpected fact that emerged in the study of the masses of architectural ornaments recovered from the site is that the decoration does not support the legend that Qaleh-i Yazdigird was a remote military outpost built in Sasanian Iran in the 7th century. In fact, the decorative style indicates that the palace set within a garden of paradise and protected by an elaborately fortified stronghold was a creation of 2nd-century Parthian Iran, contemporaneous with Han China and Imperial Rome.

This stylized flower-bud motif, painted in bold colours, was part of a repetitive design on a wall panel — a typical Parthian decorative element. Height of flower 12 cm.

This remnant of a brightly painted wall column carries a male figure that is obviously Parthian in inspiration and pose; he is dressed in trousers, tunic, and high-peaked hat. Height of figure 28 cm.

The artwork from Qaleh-i Yazdigird presents a rich variety of themes from both Eastern and Western artistic vocabularies. The richness belies the traditional view of the period of late Parthian history as a time of deterioration.

By the 2nd century Parthia was under attack from Rome, and central control in the empire was weak. But the Iranian highlands prospered from the decline, since they remained for the most part independent of the Parthian king of kings. Overlooking the strategic trade route through the Zagros Mountains, Qaleh-i Yazdigird was remote enough from the Parthian capital to discourage punitive missions. The stronghold may well have been the luxurious mountain retreat of a robber baron bent on plundering, or exacting booty from, caravans travelling the Silk Roads.

The pair of intertwined beasts on this capital are reminiscent of ancient Mesopotamian traditions. Height of capital 35 cm.

The decoration of this engaged column capital—a nude female holding a pair of dolphins with voluted tails—reflects Mediterranean traditions. Height of capital 47 cm.

The use of a variety of motifs, typical of the period of Parthian history when artistic ideas were as mobile as the trade, reflects the work of an architect who had been exposed to foreign influences. The lord of Qaleh-i Yazdigird would have been in a position to sponsor such an architect, as would the many other robber barons of the day. In spite of the eclecticism, however, the decorative scheme at Qaleh-i Yazdigird is totally Parthian.

The two griffins in this heraldic scene are portrayed in the archaic mode of ancient Mesopotamian art. Height of figures 12 cm. Reproduction cast.

The motif of this fragment from a frieze, showing two Cupids wrestling with a feline beast, has been represented as part of the Western Dionysiac tradition. Height of figures 20 cm.

This single griffin is portrayed with diminutive body and ornately curled wing, in a manner reminiscent of the later *senmurv* tradition of Sasanian and Islamic Persian art. Height of figure 24 cm. Reproduction cast.

The artist's reconstruction of the Dionysiac frieze was pieced together from several overlapping fragments. Reproduction cast.

42

The three figures illustrated here, along with the man in the high-peaked hat, were part of a repetitive scheme of decoration that once covered a wall column at Qaleh-i Yazdigird.

Nude female leaning against a column. Height 28 cm.

Personification of Pan. Height 28 cm.

Female in long Greek robe. Height 28 cm.

• An artist has reconstructed part of the column from diverse clues. Reproduction cast.

On the obverse of the coin is depicted a man referred to by numismatists as the "unknown king", who it is recognized issued coins, only in the Iranian highlands, about the middle of the 2nd century. Whether or not the "unknown king" was the robber baron of Qaleh-i Yazdigird, the independent minting of coins reflects the autonomy claimed by powerful lords along the Silk Roads throughout their history.

• Obverse of silver coin found by a villager in the fields of Qaleh-i Yazdigird. Diameter 1.9 cm.

This bust is repeated many times in the wall decorations at Qaleh-i Yazdigird. The style of frontal representation, bouffant hairstyle with diadem band, and enclosure in a decorated roundel is typically Parthian. It is tempting to think that the bust represents the resident robber baron.

One of many fragments of the male bust. Maximum width of bust 26 cm.

Artist's reconstruction of the male bust.

44

THREE EMPIRES

TANG CHINA

By the middle of the 7th century, political power in Asia was consolidated in the hands of strong central states — the Tang in China and Islam in the Middle East. In the West the Byzantine Empire, though severely reduced in extent, controlled much of the wealth of Europe and maintained widespread trade links. It was against the backdrop of the actions and interactions of these three empires that the drama of international trade was played out.

For more than three centuries after the fall of the Later Han Empire in 220, China remained a fragmented land of small rival kingdoms. Then in the late 6th century the kingdom of Sui reunified the country by force of arms. Although like the Qin dynasty in the 3rd century B.C., the Sui dynasty was short lived, it too set the stage for a strong, expansive empire.

Li Yuan and his son Li Shih-min ushered in a new golden age of Chinese empire when they established their clan as the ruling family of Tang in 618. Skilful military strategists, early Tang rulers secured their realm by subjugating in turn the remnants of the Sui, the eastern Turks in Mongolia, the western Turks in the Tarim Basin, the Koguryo in Manchuria, and the Paekche in Korea.

Tang garrisons were posted throughout the land to secure trade routes and maintain peace. As a result, commerce flowed unrestricted and the prices of most commodities remained comparatively low, at least in the early Tang period. Restoration of a stable central government and redistribution of land to provide an ample tax base revitalized the Chinese economy and made the state amenable to expanded trade and to new ideas.

The wealth of the imperial treasury was reflected in the opulence of the Tang court. Foreigners of many religious persuasions and from many countries arrived in China. By land and by sea came Buddhist pilgrims from India, Japan, and Korea; religious fugitives from West Asia; Jewish, Armenian, and Arab merchants from the Middle East; and traders in spices and gems from Arabia. Caravans from Tibet and Soghdia arrived regularly at the Chinese capital of Changan, as did envoys and embassies from all parts of the known world.

Prosperity and security fostered religious tolerance. While indigenous Daoism and Confucianism flourished, the court permitted Nestorian Christians to build a church in the capital in 628, and in 694 the emperor entertained a dialogue with devotees of Manichaeism. Buddhism, which had first come to China in the 2nd century, now thrived under imperial patronage. Buddhist missionaries and pilgrims such as the Chinese monks Fa Xian and Xuan Zhang, brought new religious icons and tracts from India, as well as India's latest theories in astronomy, mathematics, medicine, and philosophy. Indian contributions to the arts and the sciences were assiduously studied by Chinese scholars, as were Persian and Arabian ideas.

The Tang court was intrigued by all things foreign, particularly by expensive jewels from India and Arabia, entertainers and horses from Central Asia, and medicines and wild animals from India and Southeast Asia. The taste for foreign

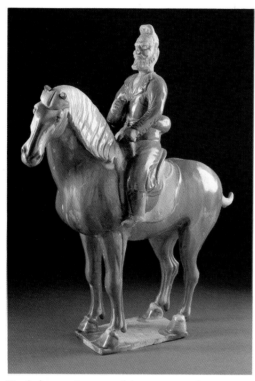

• Tomb figure of mounted foreigner, earthenware, China, late 7th to 8th century. Height 40.3 cm. Royal Ontario Museum, 918.21.329. George Crofts Collection.

luxuries spread from the court to city dwellers and the wealthy gentry, and trade grew at an unprecedented pace. Tang artists adopted ideas from the south, the east, and the west. Contemporary literature and official histories reflect the eclecticism that prevailed, and many objects survive to illustrate it. Clay tomb figures of people and animals and objects of luxury made for burial with the dead to ensure a comfortable afterlife have been unearthed by the thousands.

With economic security and international prestige established, Tang basked in a revival of art and literature. All males, even those from the lowest classes, were eligible to sit for the state examinations that were the prerequisites for administrative posts in the bureaucracy, although preparation for the examinations required years of classical study. From the ranks of the administrators rose the artists and literati whose paintings, poetry, and calligraphy set the tone for the high cultural achievements of Tang.

The 8th century was, in fact, a period of prosperity and achievement throughout East Asia, and cultural ideas moved back and forth as freely as the trade. In the first half of the century, for example, the Heian court in Japan rivalled the Tang court in China. Japan imitated Tang culture, patronized Buddhism and its arts, and generally reflected the refined aesthetics of international tastes. In the Shosoin, a storehouse attached to the Todai-ji temple in Nara, the first permanent capital of Japan, is preserved a unique treasury of Tang and other contemporary objects, the personal collection of the emperor Shomu. Some of the objects were gifts from the Tang court; some were Japanese imperial purchases. Many were made in Tang China, but others were obviously produced in Iran.

Pair of tomb figures of civil officials, earthenware, China, late 7th to 8th century. Height of each 1.1 m. Royal Ontario Museum, 918.22.12, 918.22.13. George Crofts Collection. Gift of Mrs H. D. Warren.

Tomb figure of Bactrian camel, buff earthenware, China, 7th to 8th century. Height 45.7 cm. Royal Ontario Museum, 923.24.129. George Crofts Collection.

The extravagances of the Tang court became a drain on the Chinese economy. Abuses of the money supply, land reforms, and new tax structures placed excessive burdens on the peasants. By the mid-8th century, prices and unemployment had risen drastically. The conflict between peasants evicted from the land through inability to meet taxes and oppressive landlords and merchants led to civil war. Rebellion swept the empire, and Tang rulers were unable to sustain a strong central administration. Rokshan, a regional commander of Turkish origin, marched his army through the valley of the Huang Ho and looted the Tang capitals of Loyang and Changan. Between 754 and 764, constant strife, famine, and plague reduced the Chinese population from an estimated fifty-three million to about seventeen million.

At the same time Tang authority was declining among its tributary states. In 751 the armies of Gao Xien ji, a Korean general in the service of Tang, suffered defeat at the hands of the Muslim armies near the Talas River in the Tarim Basin. It was a defeat that marked the end of Chinese control over Central Asia and the trade routes and the beginning of Islamic penetration into the region. In the west

Tomb figure of Ferghana horse, buff earthenware with cream and green glaze, China, 7th to 8th century. Height 71 cm. Royal Ontario Museum, 918.21.290. George Crofts Collection.

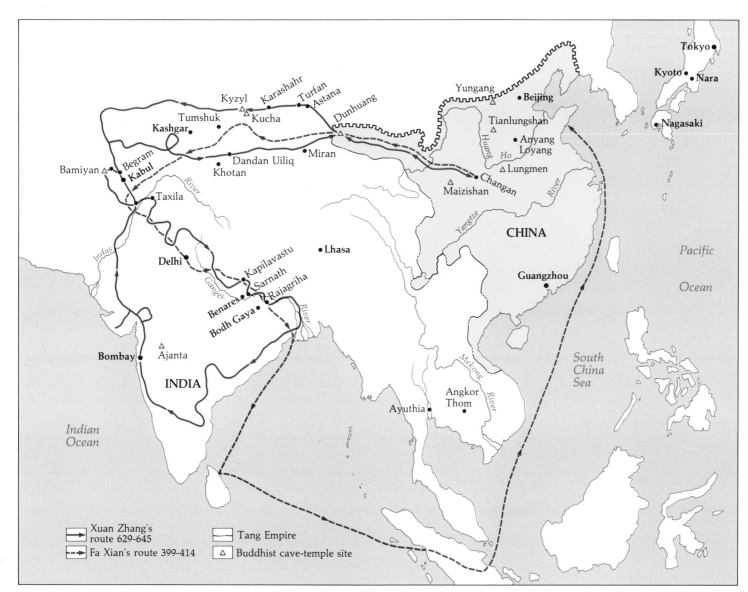

Tang China with Buddhist routes and sites.

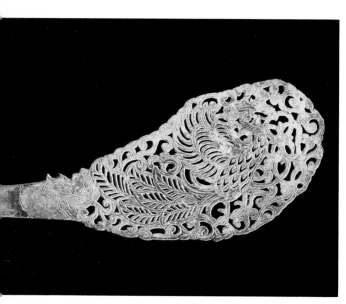

Hairpin, silver-gilt head, openwork and chased design of phoenix, China, c. 8th century. Length 32.7 cm. Royal Ontario Museum, 959.117.2. Anonymous gift.

warriors from Yunnan seized control of the direct trade routes to India and Southeast Asia. Uighur Turks attacked from the northwest. Khitans from Manchuria in the northeast and Tibetans in the west harassed the trade routes.

With two-thirds of the population annihilated, Tang China's recovery from the disruptions of the 8th century was slow. In the 9th century rising prices, natural disasters, and further rebellion continued to sap the strength of Tang. Yet the court persisted in its luxurious ways, and the peasants once again rose in resentful ferment. In 879, after laying waste vast tracts of land, the rebels massacred the foreign merchants in Guangzhou, thus cutting off a source of revenue from foreign trade. In the heyday of the Tang Empire, the presence of foreign faiths in China had been a reflection of the tolerance and brilliance of the court. By the middle of the 9th century, however, the Chinese people had come to resent the foreign presence. Buddhism, in particular, was decried as harmful to the state. One of the tenets of Buddhism required monks to beg for a livelihood, and thus they came to be regarded as unproductive and a liability to the economy. Persecution spread to other faiths, among them Manichaeism and Islam. In this environment of depression and xenophobia, strong warlords and border tribes carved out their own kingdoms with little resistance from the Tang. By the beginning of the 10th century, Tang control of China had vanished.

After the collapse of the Tang dynasty, China was again fragmented. Ten kingdoms flourished in the south and southeast. In the north an important kingdom was centred on the capital region, where five dynasties followed one another in rapid succession. Before the end of the 10th century China was once again united under the Song, who brought civil administration under firm imperial control and built up the treasury to an unprecedented extent. The Song, however, were unable to bring Central Asia into the Chinese sphere of influence. In fact, the costs of maintaining large armies for protection against its neighbours created a serious drain on the state. By the 12th century northern China was once again overrun by nomadic invaders, and the Song court was forced to flee to the south.

Box with West Asian motif of circling birds, silver and parcel gilt, China, 8th to 10th century. Length 8.0 cm, width 4.45 cm. Royal Ontario Museum, 957.152.1a–b.

Saffron robes on the Silk Roads . . .

Buddhism, a religion founded in Nepal in the 6th century B.C., became the faith of more than a third of Asia's population. Its rapid spread over vast distances throughout and beyond India coincided with existing trade patterns. Traders and missionaries carried the message by sea to Southeast Asia and southern China, and overland to Central Asia and northern China. By the 6th century A.D. Buddhism had been transmitted to Japan by way of Korea.

The diffusion of the new faith by clerics in distinctive saffron garments was part of the general flow of ideas along the trade routes. From Ajanta in western India to Bamiyan in Afghanistan, to the series of Buddhist centres in Central Asia and northern China, to Korea and Japan, a basic set of principles and a common iconography prevailed as Buddhism penetrated the cultures in its path.

The historical Buddha, the founder of the religion, is believed to have lived from c. 563 B.C. to 483 B.C. The son of a warrior-caste prince, he was given the personal name Siddhartha. The Buddha achieved the enlightenment he sought and began to teach the doctrine.

Bodhisattvas are followers of the Buddha who though well advanced on the path to enlightenment delay the final stage of Buddhahood in order to help others to attain salvation. One of the Bodhisattvas, Maitreya, is identified with a future incarnation of Buddha.

Detail of a banner showing the miracles of the Bodhisattva Guan Yin, painted silk, western China, Dunhuang, 10th century. 78 cm × 62 cm. Musée Guimet, Paris, MG17665.

On the stele, or commemorative pillar, is a depiction of Siddhartha on horseback setting out on his search for enlightenment.

While riding in the royal park, Siddhartha saw four signs — an aged man, a sick man, a corpse, and a wandering religious beggar. The first three represented the suffering of the world, with its endless cycle of birth, death, and rebirth. The contrasting serenity of the beggar caused Siddhartha to renounce his life of luxury and seek a way to defeat the cycle. After years of wandering and meditation, enlightenment came to him in the form of the Middle Way, the way of moderate detachment from earthly desires.

> What is the Middle Way? . . . It is the Noble Eightfold Path — Right Views, Right Resolve, Right Speech, Right Conduct, Right Livelihood, Right Effort, Right Recollection and Right Meditation.

> And this is the Noble Truth of Sorrow. Birth is sorrow, disease is sorrow, death is sorrow, contact with the unpleasant is sorrow, separation from the pleasant is sorrow, every wish unfulfilled is sorrow — in short all components of individuality are sorrow.

> *Samyutta Nikaya, V, 421–423*

The ultimate goal of Buddhism is *nirvana*, which when fully achieved brings cessation of rebirth.

Siddhartha in the palace, from a relief fragment, grey schist; Gandhara, 2nd to 3rd century. Height 55.88 cm. Royal Ontario Museum, 939.18.5.

Stele, grey sandstone, northern China, dated 523. 224.79 cm × 68.58 cm. Royal Ontario Museum, 949.100.

After the death of the Buddha, disciples carried his teachings beyond Nepal through India. The spread of the religion westwards to Afghanistan was hastened by the conversion to Buddhism of the rulers of the Maurya kingdom of northern India in the 3rd century B.C. In Afghanistan Buddhist iconography was to be profoundly affected by the artistic traditions that had developed in Gandhara, a former province of the Persian Empire reached by Alexander the Great in 327 B.C.

Gandharan sculpture and painting of Buddha figures imitated the type of the Western philosopher, or *togatus* figure. Draperies, formal poses, and sober expressions suggest the contemplative attitude of the Buddha. The type of the Graeco-Roman statesman served as a model for the Buddha.

Seated Buddha, black schist, Gandharan school, 1st to 2nd century. Height 61 cm. Royal Ontario Museum, 930.19.3.

Togatus figure, bronze, Roman, early 1st century. Height 12.8 cm. Royal Ontario Museum, 956.7.

Buddhism and Buddhist art with a strong Graeco-Roman influence continued to thrive in Gandhara for several hundred years after the fall of the Kushan Empire in the 4th century. The Buddhist monastery site at Hadda—which encompasses a series of relief-decorated burial mounds for relics of the Buddha—is one of the largest known.

It was probably at the Buddhist site of Bamiyan on the north-south silk route between Turkestan and India that the tradition of colossal Buddhas began. With the patronage of nobles and wealthy merchants, huge images for veneration were carved into the cliffs. Adjacent caves provided shelter for monks, pilgrims, and other wayfarers.

Attendant of the Buddha, stucco, Afghanistan, Hadda, 5th to 6th century. Height approximately 2.5 m.

The Great Buddha, carved into conglomerate cliff, Afghanistan, Bamiyan, 4th to 5th century. Height approximately 53 m.

Cave site, western India, Ajanta, c. 5th to 9th century.

In the 19th century British military explorers discovered a series of caves cut into the side of a deep ravine at Ajanta. The caves, which had been commissioned by Indian Gupta kings between the 4th and the 7th century, contained Buddhist monasteries and shrines decorated with wall paintings and sculptures depicting didactic tales and events from the life of the Buddha. By the 12th century the caves had fallen into disuse. Their relative inaccessibility, which had made them an ideal site for meditation, also led to their long period of isolation.

During the reign of the Gupta kings, a native Indian style of Buddhist art had evolved. Frankly sensual, its images were part of the tradition of pre-Buddhist fertility figures. The main icon in Ajanta Cave I displays typical attributes—full lips, a languid expression, half-closed eyes, strong but subtle modelling, and withal an aura of contemplation. The Gupta style was one of those transmitted to Southeast Asia.

Bodhisattva with lotus, wall painting, western India, Ajanta Cave I, c. 6th century. 1.30 m × 0.91 m.

Buddha, western India, Ajanta Cave I, main shrine, c. 6th century. Height approximately 3 m.

At Kakrak, near Bamiyan, a series of wall paintings illustrates both the continuity of Indian prototypes such as those at Ajanta and the beginning of a new iconography. The mandala—a circular or square arrangement of Buddhist figures within a cosmic context—was primarily a focus for meditation.

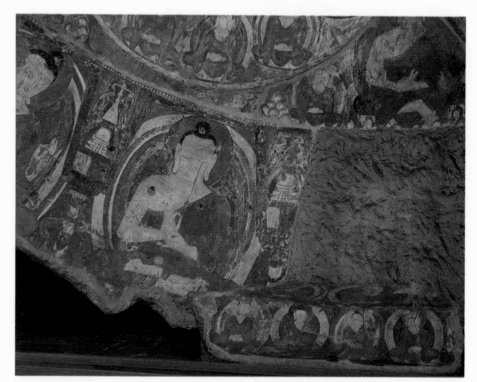

Mandala, wall painting, Afghanistan, Kakrak, c. 5th to 6th century. 1.75 m × 1.49 m. Formerly in the Kabul Museum; present location unknown.

Female divinity, fragment of a wall painting, Eastern Turkestan, Duldur Aqur, 6th to 7th century. 42 cm × 32 cm. Musée Guimet, Paris, EO1122.

Buddhist sites discovered in Central Asia early in the 20th century add to our knowledge of the trade routes and of the art that was transported along them. The oasis city-states, the marketplaces of the trade networks, were fertile grounds for exchange of artistic ideas between East and West. The resulting eclecticism in the art of such cave sites as Duldur Aqur reflects both sophistication and originality. Acts of piety in the form of donations and grants ensured the maintenance of these cave sites until Islam came to dominate the region in the 9th to the 10th century.

Aquiline noses, large eyes, and high-necked, close-fitting garments point to Western influences. The city-state of Kucha, with its dependent towns of Kyzyl, Tumshuk, and Duldur Aqur, was the centre of the only Indo-European enclave in Central Asia. The art of the region perpetuated the style of Gandhara, but incorporated some Chinese elements.

By the 8th century further Chinese influences can be seen in the full-faced figures clad in graceful, linear drapery that characterized Tang dynasty court art.

Two devotees, fragment of a wall painting, Eastern Turkestan, Duldur Aqur, 8th century. 29 cm × 22 cm. Musée Guimet, Paris, EO1123b.

Standing Buddha, wood, Eastern Turkestan, Tumshuk, 5th to 6th century. Height 23 cm. Museum für Indische Kunst, West Berlin, MIK III 8031.

The oasis city of Dunhuang at the eastern edge of the Tarim Basin was Buddhism's entry point into China. Between the 3rd and the 10th century the numerous caves dug into the sides of cliffs made this remote frontier area a major pilgrimage site. Here Indian metaphysics and Central Asian art styles confronted Chinese traditions.

As Buddhism spread through China, other great cave sites were created. A colossal Buddha carved into the sandstone cliffs at Yungang evokes the colossi of Bamiyan.

The impact of Buddhism on the arts of China was dramatic. The need for images in temples and at monastic centres transformed sculpture into the most important medium of artistic expression. On the other hand, humanistic Chinese traditions affected Buddhist arts, particularly during the Tang dynasty. The full-faced sensual figure style, with its brilliant colour schemes, developed at the Tang court, influenced Buddhist artists working at Dunhuang and other sites under the patronage of wealthy Chinese devotees.

Colossal Buddha, carved into sandstone cliff, China, Yungang, Cave 20, 5th century. Height 13.7 m.

Cave site, western China, Dunhuang, c. 9th century.

58

In addition to monumental images produced for public viewing, private devotional icons were created. Gilt-bronze altar groups were sometimes presented to temples as pious acts on the part of the donors. Such pieces were also transported to Korea and Japan, where they influenced local artistic traditions.

The lacquered wooden figure of Miroku, the Japanese Maitreya Bodhisattva, reflects strong Chinese affinities in the tall coiffure, the corpulent body, and the clinging drapery—all characteristic of late Tang dynasty style.

◆ Altar group, gilt bronze, China, 8th century. Height overall 31.4 cm. Royal Ontario Museum, 958.81a–c.

Maitreya, Buddha of the future, lacquered wood and gold leaf, Japan, Kamakura, 13th century. Height 1.08 m. Royal Ontario Museum, 939.17.30. Bequest of Reuben Wells Leonard. ◆

59

Between the 9th and the 14th century Buddhist savants developed a complex metaphysical system called Tantric Buddhism. The new theory paralleled comparable views in Hinduism. The complexity of the system was reflected in the iconography. The medieval styles of the southern Indian Cola and northern Indian Pala dynasties were instrumental in formulating Tantric Buddhist art in Java and the Himalayan region

• Standing Buddha, bronze, southern India, Nagappattinam, 9th century. Height overall 40.8 cm. Royal Ontario Museum, 957.152.2.

• Buddha, bronze, Java, Srivijaya kingdom, 9th century. Height 30.5 cm. Royal Ontario Museum, 972.82.

• Maitreya, gilt bronze, Nepal, 18th to 19th century. Height 51.9 cm. Royal Ontario Museum, 918.39.3. George Crofts Collection.

60

BYZANTIUM

In 330 Constantine the Great, the first Christian emperor of Rome, dedicated Constantinople, his New Rome, as the capital of the East Roman Empire. Built on the site of the old Greek trading city of Byzantium, Constantinople overlooked the Golden Horn of the Bosphorus, the gateway between Europe and Asia; the new capital was ideally situated both for trade and for defence. Within two centuries it became the most prestigious city in Europe, and for the next millennium it rivalled the great capitals of the world.

By the 6th century the population of Constantinople approached one million. The city's streets were lined with scores of buildings—among them magnificent baths, churches, and imperial palaces aglow with gilded mosaics— and countless shops stocked with all manner of imported goods. In imitation of the splendour and pomp of the Orient, the aristocrats surrounded themselves with lavish trappings. Wealth from land holdings and trade ventures permitted them to enjoy a luxury reminiscent of the most affluent days of Imperial Rome. While the citizens displayed their wealth in rich and ornate dress, the emperors adorned the capital with magnificent monuments.

Constantinople's wealth stemmed from wheat and linen produced in Egypt, silk fabrics woven in Syria of Chinese yarn, and metals mined north of the Black Sea. Before the advent of Islam, the city controlled maritime trade in the Mediterranean and Black seas, and maintained overland trade links with the Orient through Iran. The Byzantine economy was a blend of private enterprise and state-regulated industry, with the state the ultimate arbiter. Factories owned by the government produced most of the goods required by the army, the bureaucracy, and the court. When a black market developed for silks and dyed textiles, which were proscribed to all save the highest officials and members of the imperial family, the emperor simply lowered prices until competition fell away, and then raised them again.

Control of the economy was achieved and maintained only through rigid measures. Not all rulers were successful. Diocletian, for example, had tried to curb soaring inflation in the Mediterranean region with his edict of 301, which specified maximum prices and wages. Like many such measures, however, it was unenforceable. His successors ended the debasing of coinage, regularized taxation, and took other measures to increase confidence in the state.

Imperial control of commerce was absolute. It was only to be expected that the state should regulate imports and exports, but the state also stipulated conditions and hours of work and wages. Linen drapers, for example, were not permitted to sell silk, fishermen had to register their catches, goldsmiths were fined for hoarding gold, and leather workers were forbidden to tan hides. Since goods were sold directly to the consumer, there were no middlemen, and as a consequence, merchants enjoyed no special status.

Each trade guild was assigned to a particular quarter of the city for the conduct

Follis of Diocletian, bronze, obverse with head of Diocletian, Roman, 308–310. Diameter 2.5 cm. Royal Ontario Museum, 964x228.114.

of its business. In the 10th century the prefect of Constantinople, the highest official in the capital, who was in charge of economic affairs, issued *The Book of the Prefect*, a compilation of ordinances governing the trade guilds. The ordinances were thoroughly restrictive, not to say cruel in some instances.

> If a raw-silk dealer is caught travelling to buy silk, he is to be expelled from the guild.
>
> The raw-silk dealers must not sell unworked silk in their homes, but in the market, so that the silk may not be forwarded secretly to those who are forbidden to buy.
>
> The raw-silk dealers are not to have a licence to spin silk, but only to buy and sell it. Whoever transgresses the provision shall be punished by being flogged and shaved.

Strict regulation resulted in a level of quality control that established Byzantium as a leading manufacturer of first-rate goods. From Byzantine workshops came figured silks, jewel-studded reliquaries, and works in gold and enamel that brought the state renown throughout the world — a renown that was enhanced by the visits of magnificently attired Byzantine ambassadors to the courts of western Europe and the Middle East.

What was remarkable about Byzantium was that often political realities were not reflected in the economy. The fact is that the 7th century saw the beginning of Byzantium's territorial decline. Although the empire had survived attacks by Goths, Huns, Vandals, and Sasanians, its territories were steadily reduced. Syria, Palestine, Egypt, and North Africa fell to Islam. The Slavic peoples of the Balkan Peninsula hampered communication between Byzantium and its Italian possessions. By the 8th century piracy in the Mediterranean was once again a major threat to trade, as was the Viking expansion in the north a century later. In the 11th century the expansion of the Normans into Sicily and southern Italy threatened Byzantium's privileged position in Mediterranean trade. And yet as late as the 12th century, Benjamin of Tudela, a widely travelled Jew, observed: "Wealth like that of Constantinople is not to be found in the whole world."

For centuries Byzantium seemed to hover on the brink of disaster. While imperial territorial holdings were being reduced, however, ostentation and extravagance persisted. Until the 11th century Byzantium was the chief emporium of the Christian world. The state's ownership and control of mines, factories, and cultivation and its practice of taxing products sold in its markets enriched the treasury. International confidence in the Byzantine currency was strong.

The real decline came when other trading nations began to build up their economies at Byzantium's expense. After the Norman expansion into Sicily, Byzantium turned to the Venetian navy for help. The state soon found itself awarding trade concessions to Venice and other Italian cities in order to preserve its position. The emergence of the Italians as the dominant traders in the West was reinforced during the Fourth Crusade. Mounted in 1202 with the blessing of Pope Innocent III, the expedition never reached the Holy Land. It was to go by sea in a

Sword of a Crusader, from the arsenal of Constantinople. The Arabic inscription was
added by the Muslim captors. Length of blade 92.5 cm, width 5.8 cm; length of tang 24.8 cm;
length of crossguard 28.5 cm. Royal Ontario Museum, 930.26.45.

Port of Venice, handcoloured woodcut, Michael Wolgemut (1434–1519), Germany, Nuremberg, 1493; in *Weltkronik*, from a leather-bound fragment of the German edition containing 121 of the original 260 leaves. Each leaf 41 cm × 28 cm. Art Gallery of Ontario. Courtesy the American Friends of Canada Committee, Inc.

specially mobilized Venetian fleet that was to be paid for by the Crusaders. When it became clear that the Crusade was unable to meet the costs of transportation, the Venetians agreed to forgo remuneration if the Crusade would capture the Hungarian city of Zara on the Adriatic Sea. While the expedition was in Zara, Alexius Angelus, the son of the deposed Byzantine emperor Isaac II, appeared before the leaders to petition their help in regaining the throne from his uncle. Venice viewed the scheme as an opportunity to establish itself in Constantinople, one of the great commercial centres of the world. The mission was successful and the throne was restored to Alexius, but then he reneged on the payments he had promised. The Crusaders stormed Constantinople and pillaged it, with the result that many of its treasures and relics were dispersed through the towns and cities of Europe. The capital itself, however, survived, even though it now existed in the shadow of a new threat emanating from the presence of the Seljuq Turks, who had entered the Middle East from Central Asia and had conquered Byzantium's territories in Asia Minor in 1071.

The golden age of Tang China . . .

In the 7th and 8th centuries Tang China was remarkably receptive to new people, new thoughts, and new goods. The empire accepted, and often adapted, all manner of objects brought to China by embassies, merchants, and pilgrims from Sasanian Iran, the Mediterranean lands, India, Eastern Turkestan, and Southeast Asia.

Foreigners fascinated the people of Tang China. Among the grave goods interred with nobles to accompany them into the next life are representations of merchants from many lands. Although it is difficult to assign precise origins to the persons depicted, the features are usually those of peoples from regions to the south or the west of China.

Figure of a West Asian wine merchant, three-colour glazed earthenware, China, late 7th to 8th century. Height 36.1 cm. Royal Ontario Museum, 918.21.7. George Crofts Collection.

Caravans of camels bearing exotica to and from Tang China plied the Silk Roads. The cantankerous beasts of burden were endowed with extraordinary endurance. In addition to almost two hundred kilograms of cargo, each camel carried food and drink for the caravaners.

♦ Bactrian camel, straw-coloured glazed earthenware, China, 7th century. Height 38.2 cm. Royal Ontario Museum, 918.21.297. George Crofts Collection.

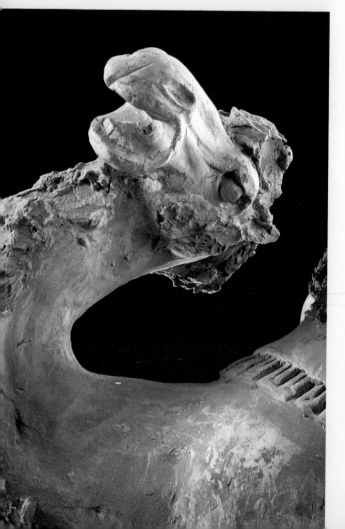

Bactrian camel, earthenware with traces of pigment, China, 7th century. Height 56.5 cm. Royal Ontario Museum, 918.21.193. George Crofts Collection.

These tomb figures reflect the taste of Tang rulers and their nobles, who were the chief recipients of all things foreign. Tang rulers sometimes employed foreign mercenaries, who continued to use their own armour. A Mediterranean origin for the two depicted here is indicated by the lionskin headdress, which is associated with Herakles, and by the gorgoneion on the shield. Attendants from far-off lands—sometimes hired, sometimes purchased as slaves, and sometimes captured in battle—lent colour to Tang festivities.

• Warrior with lionskin helmet, buff earthenware, green glaze, with traces of pigment, China, 7th century. Height 58.7 cm. Royal Ontario Museum, 918.21.371. George Crofts Collection.

Guardian figure, grey earthenware with white slip, China, 7th century. Height 43.8 cm. Royal Ontario Museum, 924.2.10. George Crofts Collection.

Pair of attendants, grey earthenware with traces of pigment, China, 6th to 7th century. Height 41.9 cm. Royal Ontario Museum, 920.1.25–26.

Although the Han had acquired breeding stocks of the magnificent horses from the pasturelands of Ferghana by the 1st century B.C., noble and wealthy Chinese continued to import outstanding animals. In Tang times an imported Ferghana horse cost about forty bolts of silk, but the prestige implicit in ownership of such a fine steed more than compensated for the high price.

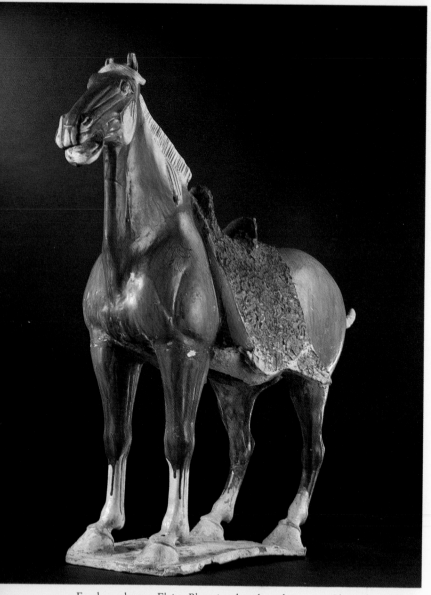

Ferghana horse, yellow, brown, and green glazed earthenware, China, late 7th to 8th century. Height 62 cm. Royal Ontario Museum, 918.21.284. George Crofts Collection.

◆ Ferghana horse, *Flying Phoenix*, glazed earthenware, China, late 7th to 8th century. Height 75.5 cm. Royal Ontario Museum, 918.22.6. George Crofts Collection. Gift of Mrs H. D. Warren.

Ferghana horses were prized for their intelligence, as well as for their fine appearance. The sculptors of the tomb models obviously delighted in capturing the spirit and grace of these superb animals.

Ferghana horse, buff earthenware with traces of pigment, China, 7th to 8th century. Height 67.5 cm. Royal Ontario Museum, 918.21.369. George Crofts Collection. Gift of John Trumbell Warren Band, Jr.

Ferghana horse, dappled glazed earthenware, China, late 7th to 8th century. Height 72.5 cm. Royal Ontario Museum, 918.21.289. George Crofts Collection.

In Tang times merchants from the Middle East reintroduced grape wine and viniculture to China. The wine became an instant vogue. Ewers, cups, and bottles that imitated Western prototypes proliferated. After the fall of the Tang dynasty, however, the Chinese reverted to the traditional rice wine.

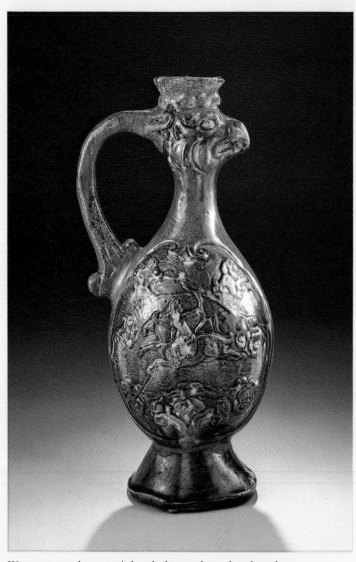

♦ Wine ewer with rooster's head, three-colour glazed earthenware, China, late 7th to 8th century. Height 34.3 cm. Royal Ontario Museum, 910.40.2. Gift of Sir Edmund Walker.

Wine ewer, white glazed porcellaneous stoneware, China, 8th century. Height 23.3 cm. Royal Ontario Museum, 920.71.1. Gift of Mrs H. D. Warren.

Eclectic motifs in the decoration of Tang wine vessels reflect the flow of cultural ideas. The cock's head is common in Persian iconography, although its exact meaning is unknown. The ewer of white stoneware is a simplified version of a silver early Islamic prototype.

The motif of the Bacchic reveller owes its inspiration to the Mediterranean region, although the Tang artist who copied it from a Western prototype may have been unaware of its significance. The Sasanians borrowed the rhyton, or drinking cup, from even earlier traditions and transmitted it to Tang China. Rhytons were made of precious metals as well as of ceramic.

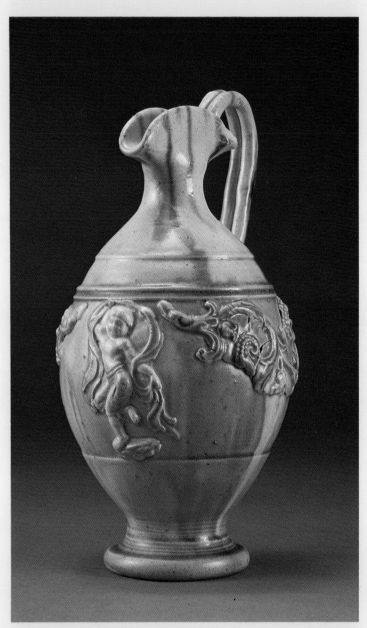

Wine ewer with Bacchic dancer, three-colour glazed pottery, China, late 7th to 8th century. Height 24.15 cm. Royal Ontario Museum, 920.1.83.

Ox-head rhyton, light green glazed earthenware, China, 7th to 8th century. Height 8.8 cm. Royal Ontario Museum, 927.19.7. Bishop White Collection.

When foreign objects that the people of Tang China coveted were unavailable, or in short supply, indigenous artisans reproduced them. Often Western motifs were copied for the sheer pleasure of variety. Textiles, ceramics, wood carvings, metalwares, and jewellery all bear witness to the Tang delight in exotica.

Wine goblet, gilt bronze, China, 7th to 8th century. Height 6.5 cm. Royal Ontario Museum, 950.36.3.

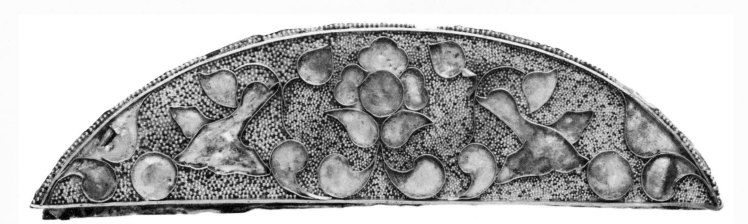

Comb top, gold filigree, China, 8th century. Height 1.9 cm. Royal Ontario Museum, 959.120.1. Anonymous gift.

The birds decorating the comb top are reminiscent of Persian motifs. The gilt work on the silver bowl is in the Sasanian manner. And the wildly dancing figure on the bottle reflects Hellenic Bacchic revels.

Bowl and cover, chased and gilt silver, China, 8th to 9th century. Height 9.8 cm; diameter 24.7 cm. From the Lee of Fareham Collection, on loan to the Royal Ontario Museum from the Massey Foundation. L960.9.129.

Pilgrim bottle, green glazed earthenware, China, 7th to 8th century. Height 12.7 cm. Royal Ontario Museum, 920.20.2. George Crofts Collection.

The opulence reflected by the Tang
court lady is also intrinsic to Chinese
Buddhist art of the Tang Empire. The
devotional Bodhisattva is as sensuous as
the secular representation.

Bodhisattva, grey sandstone, China, 8th
century. Height 69.85 cm. Royal Ontario
Museum, 953.127. Purchased with funds
from the Reuben Wells Leonard Bequest.

Tang court lady, buff earthenware, yellow,
brown, and green glaze, China, 8th century.
Height 30.5 cm. Royal Ontario Museum,
918.21.539. George Crofts Collection.

ISLAM

The phenomenal rise of Islam in the Arabian Peninsula was to have a resounding influence on political, economic, and cultural development throughout the West. What began in Medina in 622 as a modest religious movement predicated on the teachings of the Prophet Muhammad soon developed into a civilization that came to dominate the regions that had comprised Sasanian Iran and Byzantine Syria, Palestine, Egypt, and North Africa. Within a century Islamic conquest extended from the Pyrenees in Spain to the Ferghana Valley on the northwestern borders of China. Both as a political power and as a cultural force, Islam dominated territories more extensive than those of any empire since the time of Alexander the Great. A concomitant of that power was control of trade between East and West.

Although Muhammad could not be succeeded as a prophet, at his death his temporal powers passed to successors called caliphs. The first of these were men who had been closely associated with the prophet and continued to govern Islam according to his dictates. Before long, however, bloody battles were being fought over the rightful claim to succession. In 661 the Umayyad caliphate was established in Damascus; in 750 the Abbasids overthrew the Umayyads and a few years later made Baghdad their capital. A branch of the Umayyads founded an emirate in Spain.

Many of the inhabitants of Arabia, where Islam originally took root, were nomadic Bedouin tribesmen unaccustomed to luxury. Their conquests, however, gave them a taste of cosmopolitan capital cities. In the conquered territories, the Arab invaders became the new aristocracy, heirs to enormous wealth derived from extensive land holdings. In the Syrian countryside the leading Umayyad families

Koran, ink on paper, Iran, 10th century. Each leaf 16.19 cm × 12.07 cm. Royal Ontario Museum, 910.186.1. The Koran, the book of God's revelations to Muhammad, provides Muslims with both a spiritual and a secular guide.

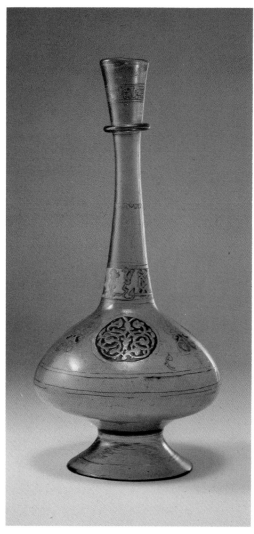

• Bottle, uncoloured blown glass, polychrome enamel, gilt, Syria, late 14th century, said to be from a mosque in China. Height 32.2 cm. Royal Ontario Museum, 924.26.2.

built palaces whose architecture and decorative schemes borrowed ideas from both Byzantine and Sasanian traditions. Extravagance in every form became an integral part of palace life. In the 9th century, Abbasid Baghdad was the marketplace of the world. Luxury goods arrived regularly from the East—by caravan and aboard the ships of the empire. In a 9th-century text by Ibn Khurdadhbih, called *The Book of the Routes and the Kingdoms*, the role of Jewish merchants in the trade of the Muslim world receives special mention: "These merchants speak Arabic, Persian, Roman, Frankish, Spanish, and Slavonic. They travel from the East to the West and from the West to the East by land as well as by sea."

The enormous resources of the lands controlled by Islam were reflected in the splendour of the court. A Byzantine ambassador to the caliph in Baghdad in 917 found an opulence reminiscent of his own imperial court.

The number of curtains which hung in the palaces of the Caliph al-Muqtadir totalled 38,000. These consisted of gold brocade curtains embroidered with gold, and magnificently adorned with representations of goblets, elephants, horses and camels, lions, and birds. The curtains included large drapes of single and variegated colours from Basinna, Armenia, Wasit, and Bahnasa, as well as embroidered drapes from Dabiq. Included in the total of 38,000 curtains were 12,500 brocade curtains embroidered with gold as previously described. There were 22,000 rugs and carpets from Jahram, Darabjird, and Dawraq. They were placed in the corridors and courtyards where the generals and the Ambassadors of the Byzantine Emperor passed. These extended from the new Bab al-Ammah to the very presence of the Caliph al-Muqtadir. However, this total did not include the carpets from Tabaristan and Dabiq in the alcoves and audience halls which were to be seen and not walked upon.

History had, of course, seen earlier extravagant displays of luxury. Before Islam absorbed the Sasanian Empire and large segments of the Byzantine, trade between Mesopotamia and the Mediterranean world largely comprised an exchange of luxury items. Even fine fabrics, rare furs, perfumes, aromatics, spices, gold, and jewels, however, were not the exclusive prerogative of kings and emperors. Aristocrats and wealthy merchants also indulged extravagant tastes, and transcontinental traders encouraged the practice. In the arduous and perilous transport of goods over caravan routes, a kilogram of grain, for example, would have been as costly to carry as one of gems, but what a difference in the profits from the two. Since commercial interests were best served by the highest possible returns on invested capital, bulk goods played little part in the overland trade.

The Islamic conquest, however, radically changed the pattern of trade. Muslim successors of the earlier Iranian and Arabian sailors entered the Indian Ocean trade in increasing numbers. Maritime trade made shipping of bulk commodities feasible and vastly expanded the potential for merchandising. After the middle of the 8th century traders established direct contact between the Abbasid caliphate in Baghdad and the Tang court. Merchant ships made regular voyages down the

View from the Grand Mosque, Zabid, Yemen Arab Republic. In an Islamic city, houses, markets, and mosques are closely interwoven in the neighbourhood fabric.

Persian Gulf to the Indian Ocean and then across it to India, Southeast Asia, and China, traversing the longest and most important sea route of the early medieval period. The voyage from Basra to Guangzhou took eight months, or even longer. Despite the high level of technical achievement in China and India, neither the Chinese nor the Indians were seafarers of this order. International maritime commerce remained largely in the hands of Muslim merchants until the arrival of Europeans in the Indian Ocean eight centuries later.

It is sometimes argued that Islam is really a religion for urbanites, even though it originated in a region peopled mainly by Bedouin nomads. The argument runs that two of Islam's principal doctrines—community prayer on Fridays and alms-giving—are more easily maintained by city dwellers. Although the contention may be only a convenient point of view for scholars, it is true that Islam fostered the growth of cities to an extent unprecedented since the time of Alexander the Great. Merchants were integral to the fabric of society. In Muslim cities, prefects of police and market superintendents who ensured the use of standard weights and measures were among the highest officials. They were also responsible for the maintenance of public morality.

This high degree of civic and commercial organization is particularly significant. From the 9th century on, the main bases of power changed frequently. Egypt was set against Iraq; Morocco and Spain went their own ways; Iran gave rise to her own dynasties. Various zealous religious movements flourished in Arabia and exported their ideas. Through all the political upheavals the cities often survived, mainly because the pattern of city-states developed in the West was not paralleled in the Muslim world. Islam's cities were subordinate to a caliph or a sultan, and were

Old bazaar, Isfahan, Iran. A 16th-century tiled shrine, a coppersmith's shop, and a packsaddle shop exist side by side.

administered by a governor appointed by the head of state. Thus a change of authority was accomplished fairly easily; the rule of the city merely changed hands, in much the same way as ministries change hands today when a government falls. That was one of the reasons that trade was not interrupted when Islamic regimes changed.

The ornate works of art produced in the workshops of the medieval Islamic world and the extravagantly decorated tombs of many of the sultans and their families hardly reflect Muhammad's teachings. The prophet had specifically discouraged the use of gold and silver vessels and had recommended burial in simple, unadorned tombs. And yet the practices of the court were not representative of the way of life of most city dwellers. While a thriving trade in exotic goods existed, the bulk of the trade catered for the needs and wishes of a middle-class consumer society. In a 9th-century treatise entitled *The Investigation of Commerce,* al-Jahiz lists typical imports into Iraq from various countries.

From Armenia: Packsaddles, carpets, and fine mats.
From Oman: Pearls.
From Isfahan: Honey, quinces, salt, saffron, soda, white lead.
From Samarkand: Paper.
From Egypt: Trotting donkeys.
From Yemen: Felts and black hawks.
From India: Rubies, ebony, and coconuts.
From Khorezm: Musk; ermine, marten, and fox furs; and very sweet sugar cane.

78

The extensive conquests of Islam resulted in a wide exchange of cultural ideas. When Islam came face to face with China in the mid-8th century, the West learned for the first time of rag-paper. Chinese paper-makers were taken as prisoners of war to Samarkand in 751. Chinese silk-weavers were brought to Iran, where the climate was found to be suitable for sericulture. Their arrival heralded the beginning of a silk industry in many Iranian cities. A gift of twenty pieces of imperial porcelain from the Chinese emperor to the caliph in the 9th century was to prove of great significance throughout Islam and the West. The porcelain found immediate favour, and potters in the Muslim world were quick to exploit the new market demand for it. Lacking kaolin clay—the essential ingredient for porcelain—they imitated the Chinese luxury wares by putting a white glaze over ordinary earthenware vessels. The imitations were far inferior to fine Chinese porcelain, but they were suitably fashionable in appearance for consumers who either did not have access to porcelain vessels or could not afford them. The apogee of creativity in the production of ceramics in the Muslim world was the period of the Seljuq Turks in Iran in the 11th and 12th centuries. Seljuq artisans adopted the technology of the Chinese and unabashedly exploited every artistic decorative scheme known to them to produce a wide range of ceramic objects.

The political attitudes of the Seljuqs had equally far-reaching implications. In 1055 they overpowered the Abbasid caliphate of Baghdad, although they retained the caliph as titular head of the realm of Islam. The Seljuqs brought new vigour to the Middle East, but they also brought change. It was they who were to obliterate some of the more radical of the religious movements, and it was they who were zealous in promoting orthodoxy by establishing Sunni schools. Christian pilgrims to the Holy Land felt the impact of the change. Their harsh treatment at the hands of the Seljuqs became the excuse—if not the real reason— for the Crusades.

The yellow, brown, and green glazed wares of Tang China were imitated in the Middle East and the West long after the dynasty had been eclipsed. Stemmed dish (foreground), glazed earthenware, China, c. 9th century. Height 6.7 cm, diameter 20.1 cm. Stemmed cup (background left), glazed earthenware, incised, Syria, 13th to 14th century. Height 10.1 cm, diameter 30.1 cm. Stemmed cup (background right), glazed earthenware, incised, Cyprus, 13th century. Height 10.0 cm, diameter 10.4 cm. Royal Ontario Museum, 927.19.101, 908 x 25.47, 962.236.2.

• Bowl with Turkish or Persian prince, quartz compound fabric, lustre painted, Iran, late 13th to 14th century. Height 8.6 cm, diameter 19.6 cm. Royal Ontario Museum, 972.339.

THE CRUSADES

In the 11th century, renewed expansion of Islam under the Seljuq Turks spurred Europe to a counter-movement that by a twist of fate restored the Mediterranean to the pivotal role in world trade that it had ceased to enjoy for several centuries. The early Abbasid caliphs had promised the West that Christian pilgrims would continue to have access to their holy shrines in Palestine. Cooperation between the Christians and Muslims was especially strong when the Fatimids of Egypt gained supremacy in the region. A schism within Islam made the Fatimids the avowed enemies of the Baghdad caliphate of the Abbasids. To foster trade, the Fatimids turned to non-Muslim powers in the eastern Mediterranean. Even when the half-mad Fatimid caliph al-Hakim ordered the destruction of the Church of the Holy Sepulchre in Jerusalem, Muslims contributed generously to the restoration of Christendom's revered shrine. Europe, however, became alarmed.

The alarm grew when the Seljuqs overran Byzantium's territories in Asia Minor and went on to capture Palestine from the Fatimids. Christian pilgrims to the Holy Land began to return to Europe with accounts of oppression and desecration. Simeon, the patriarch of Jerusalem, appealed for help to Pope Urban II, whose ultimate response to the plea was the First Crusade of 1095. The Crusades, which continued intermittently for two centuries, led to Europe's resumption of a major role in the East-West trade.

By the end of the 11th century Islam's possessions in western Europe had begun to repudiate Arab rule, though not Arab culture. Roger de Hauteville of Normandy had taken Sicily from the dynasty of Tunisian Arabs who had seized it from Byzantium in 827. Yet the administration, the art, and the learning of Sicily were still heavily influenced by Islamic traditions. Cultivation of sugar cane, flax, and olives had been introduced, and a silk-weaving establishment existed at the royal court in Palermo.

Roger and his son Roger II, who succeeded him, continued to maintain a court that was more Eastern than Western. In fact, the Norman court of Sicily was instrumental in transmitting Arabic art and learning to the rest of Europe. Among the savants at the court of Roger II, for example, was Idrisi, the most important geographer of the period.

In Spain the flowering of the Muslim occupation in the 9th and 10th centuries completely transformed the culture. Even though many Spaniards kept their Christian faith, they adopted Islam's customs, manners, architecture, and learning. Finally, however, in 1030 the Umayyad caliphate of Spain succumbed to divisive forces and was fragmented into many small kingdoms. Before long, Christian kings were attempting to wrest Spain from the Muslims. In 1085 Toledo was taken, and the drive to expel Muslim rule was under way.

Although Islam had never penetrated beyond southern Italy, the merchants of Genoa, Amalfi, Pisa, and Venice were eager to end Muslim domination of the

Portrait of a Crusader, in *Histoire des chevaliers hospitaliers de S. Jean de Jerusalem*, volume 2, Rene Aubert de Vertot, Paris, 1726. Thomas Fisher Rare Book Library, University of Toronto.

eastern Mediterranean. They foresaw enormous profits from trade with the East, if only they could establish trading outposts in the Levant.

Thus there were many forces at work in Europe, but what attracted most knights and peasants to the Crusades was the acknowledged purpose of securing the Holy Land for Christians. Because both the English king and the German king were under orders of excommunication from the Church, the First Crusade was largely a French enterprise. In fact, the large French presence led the Muslims to label all Europeans *Franks*. The French contingents took an overland route along the Danube to Constantinople; the Normans from Sicily went by sea. From Constantinople the combined armies set off through Asia Minor. After several battles and untold hardships, the First Crusade captured Jerusalem and established the Latin Kingdom. The Muslims retained control of Aleppo, Damascus, and Emesa.

The Second Crusade in 1146 came about because of Muslim encroachment on the Latin Kingdom. Then in 1187 Salah al-Din, the sultan of Egypt known in the West as Saladin, took Jerusalem. The Third Crusade was mounted in 1189, with Richard the Lionheart as one of its leaders. Although Jerusalem was not recaptured, Tyre, Acre, and ports as far south as Jaffa remained in the hands of the Christians, and Saladin agreed to renew the right of access to Jerusalem for Christian pilgrims.

The Fourth Crusade reflects little glory on its leaders. It is noteworthy, however, for the opportunities it afforded the Venetians for commerce in Byzantine territories. There were several subsequent crusades, but Jerusalem was never retaken. In 1291 Acre, the last Christian stronghold in the Holy Land, fell to Muslims, and the great European pilgrimage ended. For a brief period, then, the Crusades established strongholds in the Holy Land, but they were unsuccessful in reclaiming it for Christendom.

The Crusades, however, brought unplanned results, notably the emergence of Europe from the isolation of the preceding centuries and the resumption by the West of a principal role in the East-West trade. Crusaders developed a taste for Eastern goods, and soon European merchants had a thriving market for spices and sugar; satins, velvets, muslins, and damasks; tapestries and carpets; gems; face powders; and scents. The settlements of the Latin Kingdom gave Western merchants a base from which to venture directly into the Eastern trade. Although they were prevented from operating in the Indian Ocean, Italian merchant fleets gained control of the eastern Mediterranean and were effective in increasing Europe's access to the exotic goods of the East. The result was a level of commerce unmatched since the most active days of Imperial Rome.

With expanded commerce came untold other benefits. Traders were vehicles for the acquisition and transmission of Islamic knowledge. The accumulated learning of ancient Greece, Babylonia, and India, which had been lost to Europe for many centuries, began to seep back into the West from the libraries of Islamic universities.

NEW ROUTES TO THE EAST
AND A NEW WORLD

OVERLAND TO ASIA

At the beginning of the 13th century, Europe was still confident that Jerusalem could be regained from the Seljuq Turks. A legend began to circulate about a man named Prester John, who was believed to rule a Christian kingdom somewhere beyond Islam. Europeans reasoned that if they could establish a link with Prester John, perhaps Islam could be outflanked and its powers dissipated. For the next three centuries, the desire for direct contact with the East remained the obsession of both Christian missionaries and European traders.

The Crusades had brought western Europe out of the isolation of the preceding centuries. Merchants were all too keen to capitalize on the growing taste

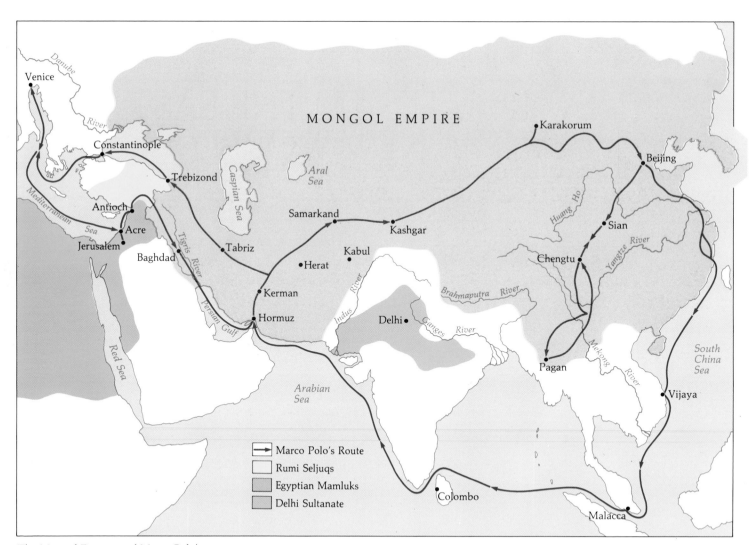

The Mongol Empire and Marco Polo's route.

Map of Africa locating Prester John's kingdom in Ethiopia, engraving, in *Theatrum orbis terrarum*, Abraham Ortelius, Belgium, Antwerp, 1583. Thomas Fisher Rare Book Library, University of Toronto.

for Eastern goods brought back by the Crusaders, but they had little opportunity to engage in direct trade with the East. Islam held a monopoly on the Middle Eastern trade routes — both the land and the sea routes.

It was just at that time that ominous new events occurred. Early in the 13th century Mongol tribesmen began to sweep across Asia. Although they were eventually prevented from penetrating the Mediterranean region by the Muslim Mamluks of Egypt, a northern flank of the armies did advance into Russia and went on to ravage Poland, Romania, and Hungary. Yet, ironically, the onslaught provided another opportunity for Europeans to establish contact with East Asia.

The remarkable rise of the Mongols began in the vast steppes north of the Gobi Desert, where they emerged as the dominant force among the many nomadic tribes of the region. The charismatic new leader took the name Genghis Khan and was proclaimed Great Khan of all the Mongols in 1206; he established his capital in Karakorum. With Mongolia effectively unified, he proceeded to subjugate northwestern China. The sack of Beijing, the Jin capital, in 1215 led to the eventual downfall of that dynasty in 1241. A Mongol army attacked the Muslim forces of Khorezm and successfully laid siege to the trading centres of Bukhara and Samarkand. In the spring of 1221 Genghis Khan began the systematic conquest of Afghanistan and Iran. Wanton violence against the conquered inhabitants soon made the Mongol name synonymous with brutality and destruction.

When Genghis Khan died in 1227, his sons inherited his territories. The third

son, Ogodai, was confirmed as the Great Khan in 1229. It was during his reign that the Mongols launched their second wave of expansion. By 1231 they had overrun Iran; by 1241 they had invaded Russia and advanced into Poland, Hungary, and Romania. Vienna was their next target, but in 1241 Ogodai died and according to custom all Mongol commanders were recalled to Karakorum to participate in the proclamation of the new Great Khan. The interlude, however, was short lived. The new ruler continued to consolidate Mongol control of Asia. The sack of Baghdad in 1258, which brought the end of the Muslim Abbasid caliphate, was followed by the fall of Aleppo and Damascus. The final halt to the onslaught came when the slave-caste armies of the Mamluks made a firm stand in Egypt and turned the Mongol tide.

In East Asia, however, the conquest of China continued. In 1260 Kublai Khan became the paramount leader of the Mongols. It was he who overran the Song territories in South China and brought all of China under Mongol control by 1279. The Mongol Yuan dynasty which he established was to rule China until 1368, when it was replaced by the Ming dynasty. In contrast to the carnage of the preceding decades, the rule of Kublai Khan was civilized. He had a great curiosity about the ways of foreigners and about Christianity; his own mother was a Nestorian Christian, as were many Central Asian tribesmen. With vast stretches of Asia under Mongol control and tolerance shown towards foreigners, Europeans were at last able to venture forth on their quest for direct routes to the East.

Europe had been braced for a Mongol onslaught when the armies returned to Karakorum in 1241. Pope Gregory IX had actually called for a crusade against the Mongols. A few years later Pope Innocent IV resorted to diplomatic measures. In

• Cross-shaped stamps, bronze, China, Nestorian Christian, 11th to 14th century. Lengths 5.7 cm (left), 7.1 cm (top right), 5.0 cm (bottom right). Royal Ontario Museum, 960.243.5, 960.243.2, 960.243.17. James Menzies Collection.

• Friar Rubruquis meeting the Mongol Batu, engraving, in *Voyages faits principalement en Asie dans les XII, XIII, XIV, et XV siecles, par Benjamin de Tudele, Jean du Plan-Carpin, N. Ascelin, Guillaume de Rubruquis, Marc Paul Venitien, Haiton, Jean de Mandeville, et Ambroise Contarini*, Pierre de Bergeron, The Netherlands, The Hague, 1735. Thomas Fisher Rare Book Library, University of Toronto.

1246 he dispatched an overland mission to the court of the Great Khan in Karakorum. Led by Johannes di Plano Carpini, a Franciscan contemporary of Francis of Assisi, the mission followed a route from Germany down the Danube River and then north of the Caspian and Aral seas and east to Karakorum. The response to the pope's embassy was not encouraging, but Carpini's account of the journey helped to revise Western views of the East. The treatise, which encompassed the geography, the climate, the customs, and the religions of the regions traversed, was the first Western work since the time of Strabo and Pliny the Elder to provide a comprehensive description of Asia. A few years later Louis IX of France sponsored another mission, which was led by a Dutch Franciscan monk named William of Rubruquis. Although Carpini and William of Rubruquis failed to obtain treaties with the Mongols, they have the distinction of being the first Westerners recorded to have journeyed as far east as Karakorum. Both mentioned that they saw Western residents in the capital. Some may have been prisoners of war, but others were undoubtedly adventurers and merchants who had wasted little time in taking advantage of the political stability of the region. Since the primary interest of the merchants was trade, they left no written records.

The great adventure of the period, which is dramatically recorded, was undertaken by a Venetian trading family named Polo. The Venetians, who controlled the eastern Mediterranean and the Black Sea, stood to reap particular advantage if they could extend their trade to East Asia. Marco Polo's father and uncle — Niccolò and Maffeo — made a journey to the East and reached the capital of Kublai Khan in 1266. Curiosity about the West prompted the Eastern ruler to send the two men back to Europe with messages for the pope, and a request for one hundred Christian monks. In 1271 Niccolò and Maffeo set out again for the court of Kublai Khan, accompanied by Marco and not one hundred but two monks. For

The caravanserai at Bisitun in Kermanshah province, Iran. All along the Silk Roads, caravans and travellers stopped for rest in the security of caravanserais like this one.

the next seventeen years Marco Polo travelled widely in China—his Cathay—and also in Thailand, Burma, and Sri Lanka. His account of the journeys, entitled *The Description of the World*, became one of the most popular books in the West. He described Beijing as grander than any city in the West, and gave a glowing account of the palace.

> The roof of the palace itself is very high. The walls of the halls and chambers inside are all covered with gold and silver and decorated with pictures of dragons and birds and horsemen and various breeds of beasts and battle scenes. The ceiling is similarly decorated—nothing but gold and pictures everywhere. The hall is so vast and so wide that a meal might be served there for more than six thousand men. The number of chambers is quite bewildering. The whole palace is at once so immense and so well constructed that no one in the world, granted that he had the resources, could imagine any improvement in design or execution. The roof blazes with scarlet and green and blue and yellow and every colour, so brilliantly varnished that it glitters like crystal and the sparkle of it can be seen from far away. And this roof is strong and stoutly built to last for many a year.
>
> In the rear of the palace are extensive apartments, both chambers and halls, in which are kept the private possessions of the Khan. Here is stored his treasure: gold and silver, precious stones and pearls, and his gold and silver vessels. And here too are his ladies and concubines. In these apartments everything is arranged for his comfort and convenience, and outsiders are not admitted.

Renewed trans-Asian contacts also brought one disastrous result—the bubonic plague. News of the dreadful disease sweeping Asia began to reach European port cities in the 1330s. In 1334 the first deaths from the plague were reported in Constantinople. Within twenty years the disease had ravaged Europe and the Mediterranean regions, leaving in its wake populations reduced by more than half and economies in ruins. The origins of the plague can be traced to a region of northern China that was afflicted by famine and other natural disasters, which gave rise to a breed of infected rats. The rats transmitted the highly contagious disease to the fleas that fed on them, and the fleas in turn passed it on to human beings.

In fact, the interlude of European access to East Asia was short. The Mongol rulers of Russia, Central Asia, and China grew further and further apart, both politically and culturally. In 1368 the Chinese overthrew the Mongols, and the new Ming dynasty began to close itself off from the West. Tamerlane, who claimed to be a descendant of Genghis Khan, sought to establish a new Mongolian empire in Central Asia, but that dream ended with his death in 1405. Thus the West seemed once again to be cut off from East Asia, but European curiosity had been aroused and the determination to establish direct trade links with the East inspired exploration for sea routes.

EXPLORATIONS IN THE SOUTH ATLANTIC

Early in the 15th century Prince Henry of Portugal, known as the Navigator, began to sponsor sea voyages of exploration to "the Land of Guinea". The capture of Ceuta, a Moroccan port city opposite Gibraltar, from the Moors in 1415 had led to knowledge of the gold of the western Sahara, the only remaining Old World source of bullion still unexploited by Europeans. Under Henry's sponsorship ships set sail into the Atlantic to search for ways to secure entry into the established Muslim overland trade in gold, ivory, and slaves. The discovery of Madeira and the Canary Islands helped to dispel some of the fears of sailing uncharted seas and to encourage further exploration. Settlement of the islands led to dreams of empire and riches. Sugar cane transplanted from Sicily flourished in the islands and bountiful crops enriched imperial treasuries. The cultivation of sugar cane, which required large work forces, also eventually stimulated a trade in slaves from West Africa.

The fall of Constantinople to the Ottoman Turks in 1453 and their subsequent control of the eastern Mediterranean gave new impetus to the European search for sea routes to the East that would circumvent the Muslim block. In an attempt to retain the lead in maritime exploration in the face of Spanish challenges, Portugal

Johannes Stadius departing from Lisbon, engraving, in *Grands voyages*, volume VII, Théodore de Bry, Germany, Frankfurt, 1590/1624. Royal Ontario Museum, 962.79.7.

obtained a papal bull declaring that the Portuguese had a monopoly of exploration in the seas south of the Canary Islands. In 1483 Diogo Cão sailed south along the east coast of Africa as far as the delta of the Congo River, which he claimed for King John II of Portugal. Four years later Bartolomeu Dias was commissioned to find eastern sources of "gold, precious stones, pepper, cloves, cinnamon, and rhubarb". In a wild storm, Dias's ship was accidentally blown round the southern tip of Africa. His name for the area, Cape of Storms, was later changed by King John to the more auspicious Cape of Good Hope. At the same time Pero Covilhã tried to find a way to the legendary kingdom of Prester John by way of Arabia. He sailed south through the Red Sea, but then instead of turning eastwards touched land at Zanzibar. There he learned from Muslim sailors that it was possible to reach an ocean to the south and west of Africa.

Covilhã's reports inspired more thorough explorations of the Atlantic. Guided by Covilhã's information, Vasco da Gama rounded the Cape of Good Hope in 1497 by sailing far out into the Atlantic to catch the strong westerly winds that would take him clear of the tip of Africa. In Zanzibar, da Gama was granted an audience with the local sultan, who demanded bolts of prized European scarlet — fine woollen fabric produced in northern Europe and widely exported. Vasco da Gama had entered a well-established trade network, but from a different direction. The sultan had been accustomed to have his European woollen fabric arrive from northern routes that led from the Mediterranean through Egypt or Arabia.

The Portuguese soon altered the trade patterns in the Indian Ocean, and also indirectly affected many of the overland routes through the Middle East. While he was in Zanzibar, Vasco da Gama employed an Indian pilot from Gujarat who reintroduced the Europeans to the art they had lost after Roman times of sailing on the monsoon winds across the open sea to India. Without this knowledge, da Gama would probably have continued to hug the African coast and would have ended up in the Red Sea. Vasco da Gama is credited in the West as the first European to reach India by sailing round Africa. The ramifications of this discovery reshaped world trade within the next century.

Ships like banners upon the sea . . .

Early explorers ventured into unknown waters with only theories about
what the world was like to guide them. Innovations in ship design and
navigational instruments came about in response to challenges encountered in
journeying farther afield. Observations made on voyages of discovery brought
practical knowledge, which made more accurate maps possible. So it was that
expansion of sea trade was inextricably linked to the advancement of scientific
knowledge, the mapping of the oceans and the coasts, and the evolution of ships
and navigational instruments.

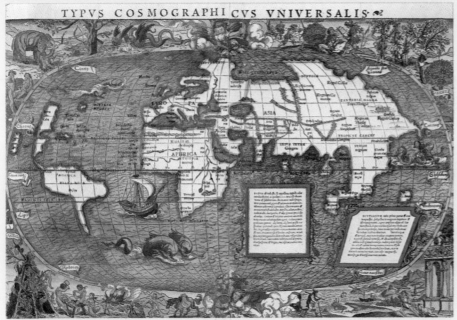

In the age of exploration, map-makers
filled the borders of their maps with
representations of themes that were
associated with the four quarters of the
globe. The border of Sebastian Münster's
map includes a standard representation for
Asia, a pepper tree (top right), and one for
the Americas, a group of cannibals in the act
of dismembering a body (bottom left).

World map ascribed to Sebastian Münster,
engraving, handcoloured, 1532. 55.0 cm × 38.5 cm.
Royal Ontario Museum, 956.186.2.

Detail from Sebastian Münster's world map
of 1532.

Detail from "A New and Accurat Map of the World", coloured engraving, anonymous, 1651. Royal Ontario Museum, 961.146.4.

The globe, a spherical representation of the world, came into vogue in the 16th century, when scientists began to reconcile the theories of the universe propounded by Claudius Ptolemy in the 2nd century with those of their contemporary Copernicus.

The globe from the anonymous map of 1651 identifies the equator, the tropics, the Arctic and Antarctic circles, the north-south meridian, and the ecliptic (the apparent annual path of the sun in the heavens caused by the seasonal variation in its noon-day altitude).

Early geographers, astronomers, and mathematicians knew more about the nature of the earth and its role in the universe than they did about the precise outlines of the lands and the seas. Their theories were not translated into practical guides for navigation until the 16th century.

Eratosthenes, a Greek geographer who became head of the library in Alexandria in 240 B.C., was a pioneer in map-making. He is credited with calculating the size of the earth and the distance from earth to sun and earth to moon. The partitions of his world map were the forerunners of coordinates of latitude and longitude. Eratosthenes' map identifies three continents—Europa, Libya (Africa), and Asia, which ends abruptly at India on the east.

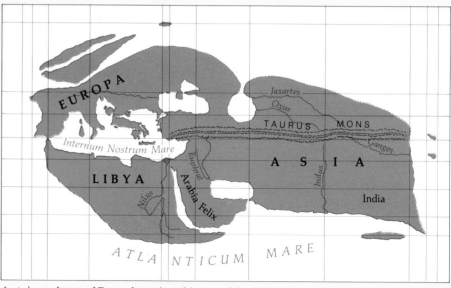

Artist's rendition of Eratosthenes' world map of the 3rd century B.C.

The work of Eratosthenes may have represented a scientific breakthrough, but his view of the world was far from accurate, and his map was of little use to the voyager. There were maps being drawn a few centuries later, however, that met the practical requirements of land travellers. They were schematic road maps, something like a modern route map for a public transportation system. Although distances were deliberately foreshortened so that the map would be of a convenient size for carrying, towns were clearly labelled. Merchants and military men travelling along the road could gauge what lay ahead.

The section of a road map illustrated here is a reproduction of a 13th-century copy of a 3rd-century Roman road map, which encompassed the world from Britain to Asia, and was drawn on a papyrus roll approximately seven metres long. Like Eratosthenes' world map, the Roman map stopped short at India on the east—at the point where the Ganges and Araxes rivers are shown entering the ocean. The 13th-century copy is known as the *Peutinger Table*; it was bequeathed to Konrad Peutinger, a German antiquarian, in the 16th century and is now in the National Library in Vienna.

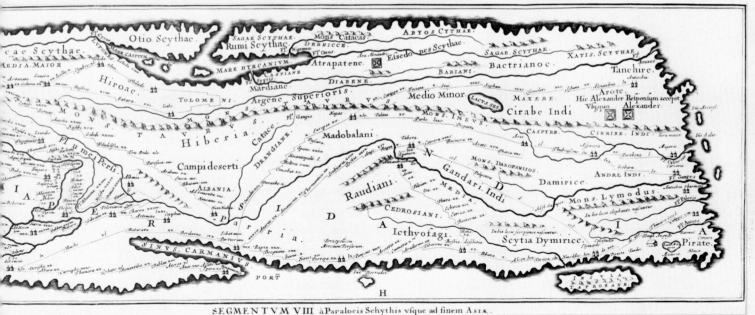

Asian section of road map, engraving, in *Histoire des grands chemins de l'empire romain*, Nicolas Bergier, Belgium, Brussels, 1736. Thomas Fisher Rare Book Library, University of Toronto.

The last significant contribution to geographic learning in classical times was the work of Claudius Ptolemy, a Graeco-Egyptian mathematician, astronomer, and geographer who practised in Alexandria in the 2nd century. Ptolemy formalized Eratosthenes' arbitrary system of coordinates of latitude and longitude.

Knowledge contained in Ptolemy's treatise *Geographia* had a profound effect on western Europe in the 15th century, when manuscript copies of the work found their way out of Constantinople during the flight of the city's inhabitants before the invasion of the Ottoman Turks in 1453. The rediscovery of the *Geographia* contributed to a phenomenal rebirth of map-making in the 16th century, as did the great voyages of discovery that extended the horizons of the known world, and the invention of printing and engraving (up to that time maps had been jealously guarded manuscripts).

Although this world map of 1541 was based on Ptolemy's world map, it reflects the more specific knowledge of the extent of Africa that was generated by the explorations of the Portuguese.

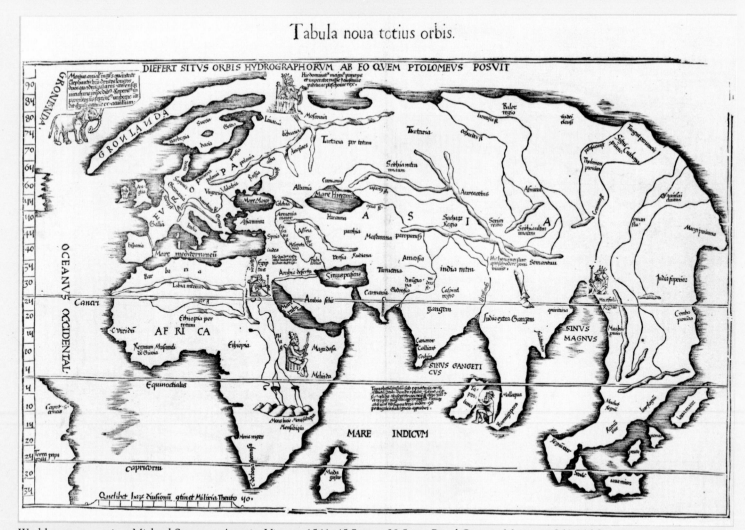

Tabula noua totius orbis.

◆ World map, engraving, Michael Servetus, Austria, Vienna, 1541. 45.7 cm × 28.5 cm. Royal Ontario Museum, 961.146.2.

94

In the late 16th century the most renowned cartographer of all time, Gerhardus Mercator, used the ancient image of Atlas supporting the globe as the frontispiece for his book of maps. Other map-makers followed his lead, and before long *atlas* was the standard term for a printed and bound collection of maps.

In 1538 Mercator published a map that identified North and South America. The name *America* had been coined in 1507 by the map-maker Martin Waldseemüller, after Amerigo Vespucci had noted in a letter that he had just visited *Terra Nova*, a New World.

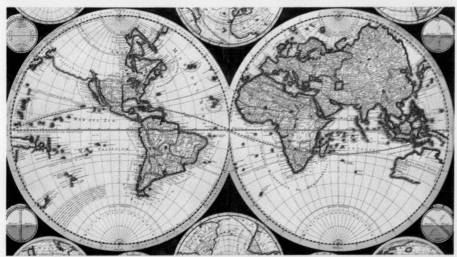

* Double hemisphere, detail from world map *Planisphaerium terrestre*, engraving, Carel Allard, The Netherlands, Amsterdam, 1706. Entire map 59.9 cm × 51.8 cm. Royal Ontario Museum, 960.223.2.

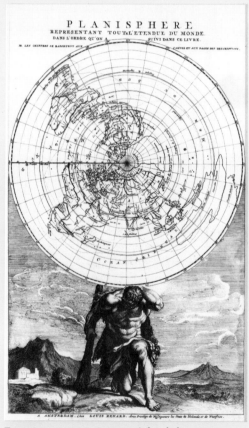

Frontispiece, engraving, in *Atlas de la navigation*, Louis Renard, The Netherlands, Amsterdam, 1739. 42.2 cm × 26.4 cm. Royal Ontario Museum, 961.18.1.

Knowledge of winds was vital to navigation. By the 14th century the wind-rose, a map symbol indicating the strength and frequency of winds from various directions in a given locality, was sometimes shown with as many as thirty-two directional points.

The personification of twelve winds on Sebastian Münster's world map of 1540 underscores their importance.

World map, engraving, Sebastian Münster, Switzerland, Basel, 1540. 34.5 cm × 25.9 cm. Royal Ontario Museum, 961.146.1.

Towards the end of the 13th century there appeared a type of harbour chart called a portolan map, which was the most practical existing chart for mariners. Characterized by networks of rhumb lines radiating from wind-roses, the portolan enabled navigators of trading vessels to determine what winds and bearings were needed to sail from port to port. Although the coastlines of portolans are dotted with place names, the interiors of the continents are largely devoid of detail. Portolan maps proliferated in the 14th and 15th centuries, and were still being used in the 17th century.

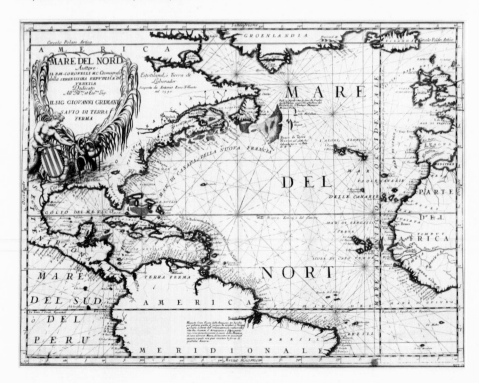

Portolan map of the Atlantic, engraving, Vincenzo Coronelli, Italy, Venice, 1695. 61.1 cm × 45.6 cm. Royal Ontario Museum, 957.192.1.

Monstra marina & terrestria, quæ passim in partibus aquilonis inueniuntur.

◆ Engraving, Sebastian Münster, 1550. 31.0 cm × 49.5 cm. Royal Ontario Museum, 958.209.7.

In spite of the advances that had been made, sea voyages in the 16th century involved very real hazards. What is more, people—even those in the scientific community—had little doubt that the remote regions of the world were filled with extraordinary creatures. Sailors encouraged these ideas with their tales of monsters encountered on the high seas.

Although labels give them the semblance of scientific verity, the fanciful creatures are all (except the lobster) creations of a 16th-century artist's imagination.

The atlas published by Abraham Ortelius carried a foreword by Gerhardus Mercator, and its maps incorporated the latest geographical information. Nonetheless, the old fears of the unknown are reflected even in this revolutionary work of science.

Detail from a map, engraving, in the atlas *Theatrum orbis terrarum*, Abraham Ortelius, Belgium, Antwerp, 1583. Thomas Fisher Rare Book Library, University of Toronto.

Because navigational instruments were still very primitive in the 16th century, explorers often owed their success to earlier experience of sailing—and sometimes to sheer luck. Familiarity with the stars was the first essential for a navigator. Difficulty arose when his ship left known waters and he was faced with differences in the relative positions of the stars. In the tropics the sun was too high in the sky to permit useful readings, and in the Southern Hemisphere the polestar, the preferred reference point of Arabian navigators, was either invisible or too close to the horizon. It was the Portuguese who discovered that the Southern Cross provided an adequate substitute for the polestar. In any case, an essential part of any exploration was the recording of observations, which would facilitate the repetition of the voyage.

  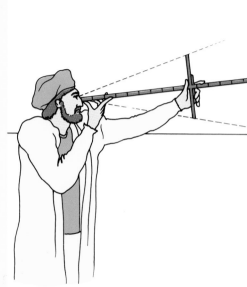

The astrolabe, an instrument used for calculating the altitude of a heavenly body, was an invention of Greek astronomers— later perfected by Persian and Arabian astronomers. Mariners used a simplified version that permitted them to take readings on a pitching deck. By measuring the angle of the polestar or the sun above the horizon, they were able to calculate the ship's latitude.

The *kamal* was a primitive Middle Eastern instrument used for the same purpose. It consisted of a plate and a string with knots in it. Each knot represented the latitude of a specific port. When a navigator took a reading at the latitude of the port, the bottom of the plate coincided with the horizon, and the top with the star. If the coincidence was impossible to achieve, the navigator knew that the ship had to sail either north or south.

With the cross-staff, which was being used early in the 15th century, readings were easier. The sliding cross had a hole at the top and another at the bottom. The navigator moved the cross back and forth until he could sight the heavenly body in the upper hole and the horizon in the lower one simultaneously. The altitude could then be read on a scale marked on the staff.

The Chinese junk was developed for trade in the South China Sea, where typhoons are frequent and violent. Separate bulkheads in the hull made the ship extraordinarily strong. Lug sails were stiffened with horizontal bamboo battens so that they could be trimmed easily in rough weather. The stern rudder, which could be raised or lowered by a windlass, permitted a sea-going junk to operate in shallow waters. In the 13th century junks were thirty metres long and according to Marco Polo had as many as four masts. Although no archaeological or literary evidence exists for the form of junks before about the 12th century, the design is believed to be quite ancient. The Chinese were content with a vessel that worked well for them and made no subsequent innovations.

With cargoes of grain and oil stored in pottery jars, the Roman merchantman plied the Mediterranean at slow but steady speeds. It was essentially a heavy barge under sail that replaced the earlier oared galleys. A three-master carried a cargo weighing between one hundred and two hundred tons. The strength of the vessel came not from ribs but from an exterior shell of planks joined together by mortises and tenons—a laborious and costly construction. The curve of the hull from stem to stern gave the ship a double-ended profile, except when an ornament such as a swan's head was added to the stern. The vessel was steered by a pair of side oars at the stern quarter.

Constellation Orion, miniature painting in a 16th-century Persian treatise on astronomy. 15 cm × 10 cm. Royal Ontario Museum, 970.268.3.

Artist's rendition of a Chinese junk.

Artist's rendition of a Roman merchantman.

Dhow is the general term for a whole range of craft used by Arabian, Persian, and East African sailors. The distinctive characteristic of most dhows was the triangular lateen sail, which was carried by a huge main yardarm, often as long as the vessel itself. The yardarm was made of several beams lashed together and supported by a massive main mast, which was raked forward to allow the yardarm to swing freely and the sail to billow out when the ship was running before the wind. Rope-sewn planks gave the vessel great resilience, so that it could be beached without damage. After the 16th century a square stern was introduced, under the influence of European shipyards in India.

Caravels carried the Portuguese on their first voyages of discovery along the Atlantic coast of Africa. The lateen sail, which was introduced to the Mediterranean in the 7th or the 8th century, allowed the caravel to sail in variable winds. About the 12th century the stern rudder was adopted from northern Europe, where it had proved to be more effective than side steering oars in rough seas. When the ship rocked, the rudder stayed in the water. Two of Columbus's ships on his voyage of 1492 — the *Nina* and the *Pinta* — were caravels.

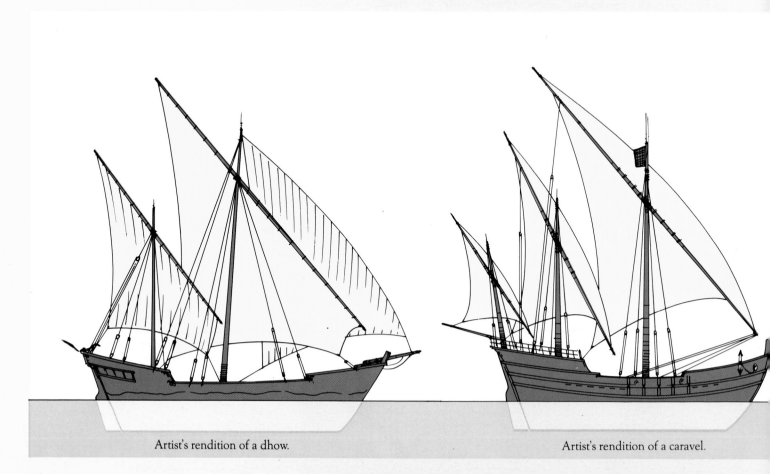

Artist's rendition of a dhow.

Artist's rendition of a caravel.

In addition to the usual high stern, the carrack had an exaggerated forecastle set over the bow. The vessel, which carried a large mainsail for running before the trade winds, was designed for strength and stability on long voyages. The carrack was the standard European merchant vessel of the 15th and 16th centuries. Columbus's *Santa Maria* was a carrack.

As European countries vied for supremacy on the seas, many of their carracks were fitted out with cannons, since the ships had to double as men-of-war. Manoeuvrable galleons eventually took on the fighting role, and the trade vessel developed into what was called the East Indiaman.

The problem of reading the angle between the horizon and a heavenly body was eased by the use of reflecting mirrors. John Hadley's octant, invented in 1732, made more precise observations possible. The mechanics of the instrument involved two mirrors. The sun was reflected by the first mirror onto the second, through which the horizon could be sighted at the same time. When the reflected images converged, a moving arm gave the reading of the angle.

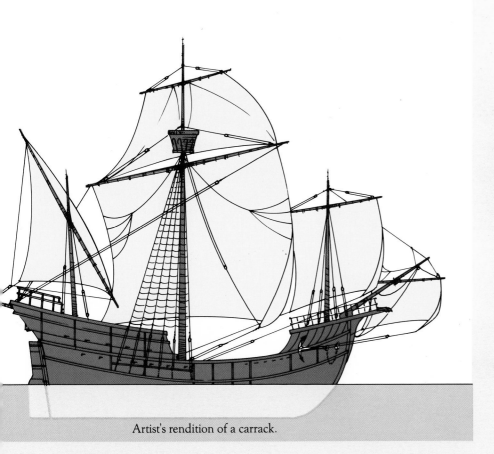

Artist's rendition of a carrack.

Designed for the long China run and rigged for speed, the clipper was capable of covering 500 kilometres a day. The first true clippers, developed in the 1840s, measured 70 metres in length and rated 750 tons. The *Great Republic*, the largest American clipper ever built, was registered at 4550 tons.

Dismayed by the loss of the monopoly of the tea trade, the British developed their own clipper in 1850. Although the British clipper was smaller than the American, it was made of better-cured timber and consequently performed better in rough seas. British clippers thus met the challenge of the American vessels, until sailing ships began to give way to steam-powered vessels.

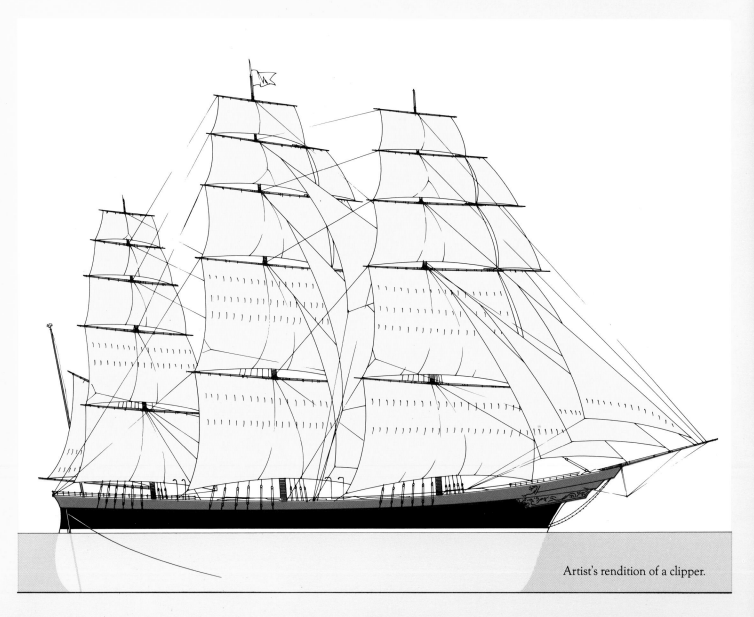

Artist's rendition of a clipper.

A NEW WORLD

Towards the end of the 15th century the growing rivalry between Portugal and Spain received an added fillip when a Genoese sailor now known as Christopher Columbus took his "Enterprise of the Indies" to King Ferdinand V and Queen Isabella. Their marriage in 1469 had united the kingdoms of Aragón and Castile, and they then devoted their energies to expelling the last of the Muslims from Spain.

After eight years of supplication, Columbus, who firmly believed that he could reach India by sailing west, was granted a subsidy by Ferdinand and Isabella to cross the western ocean to Cipangu (Marco Polo's Japan) and bring back cargoes of pearls, precious stones, gold, silver, and spices. He also managed to secure from the monarchs a guarantee in writing that he would receive ten per cent of the value of

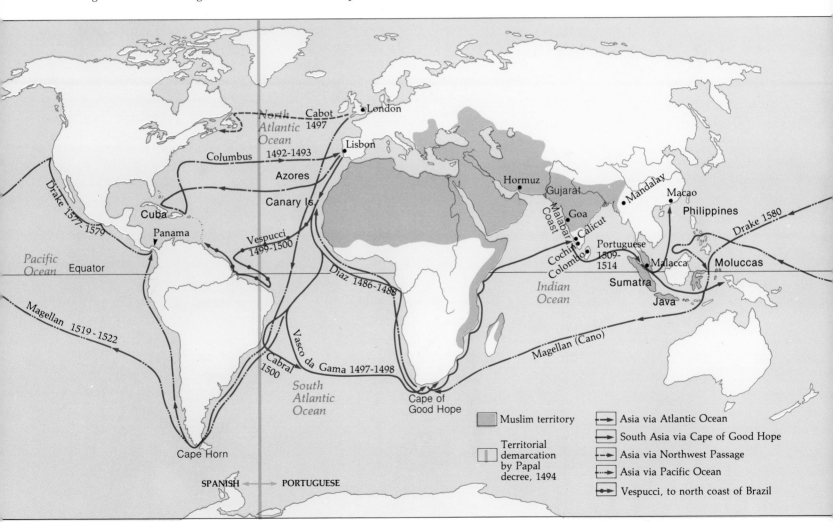

Voyages of discovery prompted by the Western desire to circumvent the Muslim blockade of access to East Asia by overland routes.

the goods he brought back. The landmark date of 1492, the year in which Columbus sailed, was also celebrated in Spain for the downfall of the last Muslim principality, when the fortress of the Alhambra in Granada fell to Ferdinand and Isabella.

Columbus was right, of course, about lands to the west, but they were not the lands he dreamed of. Many contemporary geographers had begun to accept the view that the world was spherical. Columbus's beliefs stemmed from the sailing knowledge he had gained during his years as a sugar buyer in the Portuguese islands off the coast of Africa. He had seen tell-tale signs of other lands, such as large tree trunks floating in the South Atlantic. His real inspiration, however, came from the apocalyptical book of Esdras, in which it is stated that the earth is round and consists of six parts of dry land and one part of sea. With the words of Esdras as a guide, and using an erroneous measurement for a degree of longitude, Columbus calculated that Asia would be located just about where in the end he discovered America. Columbus had seriously miscalculated the circumference of the globe, but until his death he remained convinced that when he reached the Bahamas and claimed them for Spain he had sailed round the world to the East.

Columbus's apparent success in discovering a new route to the East intensified the rivalry between Spain and Portugal for empire and trade monopolies. Now Spain secured a papal bull, which granted her territorial rights west of a line of demarcation set about five hundred kilometres west of the Azores. In 1494, after some dispute, Spain and Portugal signed the Treaty of Tordesillas, which gave Portugal claim to Africa and India, and Spain claim to the New World, although the new north-south line of demarcation also gave Portugal claim to the eastern portion of Brazil. While the treaty was intended to settle rights of sovereignty over

Padrones column, engraving, in *Grands voyages*, volume II, Théodore de Bry, Germany, Frankfurt, 1590/1624. Royal Ontario Museum, 962.79.2.

the world's resources, it also ensured the universality of the Roman Catholic Church. Although commercial aims often overwhelmed missionary goals, Catholic principles and the desire to convert nonbelievers initially guided and encouraged Spanish and Portuguese exploration. The climate was to change, of course, with the Reformation in the 16th century.

As discoveries of new lands proliferated, other nations entered the race. In 1496 an Italian explorer known as John Cabot persuaded Henry VII of England to authorize a voyage across the North Atlantic. Cabot sailed from Bristol in 1497 and reached Newfoundland and Nova Scotia. Like Columbus, he firmly believed that he had sailed round the world and reached the East.

Spain's hopes of reaching Cathay by sailing westwards were dashed, however, when Vasco Núñez de Balboa crossed the Isthmus of Panama only to discover the Pacific Ocean in his path. He claimed the Pacific and all the shores washed by it for Spain, though the economic potential of the New World was not recognized until some decades later. It was the desire for commerce with the East that was the driving force behind voyages of discovery in the early 16th century.

Portugal, which had an advantage in the monopoly of the South Atlantic and the route round the Cape of Good Hope, was able to buy navigational information from opportunist traders in the Indian Ocean and quickly established a trading network. First Portugal set up fortified bases on the coast of Africa, where ships could be repaired and take on food and fresh water. The next step was to acquire trading stations near major ports on the Asian coastline. For the most part, these were taken by force of arms and remained manned by an armed contingent. In 1507 a Portuguese commander named Afonso d'Albuquerque seized the island of Hormuz at the entrance to the Persian Gulf. The island provided a base from which to expand into the Indian Ocean and also access to the goods moving along the Middle Eastern trade routes to Syria and Turkey. Portuguese control brought untold wealth to the island, whose glory was celebrated in poetry: "If the whole world were a ring, Ormuz [sic] would be a gem in it." In 1510 the Portuguese took Goa, on the west coast of India, and thereby ensured a supply of Indian cotton and silk textiles for trade in Southeast Asia. The rapid territorial conquests of the Portuguese were crowned when in 1511 Albuquerque captured Malacca on the west coast of the Malay Peninsula; Malacca was to become a major entrepôt for the East Indies and China trade.

And still Portuguese triumphs continued. In 1526 Babur, a descendant of Tamerlane who had established a kingdom in Afghanistan, launched an invasion of India. Having occupied Delhi and Agra, Babur founded the Muslim Mughal Empire of northern India. Western powers were now obliged to negotiate with the court at Agra for permission to trade along the coast of India. Impressed by the prowess of Portuguese ships on the high seas, the Mughals in the 1530s granted Portugal trading rights in Bengal. By the 1540s Portugal had developed a trading network with Thailand, Burma, and Cambodia, and had entered the East China Sea to trade with Japan.

In the 16th century the power of the Ming dynasty, which had given China more than two centuries of orderly government and social stability, was declining. In the early years of the dynasty China had undertaken several seafaring expeditions to Southeast Asia, Sri Lanka, and East Africa, but by the middle of the 15th century the voyages had ceased. Ming China returned to a traditional pattern of land-centred self-sufficiency. Trade with outside powers continued, but Ming China preferred to regard it as tribute from other states. In spite of the proscriptions of the Ming court, however, private vessels commanded by Chinese, Japanese, and Malaysian merchants continued to conduct a brisk trade throughout Southeast Asia.

When Portuguese merchants reached the coast of southern China in 1517, they were received with little enthusiasm. Their undisciplined behaviour confirmed the Chinese stereotype of foreign merchants as barbarians. Portuguese persistence and naval superiority prevailed, however, and Portugal was permitted to build a trading station at Macao near the port city of Guangzhou in 1557. The trading stations at Goa and Macao became major entrepôts in the Portuguese trade with Asia. From these centres crown-appointed governors controlled the commerce that made Portugal into a strong, rich empire.

New discoveries and the details of their achievement remained matters of national security. The Portuguese *portolani* maps, which listed sequences of landfalls and the intervals between them, were jealously guarded, as were the maps and charts acquired in foreign waters. Acquisition of a Javanese chart of the East Indies, for example, led Portuguese ships to Taiwan and the port of Guangzhou. Sometimes data were deliberately misrecorded, for fear that other nations would profit from the information. Portugal, in fact, charted the Moluccas with a discrepancy of six degrees, so that the islands would be in no danger of falling beyond the territory allotted to her in the Treaty of Tordesillas.

Spain's hopes for sea routes to the Asian trade were revived when Ferdinand Magellan devised a plan to sail round South America. Unable to persuade his native court in Portugal to accept the plan, he took it to King Charles I of Spain,

Curios and natural specimens brought back to
Europe by adventurers were mounted in precious
metals to grace noble homes.

Left: Altar ornament, quartz crystal with gilt-silver ♦
mount, Italy, late 16th to 17th century. Height
16.5 cm. Royal Ontario Museum, 927.10.4.

Middle: Cup, coconut shell with gilt-copper
("latten") mounts, The Netherlands, Flanders, or ♦
England, 1612. Height 20.2 cm. Royal Ontario
Museum, 925.23.19.

Right: Cup, nautilus shell with gilt-silver mounts, ♦
Germany, Augsburg, Daniel Müller or Daniel
Michael, c. 1600 to 1630. Height 33.7 cm. Royal
Ontario Museum, 922.19.11.

- Map with portraits of the explorers Columbus, Vespucci, Magellan, and Pizarro, engraving, handcoloured, Théodore de Bry, Germany, Frankfurt, 1596. 32.5 cm × 39.0 cm. Royal Ontario Museum, 956.186.6. The map shows what was believed to be a vast unexplored continent, Terra Australis Magallanica.

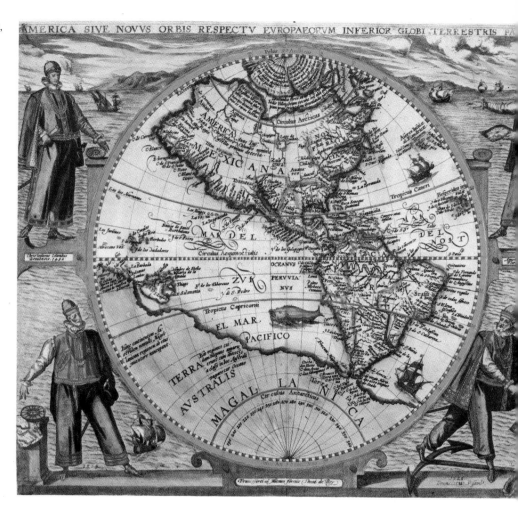

who commissioned Magellan to sail west "for the discovery of spicery". On 21 October 1520 Magellan sighted and entered the strait that bears his name. More than a month later he reached the Pacific and made a perilous crossing to the Philippines. Although Magellan himself was killed in the Philippines in 1521, one of his five vessels returned to Cádiz with a cargo of cloves, whose sale paid the costs of the entire expedition. In Manila and the Moluccas, Spain established bases that were linked to Europe by way of the Pacific Ocean and Spain's possessions in Peru and Mexico. In Mexico goods arrived by ship at the harbour of Acapulco and were transported overland to the port of Veracruz, where they were reloaded into vessels bound for Spain.

With easy access to the East via the Cape of Good Hope, Portugal continued to control the bulk of the European spice trade. And Portugal took advantage of her Indian Ocean network to thwart attempts by other powers to gain trade concessions with China, although many private Japanese and Chinese merchants supplied goods picked up in Guangzhou to the Spanish in Manila, and after 1624 to the Dutch in Taiwan.

Columbus discovering America, engraving, in *Grands voyages*, volume IV, Théodore de Bry, Germany, Frankfurt, 1590/1624. Royal Ontario Museum, 962.79.4.

At one point in the 1580s Spain actually considered an invasion of China to break the Portuguese trade monopoly. First, however, Spain had to deal with England's sea power, which was becoming a menace. In 1572 Francis Drake made the first of his marauding expeditions against Spanish possessions. In 1577 he set out again, with five ships, to raid Spanish holdings on the Pacific Coast of the New World. In his *Golden Hind*, Drake sailed through the Straits of Magellan and then set off northwards along the coast of South America. He plundered Valparaíso and captured a rich Spanish treasure ship. Using Spanish sea charts, which he had also confiscated, Drake sailed north to San Francisco, which he named New Albion and claimed for Queen Elizabeth I. He then crossed the Pacific to the Moluccas, the Celebes, and Java, and returned to England by way of the Cape of Good Hope.

Queen Elizabeth I tried at first to appease the Spanish ire, but in 1588 King Philip II launched his one-hundred-vessel-strong "Invincible" Armada. Drake, now Sir Francis Drake, commanded the English fleet assembled in response, which was augmented by tens of trading and fishing vessels. The forces met in the English Channel. The English had an advantage in the manoeuvrability of their smaller ships, and, a storm also worked against the Spanish. The defeat of the Spanish Armada halted Spain's dreams of dominance in New World and Asian trade.

THE RISE OF TRADING COMPANIES AND COLONIES

WINDS OF CHANGE

When Martin Luther posted his historic articles on the door of the church in Wittenberg in 1517, he was calling for debate on practices and doctrines of the Roman Catholic Church that he felt were inimical to true spirituality. His action, however, sparked a full-scale revolution against the worldly power of the Church in Rome. Before the movement known as the Reformation ended, Protestantism was established and Europe was fragmented into bitterly opposed religious camps.

In the 1530s Henry VIII of England repudiated the authority of the pope and made himself head of the Church of England. Parliament decreed that allegiance to the pope was treasonable, and church lands were confiscated. In the Scandinavian countries, too, the monarchs welcomed the opportunity to end the interference of the Church in matters of state, and Protestantism was established with little struggle. In Germany, where Martin Luther had provoked the revolt, the issue was not fully resolved until the end of the Thirty Years' War a century later. The desire for religious freedom helped to unite the people of the Netherlands in their determination to be free of the domination of Spain. Independence for the northern provinces also came with the treaty that ended the Thirty Years' War.

The response of the Roman Catholic Church—known as the Counter Reformation—stemmed the tide of Protestantism in Portugal, Spain, Italy, Sicily, Hungary, Austria, Bohemia, and Poland. Internal reform of the Church, educational programmes of the newly founded Society of Jesus (Jesuits), and suppression through the Inquisition were all instrumental in halting the spread of Protestantism in those countries.

At the roots of the Reformation were the social, economic, and political realities of an outdated medieval order derived from the Holy Roman Empire, and the indisputable authority of the Church in Rome. The rise of cities and the revival of classical learning, which were characteristic of the Renaissance, unleashed new social ideas and aspirations that created powerful economic and political forces. Nations were forged where before there had been petty kingdoms with constantly changing boundaries. This spirit of nationhood gave rise to a climate of independence that transformed Europe and its interaction with the rest of the world.

Throughout the 16th century the Portuguese monopoly of the Asian spice trade remained the dominant influence on European markets. Until 1580 Dutch merchants handled most of the spice trade with northern Europe; they collected supplies at the port of Lisbon and resold them through the port of Antwerp. When Spain annexed Portugal in 1580, Dutch merchants were no longer welcome in Lisbon. The cost of spices in Amsterdam and London rose sharply, since the two cities were reduced to limited supplies, which had to be trans-shipped from other ports. Private Dutch merchants responded by outfitting their own fleet, which in 1595 sailed south into the Atlantic and round the Cape of Good Hope to try to establish direct dealings with the spice merchants of the East Indies. The success of the enterprise—the ships returned to the Netherlands with large cargoes of spices

Rug, polychrome knotted wool pile, Turkey, late 17th century. 214.5 cm × 173.0 cm. Royal Ontario Museum, 979.280. Gift of Mrs John Alexander Wilson in memory of Dr Veronika Gervers.

and other merchandise – demonstrated the vulnerability of Portugal's rights in the South Atlantic and of her monopoly of the spice trade. Ports in northern Europe – London, Amsterdam, Copenhagen, and Stockholm – soon became important centres of trade and commerce.

Throughout the latter half of the 16th century, English privateers, licensed by the crown, harassed the Atlantic sea lanes. They disrupted Spanish and Portuguese trade with the Americas and with Asia, and spread religious dispute into the world of commerce. England's first attempts to establish direct trade with the East Indies, however, were less successful, even though Francis Drake had reached the spice islands in 1579. Nonetheless, direct trade with the East continued to be the goal not only of England but of other European trading nations. The ambition was fuelled by accounts of the astonishing riches of the East, such as Richard Hakluyt's description of the cargo of the *Madre de Dios*, which was captured by the English off the Azores in 1592.

Armada medal, obverse with Elizabeth I, bronze, England, 1589, possibly designed by Nicholas Hilliard. Height 4.7 cm, width 4.3 cm. Royal Ontario Museum, 930.8. Gift of Mr H. R. Jackman.

> . . . the principall wares after the jewels (which were no doubt of great value, though they never came to light) consisted of spices, drugges, silks, calicos, quilts, carpets and colours &c. The spices were pepper, cloves, maces, nutmegs, cinamom, greene ginger; the drugs were benjamim, frankincense, galingale, mirabolans, aloes, zocotrina, camphire; the silks damasks, taffatas, sarcenets, altobassos, that is, counterfeit cloth of gold, unwrought China silke, sleaved silke, white twisted silke, curled cypresse. The calicos were book-calicos, calico-launes, broad white calicos, fine starched calicos, course white calicos, browne broad calicos, browne course calicos. There were also canopies, and course diaper-towels, quilts of course sarcenet and of calico, carpets like those of Turky; whereunto are to be added the pearle, muske, civet and amber-griece. The rest of the wares were many in number, but lesse in value: as elephants teeth, porcellan vessels of China, coco-nuts, hides, ebenwood as blacke as jet, bedsteds of the same, cloth of the rindes of trees very strange for the matter, and artificiall in workemanship. All which piles of commodities . . . amounted to no lesse then 150000 li. sterling which being divided among the adventurers (whereof her Majesty was the chiefe) was sufficient to yeeld contentment to all parties.

Little wonder that by the time these goods reached England, there was considerable perplexity about the ultimate origins of many of them.

Visions of Cathay ...

The Western predilection for exotic imported goods helped to perpetuate an illusory vision of East Asia—Marco Polo's Cathay—as a mythical land of fabulous riches and luxury, where a gentle people whiled away pleasant hours in delicate pavilions set in an ethereal landscape. This fantastic vision of Cathay found expression in European decorative schemes. Western craftsmen, prompted frequently by the scarcity or prohibitive cost of oriental imports, indulged the popular China taste with their chinoiseries—objects that imitated the exotic Eastern ones, often in an exaggerated way, or that evoked the mystery and opulence of the imagined Cathay. Initially most Europeans were unable to differentiate between what was Chinese and what was Indian, Japanese, Southeast Asian, or even Middle Eastern, so that the vision combined many elements, none of which reflected a geographic reality.

Of late, 'tis true, quite sick of Rome and Greece
We fetch our models from the wise Chinese;
European artists are too cool and chaste,
For Mand'rin is the only man of taste ...
On ev'ry shelf a Joss divinely stares,
Nymphs laid on chintzes sprawl upon our chairs;
While o'er our cabinets Confucius nods,
Midst porcelain elephants and China gods.

Of Taste, James Cawthorn, 1756

The fanciful adaptation of a classic Chinese porcelain design depicting a boy on a buffalo reflects the informal, asymmetrical patterns favoured by Western decorators of chinoiserie.

◆ Plate, porcelain (bone), overglaze polychrome enamel, England, c. 1805, probably Miles Mason. Diameter 21.9 cm. Royal Ontario Museum, 936.8.2.

115

◆ Copperplate-printed linen and cotton tabby, blue design, England, Middlesex, Bromley Hall factory, c. 1765. 128.2 cm × 67.2 cm. Royal Ontario Museum, 971.6.1.

116

Fantastic representations of Cathay were sometimes based on imagery known from imported objects, but for the most part they were the inventions of Western designers. Whimsical decoration in the fashionable chinoiserie style was applied to a standard European bombé shape in this silver tea caddy by the London silversmith Eliza Godfrey.

Tea caddy, or box, and detail of lid, silver, England, London, Eliza Godfrey, 1746. Height 12.8 cm. On loan to the Royal Ontario Museum from Dr Philip G. Downs. L970.6.4.

The very few oriental luxury goods that arrived in Europe before 1600 usually found their way into the "cabinets of curiosities" of princes of the church and the state, who felt that the acquisition of these exotic novelties enhanced their status and prestige.

The inventory of objects in the collection of Henry VIII of England included this entry:

Cup of Purselaine glasse fation with two handles garnisshid with siluer and guilt the Couer garnished with iij Camewe heddes and thre garnettes.

(Cup of porcelain glass fashioned with two handles garnished with silver and gilt; cover garnished with three? cameo heads and three garnets.)

Singular examples of imported oriental wares, as well as natural specimens such as coconuts and shells, were frequently enshrined in mounts of gold and silver for display — a tradition begun by medieval European princes.

Covered dish, Chinese porcelain, with English silver-gilt mounts, early 17th century. Height 14.6 cm, length 12.7 cm, width 7.6 cm. From the Lee of Fareham Collection, on loan to the Royal Ontario Museum from the Massey Foundation. L960.9.94.

A rare Japanese silk kimono was copied by an Indian chintz painter to indulge the whim of fashionable Dutch gentlemen, who in the early 18th century wore such exotic garments as dressing gowns.

Man's dressing gown, cotton tabby, mordant-painted, resist-dyed, India, Coromandel Coast, southern region, early 18th century. Royal Ontario Museum, 959.112.

From the late 16th century on, an ever-increasing volume of East Asian luxury goods reached Europe—from China, India, Japan, and other Eastern countries producing wares in the China taste of Westerners.

European merchants—with minimum risk to capital and maximum profits in mind—began to place orders for specific goods and patterns that would make the greatest appeal to their customers. The result was a class of made-to-order goods, whose patterns and models often required Asian craftsmen to modify traditional production methods.

The Pintadoe Quilts came safe to our hands and we have disposed of some part of them in sales at 50sh/– each piece. They serve more to content and pleasure our friends than from any profit that ariseth in sales, your first cost, freight and custom being put together. Of these 60 or 100 quilts will be as many as one year will vent. Those which hereafter you shall send we desire may be with more white ground, and the flowers and branch to be in colours in the middle of the quilt as the painter pleases, whereas now most parts of your quilts come with sad red grounds which are not so well accepted here, and therefore let them be equally sorted to please all buyers.

Directive from the London office
of the East India Company
to the factor at Surat, 1643

119

Among the goods produced in Japan for the export trade were articles of furniture of European type, but finished with lacquer and decorated with oriental motifs. This portable, drop-front, multi-drawer cabinet follows Spanish or Portuguese models, although it eventually found its way to England.

Embellishment of oriental luxury goods with European coats of arms was typical for special orders negotiated by traders on behalf of wealthy clients.

Cabinet, black-lacquered wood with mother-of-pearl inlay, gilt, Japan, late 16th to 17th century. Height 53 cm, length 75 cm, width 40 cm. Royal Ontario Museum, 967.33.1. Gift of Mr and Mrs Frank H. Ferris, Jr.

• Plate with coat of arms of Italian cardinal, copper, polychrome enamel, China, 18th century. Diameter 22.6 cm. Royal Ontario Museum, 924.10.15.

Eastern embroiderers often copied European engravings of classical themes, with their identifying cartouches. On this cotton coverlet, produced for the Portuguese market, are depicted Mars and Diana (above), and the judgement of Paris (below).

• Coverlet, white cotton tabby with yellow tussah silk embroidery, India, Bengal, early 17th century. 320 cm × 251 cm. Royal Ontario Museum, 972.117.8. Gift of Mrs William W. C. Van Horne.

In the 17th and 18th centuries the vogue for oriental objects and decoration swept Europe. From the East came quantities of export goods styled in the China taste of the West. In Europe artisans and craftsmen produced a plethora of all manner of chinoiseries that combined elements of Chinese, Japanese, and Indian motifs with the prevailing baroque, and later rococo, styles of the West.

The pattern for this coverlet, made in India for the English market, was adapted from an English design in the China taste, which showed shepherds in rockeries, flowering trees, and exotic phoenixes. Three other examples of the design survive: an English crewelwork embroidery and two sets of bed furnishings made in India, one of chintz and the other embroidered.

Details from central fragment of a coverlet, cotton tabby with silk chainstitch embroidery, India, Gujarat, late 17th century. 250.5 cm × 178.5 cm. Royal Ontario Museum, 978.339.

The flowering tree was one of the characteristic motifs of the European China taste of the 17th century. European trade companies ordered coverlets decorated with the motif from Indian cotton chintz painters. English embroiderers in turn created their own versions of the celebrated theme.

In the 1640s, when China was in upheaval after the fall of the Ming dynasty, Dutch traders turned to Japan for porcelain, and a new range of wares decorated with coloured overglaze enamels was introduced into Europe. During the 18th century Japanese Kakiemon and Imari designs were copied at many European porcelain factories, including the Bow factory in England.

Plate, porcelain (soft paste) polychrome overglaze enamel, England, Bow factory, 1755–1760. Diameter 19.8 cm. Royal Ontario Museum, 936.7.9. Gift of the Ceramic Arts Club, Toronto.

◆ Curtain or wall hanging, linen satin with wool embroidery, England, early 18th century. 207 cm × 184 cm. Royal Ontario Museum, 971.227c.

The West's vision of a topsy-turvy Cathay found expression in representations of curious figures in gardenlike settings, with exotic, often disproportionately large, flowers. The imagery was reproduced in a variety of media.

• Porringer, silver with chased design, London, 1688/89. Height 11.1 cm, diameter 13.7 cm. Royal Ontario Museum, 950.82.4. Gift of Mrs F. N. G. Starr.

The brilliant colour schemes and chinoiserie designs of domestic embroidery evoked the decoration of luxury oriental imports. The totally exotic design on this coverlet was an invention of its maker.

• Child's coverlet, linen twill with wool embroidery, England, dated 1728. 130.8 cm × 139.0 cm. Royal Ontario Museum, 970.128. Anonymous gift in memory of Gerard Brett.

124

Published pattern books and manuals encouraged fanciful domestic adaptations of oriental designs and techniques. The English japanned chest imitates Japanese lacquered imports.

... with Indian or Chinese greater liberties may be taken ... for in these is often seen a Butterfly supporting an Elephant or things equally absurd; yet from their gay Colouring and easy Disposition they seldom fail to please.

The Ladies Amusement or Whole Art of Japanning Made Easy, London, 1760

Plate from A *Treastise of Japanning and Varnishing*, John Stalker and George Parker, London, 1688.

Chest, lacquered wood and gilt, on silvered stand, England, late 17th century. Height 162.5 cm, length 106.7 cm, width 47.6 cm. Royal Ontario Museum, 960.13.

125

Throughout their vogue in the 17th and 18th centuries, chinoiseries retained their aura of intimacy and hedonistic escape—whether in the ornate monuments built for French court favourites or in the less ambitious but equally sensuous chintz-hung boudoirs of English "ladies of taste". In the 17th century, exotic motifs inspired by still undifferentiated notions of the East were combined with elements of the baroque decorative arts. In the 18th century, however, chinoiserie designers deliberately threw increased authentic knowledge of the Orient to the winds and continued to celebrate the fantastic world of Cathay.

In 1746 Mrs Mary Granville Delany had her dressing room "hung with the finest Indian paper of flowers and *all sorts of birds* . . . the ceilings are all ornamented in the Indian taste, the frames of the glass and all the furnishings of the room are well suited; the bedchamber is also hung with Indian paper on a gold ground, and the bed is *Indian work* of silks and gold on white satin."

The decorative theme of the waistcoat is an invention of French chinoiserie designers, although the colour scheme and chainstitch embroidery make direct reference to oriental textiles.

Saucer, porcelain, overglaze polychrome enamel and gilt, Germany, Meissen factory, 1730. Diameter 15.2 cm. Royal Ontario Museum, 953.139.4.

Uncut waistcoat fronts, embroidered silk satin, France, late 18 century. Length 69 cm, width 56 cm. Royal Ontario Museum, 934.4.425. Harry Wearne Collection. Gift of Mrs Harry Wearne.

Detail of a mirror with pagod, gilt on pine,
England, c. 1760. 254.0 cm × 128.4 cm.
Royal Ontario Museum 961.123.90.
The Larkin Bequest.

Fragment of a curtain, woodblock-printed cotton, France, Jouy, Oberkampf factory, c. 1775.
165 cm × 97 cm. Royal Ontario Museum, 934.4.172a. Harry Wearne Collection. Gift of
Mrs Harry Wearne.

The botanical motifs of the woodblock-
printed cotton were copied by J. Oberkampf
from an Indian cotton chintz, with the
express intention of creating *indiennes* that
would be competitive in the marketplace.
The Indian original had been inspired in
turn by a Western botanical drawing of the
West Indian pineapple.

> . . . the Chinese taste, which has already
> taken possession of our gardens, our build-
> ings and our furniture, will also find a way
> into our churches; and how elegant must a
> monument appear, which is erected in the
> Chinese taste, and embellished with dra-
> gons, bells, pagods and mandarins?"
>
> *The Connoisseur*, 1755

127

Structural details such as fretwork and pagoda crestings were hallmarks of late 18th-century furniture designed in the China taste. Although lacquering continued to be used, more and more, Chinese details were added to polished mahogany pieces such as this 1840s copy of a 1750s Thomas Chippendale china cabinet.

Detail of copperplate-printed linen tabby, purple-black design, England, c. 1765. Overall 228.6 cm × 185.4 cm. Royal Ontario Museum, 934.4.416. Harry Wearne Collection. Gift of Mrs Harry Wearne.

• China case, mahogany, England, c. 1840, after a design published by Thomas Chippendale in 1753. Height 269.0 cm, length 161.3 cm, width 43.7 cm. Royal Ontario Museum, 923.20.1. Gift of the T. Eaton Company Limited.

NEW PATTERNS OF TRADE

Philip II's claiming of the throne of Portugal in 1580 did not end competition between Spain and Portugal in Asia, nor did it strengthen Spain's position in Europe. Until 1591 the two kingdoms and their empires had separate administrations. In any case, the defeat of Philip's Armada marked the decline of Iberian authority. Northern Europe was quick to take advantage of the diminished power of Spain and Portugal. In 1600 a group of London merchants subscribed £72,000 to found the London East India Company, which was to have exclusive rights to trade in East Asia. Elizabeth I affixed her seal to the charter on the last day of the year. In 1602 the Netherlands followed suit with a larger and better-financed company, which was chartered as the Vereenigde Oost-Indische Companie and came to be known as the Dutch East India Company. Before the end of the century other European nations had also established East India trade companies. This new system of privately owned commercial enterprises, in which capital risk was shared jointly by the stockholders, differed significantly from the system of royal patronage that controlled Spanish and Portuguese commerce.

In 1601 five English ships laden with gold and silver coins, iron, tin, and lead to the value of £30,000, as well as a large quantity of woollen broadcloth, set sail for East Asia. The ships returned to London in 1603 with cargoes of spices worth more than a million pounds. A number of merchants remained in the East to set up a trading post, or, as it was termed, a factory. The decision to build it in Sumatra was abandoned in the face of Dutch competition; the factory was finally established at Bantam. The English trade goods, including wrought iron and woollen broadcloth, met with little success in the spice islands, but the merchants soon discovered that there was a great demand for Indian cottons. By 1608, when the London East India Company embarked on its third trading voyage, the London office had directed the company's ships to call in India for supplies of cotton before going on to the Moluccas. Thus the English fell into the "three corner" trading pattern of the Portuguese, who had learned it from Eastern merchants. European bullion was taken to India and exchanged for Indian cotton and silk fabrics, which in turn were traded for cinnamon, pepper, cloves, and nutmeg in Malacca, Sumatra, and the Moluccas. The spices were then taken to Europe for sale, and the cycle began again. Variations on the basic "three corner" pattern included trade along the west coast of Africa, where Indian cottons, the so-called Guinea cloths, were bartered for slaves, who were sold in the sugar plantations of the New World.

From the outset, Dutch, Danish, and English trading companies—and later French, Swedish, and Prussian—established intermediate bases in Africa, Asia, and America, like those of the Portuguese and Spanish. Most of the bases were fortified to protect traders from aggression by other Europeans. Many, such as the Dutch settlement at Capetown, which had originally served as a site where trade ships were repaired and food and water supplies were replenished, grew into permanent colonies.

Plate, porcelain, China, late 16th to 17th century. Height 9.9 cm, diameter 49.3 cm. Royal Ontario Museum, 908.14.3.

Although the trading stations founded by the chartered companies in the 17th century resembled those established in the 16th century by Spain and Portugal, their administrations were different. Whereas the Spanish and Portuguese stations were governed by royal appointees, whose interests lay in quickly amassing large profits for their monarchs, those founded by the chartered trading companies were in the hands of a factor or director, who was appointed by the board of the company and was directly responsible to it.

With high profits at stake, rivalries flared up between European trading nations. Religious differences provided convenient justification for aggression. While the English were more likely to be satisfied to coexist with other trading nations, especially with the Portuguese, the Dutch actively and by force of arms tried to exclude others. For them competition allowed of no compromise, and any activity that ensured advantage seemed to be justified.

In 1604 the Dutch captured a Portuguese carrack, the *Catharina*, off the coast

◆ Sugar caster, porcelain, underglaze blue, silver mounts (Dutch, dated 1853), China, early 18th century. Height 16.5 cm, diameter 9.0 cm. Royal Ontario Museum, 949.242.

of Malaya and took her cargo of more than one hundred thousand pieces of Chinese porcelain to Amsterdam, where it was sold at public auction. The porcelain, which became known as *kraak* (a corruption of carrack), created a great stir in northern Europe. Although the aristocracy and the nobility, including King James I of England, were among the purchasers, the quantity was large enough to permit the wealthy middle class to acquire some pieces. Soon there was a growing demand for porcelain, which the Dutch East India Company sought to meet by including increasing quantities of ceramics in its shipments.

Chinese porcelain had found instant favour with European nobility when Portuguese traders first brought it back to Europe at the beginning of the 16th century. Portugal capitalized on the new taste, and by the 1520s the king had decreed that one-third of the cargo of a ship returning from the East might comprise porcelain. By the 1580s six shops along Lisbon's luxury shopping street, the Rua Nova dos Mercadores, specialized in porcelain. Until the Dutch sale of the cargo of the *Catharina*, however, porcelain had remained exclusive to the nobility and the aristocracy.

The Dutch East India Company was quick to exploit this development in the marketplace and to create a popular fashion. The company began to order porcelain vessels from its trading stations in the East in 1614; the requisition of 1620 reflects the demand for the wares.

> Of the largest dishes 500, one size smaller 2000, one size smaller still 4000, double butter dishes 12,000, single butter dishes 12,000, fruit dishes 3000, half-sized fruit dishes 3000, caudle-cups 4000, half-sized 4000, clapmutsen 1000, half-sized clapmutsen 2000, saucer-dishes 8000, table-plates 8000, other small things as they come, but small brandy cups we do not want at all.

Concern for ready sale and quick profit, with minimal risk to capital investment, led merchants to request specific forms based on European models, and thus there came into being a class of porcelain made to order for the Western market.

When in the 1640s political upheaval disrupted the manufacture of porcelain in China, Dutch traders turned to Japanese kilns near Arita for the supplies of porcelain they required to satisfy the European demand. In changing the source of supply, the Dutch also introduced new styles of ceramic decoration to the West. On many of the Japanese wares, coloured enamels were applied over the glaze. European potters soon began to imitate the Imari and Kakiemon styles of Japanese ceramics. In the 1670s, after the Manchu had overthrown the Ming dynasty, China resumed the production of porcelain, and Chinese potters also copied the Imari and Kakiemon styles.

The vogue for porcelain led to European manufacture of imitations. Lacking the technical knowledge of the Chinese method of manufacture, potteries at Delft used a tin-glazing technique to produce a white vessel to which cobalt decoration was applied. England, France, and Germany also produced imitations of Chinese porcelain wares.

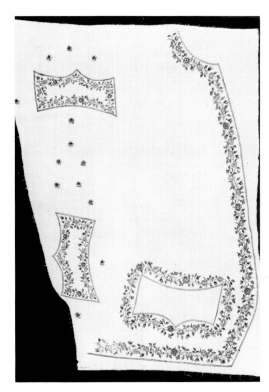

During the 17th century other traditional patterns of trade with Asia changed. By the 1640s mordant-painted and resist-dyed cotton fabrics called chintzes had become a major focus of India's trade with Europe. These cotton fabrics, first introduced by the Portuguese, were admired in Europe not only for their comfort and exotic origin, but also because the dyers in India had perfected brilliant washable colours that were far superior technically and aesthetically to any available in Europe at that period. Throughout the 1650s the Dutch and the English developed Western markets for fine chintzes and muslins, and by the 1660s orders for specific designs were being sent to Indian chintz painters to be copied. The directive of the London office of the East India Company to its factor in 1683 reflects the extent of the vogue.

> You cannot imagine what a great number of the chintzes would sell here, they being the wear of gentlewomen in Holland. Make great provisions of them beforehand; 200,000 of all sorts in a year will not be too much for this market, if the directions be punctually observed in the providing of them....
>
> Send us therefore 100 suits of painted curtains and vallances ready made up of severall sorts and prices, strong, but none too deare, nor any over mean in regard; you know that only the poorest people of England lie without any curtains or valances and our richest in damask, etc. The vallance to be 1 foot deep and 6½ yds. compass. Curtains to be from 8 to 9 feet deep, the 2 lesser curtains each 1½ yds. wide, the 2 larger curtains to be 3½ yds. wide. The tester and Headpiece proporconable. A Counterpane of the same work to be 3½ yds. wide and 4 yds. long, halfe of them to be quilted and the other half not quilted. Each bed to have to it 2 small carpets 1½ yds. wide and 2 yds. long. Each bed to have 12 cushions for chairs of the same work; by the ships you shall have a variety of patterns and further directions, but be doing what you can in the meantime.

The French trading company, Compagnie des Indes Orientales, was founded in 1664 as part of the general reorganization of the French economy, which was aimed at strengthening the monarchy. From the Compagnie the king was able to acquire the best oriental luxuries at reasonable prices, although his courtiers, conforming to the fashion set by the court at Versailles, were obliged to compete with one another for the costly Asian imports. The result was that the state treasury was enriched at the expense of the personal fortunes of the nobility. The founding of the Compagnie coincided with the first European vogue for chinoiseries, most of which were created as royal diversions. The *Trianon de porcelaine* built by Louis XIV in 1670 for his mistress Madame de Montespan was decorated with glazed tiles and hung with silk curtains. This novel conceit was imitated in a host of chinoiserie pavilions at other royal residences throughout Europe. Court masquerades and other entertainments were conceived to celebrate the chinoiserie style.

The dramatic increase in the volume of Asian trade goods brought to Europe in the 1670s and 1680s provoked an inevitable reaction among local producers and

Dress, cotton, glazed, Indian hand-painted and resist-dyed, called chintz, France, late 18th century. Royal Ontario Museum, 959.80a–b.

manufacturers, whose goods were forced to compete with imported wares. As Indian cottons revolutionized high fashion and consumer patterns, workers and supporters of the wool and silk industries agitated for laws banning the importation of Eastern textiles. In 1686 the French government was obliged to enact a prohibition. A similar prohibition in England a few years later was largely ineffective, since the entry of chintz for purposes of re-exportation was still allowed, and there were numerous ways for people in England to circumvent the law. A subsequent law in 1720 attempted to resolve the problem by banning the use of chintz for furnishings and clothing. In the Netherlands the overlapping commercial interests of the Dutch East India Company and the cloth industries forestalled such laws.

The use of chintz continued in the Netherlands; in fact, chintz eventually became part of the regional costume in several areas in the north. In England, the fashionable managed to elude customs officials and continued to enjoy the forbidden fruits of the East. The ban in France was lifted only in 1759, when printed fabrics from the factories at Jouy, Nantes, Orange, and other French centres were becoming competitive.

In 1628 the Dutch introduced the "China drink" called *cha* to Europe. At first the high cost of tea limited its consumption to the very wealthy—a fact that is reflected in the imported porcelain and silver vessels that were first used for brewing and drinking tea. In 1664 the London East India Company gave Charles II a gift of about one kilogram of tea, which suggests that it was still a rare and costly novelty from the East. By the end of the century, however, the demand for tea had increased to such an extent in England that imports climbed to an annual average of some nine thousand kilograms, and the price dropped accordingly to about thirty-five shillings a kilogram. During the 18th century tea became more and more popular in England, until it gradually replaced ale and beer as the leading drink of the people.

As the trade expanded, colonization became a means of ensuring trade monopolies, and it also created outlets for the expanding volume of goods manufactured in Europe. Groups at variance with the established religions of their countries, or unable to make a decent livelihood, began to emigrate to the colonies. Increasingly the colonies became suppliers of raw material and inexpensive labour for the mounting demands of a complex global trade.

Growing colonial populations and consequent new markets yielded revenues to the stockholders of private trading companies, investment capital for European manufacturers, and taxes for national governments. Unhappily, slavery and prejudice followed in the wake of commercial development. In the 16th century cargoes of slaves bound for the plantations and the mines of European colonies loomed large in European commerce.

◆ Coverlet, cotton tabby, mordant-painted and resist-dyed, India, early 18th century. 270 cm × 221 cm. Royal Ontario Museum, 961.7.6.

THE CHANGING FACE OF ASIA

Japan

When Portuguese sailors first appeared in Japan in 1542, the country was in the midst of a long and bitter civil war. The arrival a few years later of a handful of Jesuit missionaries and the activities of the black ships of Portuguese merchants in distant Kyushu were of little significance to those involved in the intrigues and power struggles taking place at the court in Kyoto. Even the advent of Spanish Franciscans and their subsequent disputes with the Jesuits were largely ignored. The curios and Chinese trade goods brought to Japan by Western merchants were popular enough, but for the emerging military class that was trying to wrest control of the government from the traditional nobility, the real attraction was Western firearms.

By 1590 three great warriors—Nobunaga, Hideyoshi, and Ieyasu—had unified Japan. While Hideyoshi ruled as regent to the shogun, the traditional military ruler, attention was focused outwards to the Asian mainland. Japan invaded Korea in 1592 and again in 1596, but the plan to build a vast empire that would include China and India was abandoned after Hideyoshi's death in 1598. Ieyasu was appointed shogun in 1603; his family, called Tokugawa, ruled Japan for two hundred and fifty years.

• Screen with Portuguese ships and traders, paper, ink and colour on gold leaf, six-fold, left of a pair, Japan, early 17th century. 147.0 cm × 334.3 cm. Cleveland Museum of Art, purchase, Leonard C. Hanna, Jr Bequest.

In the meantime, the Netherlands and England had initiated regular trade with Japan, in spite of the efforts of Portuguese and Spanish priests to have the Protestants banned. The English trading company, however, suffered disastrous losses and withdrew voluntarily in 1623.

The mission to convert Japan to Christianity achieved some success at first, among both nobles and commoners. In 1552 a Japanese convert was sent to Europe to study; he was the first Japanese to be seen in Western capitals. His appearance in Europe was highly significant for the Jesuits, since it demonstrated the potential of their Asian mission. A second group of Japanese converts visited Catholic centres in Europe between 1584 and 1586.

The Tokugawa shogunate grew suspicious of the activities of foreigners; the rulers feared that missionaries and traders might eventually bring European armies to Japan. In 1614 the shogun expelled all priests from Japan and ordered Japanese converts to Christianity to renounce the foreign religion—an edict that was crushingly enforced by massacre of Christians in 1637. Gradually Japan cut herself off from the rest of the world, and Japanese citizens were forbidden to leave the country.

By 1640 the only remaining foreign presence in Japan was a Dutch trading station, which was confined to the small island of Dejima in the harbour of Nagasaki. The island, which was closely guarded and supervised by appointees of the shogun, was a virtual prison. Although the cost of maintaining the station was high, and trade was restricted to only a few ships a year, the profit on Chinese silk, which formed the bulk of the Dutch trade with Japan, was forty-nine per cent, and profits on Indian cottons, European clocks and other mechanical devices, and American tobacco were even higher. Although the Dutch had the only Western trading station in Japan, they never held a monopoly on the trade, since private Chinese merchants were allowed to use the facilities at Nagasaki.

Jar and cover, porcelain, gilt (*Imari* ware), Japan, 19th century. Height 78.0 cm, diameter 41.5 cm. Royal Ontario Museum, 923.44.1a–b.

China

Although the Ming court did not officially recognize commerce, it actively encouraged the introduction of Western scientific knowledge by the Jesuits. In 1582 an Italian Jesuit named Matteo Ricci was assigned to China. He arrived in Macao and spent the next several years studying Chinese language and culture, thereby gaining the patronage of high officials. In 1601 he was allowed to establish a residence in Beijing, where until his death in 1610 he served the Ming court as mathematician and astronomer. Although the aim of the Jesuits—and later of other orders—to convert the Chinese court and then the empire was not fulfilled, the presence of Christian missionaries in China fostered Western ideas and to a limited extent a tolerance for Western trade.

By the 17th century the luxury-loving Ming court had become politically ineffective; it was unable to deal decisively with civil unrest or to prevent vassal tribes along the northeastern borders of China from uniting under Manchu leadership. The rebellion that erupted in China in the 1640s drove the Ming

Jesuits Ferdinand Verbiest and Adam Schall in Chinese costume, engraving, in *A Description of the Empire of China and Chinese Tartary together with the kingdoms of Korea, and Tibet: containing the geography and history (natural as well as civil) of those countries*, Jean Baptiste Du Halde, English translation, London, 1738/41. Thomas Fisher Rare Book Library, University of Toronto.

Informal portrait of first-rank official in the Qing court, oil on paper, China, 18th century (head and shoulder replacement, possibly early 19th century). 145.0 cm × 115.5 cm. Royal Ontario Museum, 921.32.74. Gift of Mrs H. D. Warren.

emperor to suicide. A Chinese commander enlisted the help of the Manchu army to quell the rebellion. Once inside the Great Wall, the Manchu not only drove the rebels from Beijing, but they stayed to claim the empire and establish the Qing dynasty.

During the period of rebellion and of consolidation of the Qing Empire, commerce was disrupted, but by the 1680s the production of luxury goods was flourishing again. The Jesuits remained in favour at the Qing court, and the earlier practice of dealing directly with Portuguese traders was maintained, although other European nations were permitted some limited facilities. The Netherlands sent several embassies to Beijing to seek formal trade agreements, but they were largely fruitless. By the end of the 17th century both England and the Netherlands had been granted trading privileges in Guangzhou. The record of trading vessels that visited Guangzhou in 1736 reflects the changing power structure in Europe: five ships from England, three from France, two from the Netherlands, one from Denmark, and one from Sweden.

Ruins of Yuan-ming-yuan pleasure palace, China, Beijing, built 1740/47, sacked in 1860 by English and French troops.

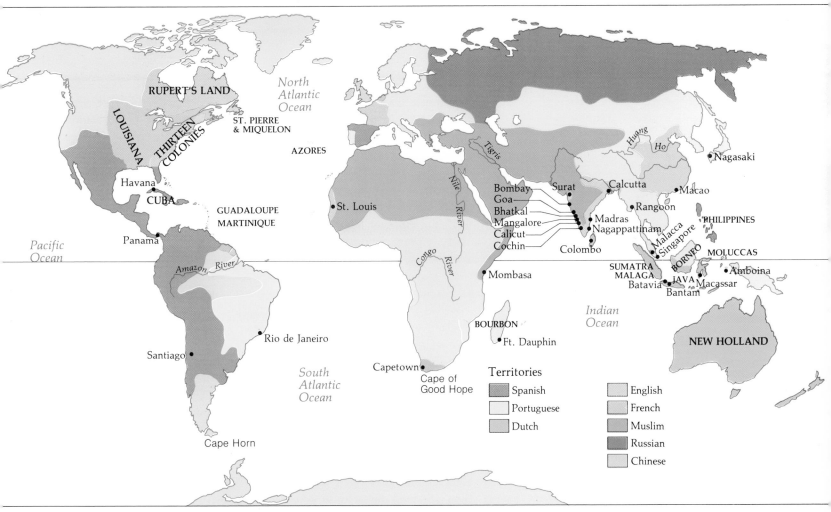

RUPERT'S LAND

LOUISIANA

THIRTEEN COLONIES

ST. PIERRE & MIQUELON

North Atlantic Ocean

AZORES

Havana

CUBA

GUADALOUPE
MARTINIQUE

Panama

Pacific Ocean

Amazon River

Santiago

Rio de Janeiro

South Atlantic Ocean

Cape Horn

St. Louis

Nile River

Congo River

Mombasa

BOURBON

Ft. Dauphin

Capetown
Cape of Good Hope

Tigris

Bombay
Goa
Bhatkal
Mangalore
Calicut
Cochin

Surat

Calcutta

Madras
Nagappattinam

Colombo

Huang Ho

Nagasaki

Macao

Rangoon

PHILIPPINES

Malacca
Singapore

SUMATRA
MALAGA
Batavia

BORNEO

JAVA
Bantam

Macassar

MOLUCCAS

Amboina

Indian Ocean

NEW HOLLAND

Territories

Spanish	English
Portuguese	French
Dutch	Muslim
	Russian
	Chinese

Imperial holdings in the 18th century.

Southeast Asia

Within a decade of their arrival in Asian waters in 1595, Dutch traders had largely wrested control of the spice trade from the Portuguese, although they still faced competition from Spain in the Moluccas. In 1619 the Dutch East India Company founded a factory on the north coast of Java at Batavia, which became the headquarters for the Asian trade of the Netherlands. England's attempts to establish trading stations in Sumatra and Java were eclipsed by the success of the Dutch, although both England and Denmark maintained a presence in Macassar until 1667.

In 1641 the Dutch drove the Portuguese from Malacca and extended their own sphere of influence to the Thai court at Ayuthia. Although the Dutch were able to thwart England's attempts to trade with the extensive Japanese settlement in Thailand, they faced competition from Muslim traders. In 1685 the French, aided by a Greek adventurer named Constant Phaulkon, who had seized political control in Bangkok, made a bid for dominance in trade with Thailand, but in 1688 Phaulkon was executed and Thailand was closed to foreigners for more than a century.

India

Early in the 17th century both the Dutch and the English trading companies challenged the Portuguese monopoly of trade in India. Unable to oust the Portuguese from their colony in Goa, the Dutch founded a trading station farther north in Surat in 1606, which was followed by one in Pulicat and another in Masulipatam in 1610. The English arrived in Surat in 1608. The Portuguese Jesuits who were in favour at the court of the Mughal Empire in Agra tried to use their influence to frustrate the plans of the Dutch and English. When the Portuguese were defeated at sea by the English in 1611, the attitude of the court changed. In 1615 the emperor Jahangir received Sir Thomas Roe, an ambassador from the court of James I of England. Roe negotiated a trade agreement for the London East India Company, which during the next decade established a trading station at Surat and another near Pulicat on the east coast.

Portuguese prestige in India continued to decline. In 1632 the Mughals expelled the Portuguese from Bengal and granted trading privileges there to England and the Netherlands. The Dutch also harassed the Portuguese in Sri Lanka and drove them from the island in 1658.

Throughout the 17th century, trade in India was affected by rebellion and unrest as the Mughals pressed their empire southwards into the Rajput kingdoms. In 1640 the London East India Company moved its factory from Pulicat to Madras. The trading colony in Bombay was transferred from Portugal to England as part of the dowry of Catherine of Braganza on her marriage to Charles II in 1662. Although England ill-advisedly supported Hindu rebels in the 1660s, her presence in India grew stronger. After 1707 the Mughal Empire declined as the power of the central government grew weak and local rulers declared independence. Political unrest created a climate in which England was able to stake claims to her own empire in India.

• Length of furnishing fabric, silk velvet, polychrome, cut and voided on compound cloth-of-gold field, bouclé d'argent, Iran, late 16th to 17th century. 222.0 cm × 74.3 cm. Royal Ontario Museum, 960.257. Gift of Mrs John David Eaton.

During the 16th century the Safavid dynasty claimed the throne of Iran, restored internal order in the country, and created a new Persian empire. Under the rule of strong Safavid shahs, the empire was once again receptive to trade goods and cultural ideas, both from the East and from the West. In 1598 Shah Abbas I established his capital in Isfahan, which became a splendid cosmopolitan centre with fine buildings, foreign residents, and markets filled with luxury manufactured goods from the West and from East Asia. The trade goods arrived overland from the north and the west, and by sea from the south. With the help of the English, the Persians recaptured the island of Hormuz from the Portuguese in 1622, and regained control of ocean traffic from the East into the Persian Gulf. Embassies from Venice, Poland, Denmark, and Russia were received at the court and sent home with lavish gifts of carpets, velvets, and jewels.

The Safavids, who embraced the Shiite branch of Islam, were unrelentingly opposed by the Ottoman Turks, who remained strong proponents of the orthodox Sunni division of Islam and regarded themselves as the upholders of the tradition of the old caliphate. While the Ottomans more than held their own against the Safavids, they began to lose ground in Europe. A European allied fleet comprised mainly of Spanish, Venetian, and papal ships delivered a stunning defeat to the Ottoman Turkish fleet at Lepanto in 1571 and put an end to the notion of Ottoman supremacy in the Mediterranean. Although the Ottomans recouped and won some military victories in the next century, their assault on Vienna in 1683, which was thwarted by allied forces of the pope, Austria, Poland, Venice, Tuscany, Malta, and Russia, actually marked the beginning of the disintegration of their empire.

West Asia

Plate, earthenware (quartz compound), Iran, 16th century. Diameter 45.7 cm. Royal Ontario Museum, 909.25.4.

141

Russia

Throughout most of the 13th and 14th centuries, the Russian steppes were controlled by descendants of Genghis Khan. Native princes, however, were able to maintain their Russian identities and by the end of the 14th century had succeeded in defeating the Mongols in open battle. This proof of Mongol frailty encouraged the Russians to make a stand against Tamerlane when he prepared to attack Moscow in his attempt to reestablish a Mongol empire.

During the 15th century the Mongol holdings became fragmented, with the result that Moscow, under the leadership of Ivan III, known as Ivan the Great, was able to begin to expand. The duchy had already become the main bastion of Eastern Orthodox Christianity after the fall of Constantinople to the Ottomans in 1453. When the city-state of Novgorod was annexed to its territory in 1478, Moscow represented a formidable power. Buoyed by this new strength, Ivan III declined to pay tribute to the Mongols after 1480, and as a consequence the Mongol Tartars were never again able to dominate Russia, although they made raids on the populace from time to time, particularly during the troubled years when Ivan IV, known as Ivan the Terrible, was ruler.

In 1613 the Romanov dynasty came to power in Russia. Under a series of brilliant rulers, a kingdom that was still medieval in culture and outlook became an empire. During the twenty-nine-year reign of Peter the Great, who became sole tsar in 1696 and emperor in 1721, internal reform and expansion brought Russia into the mainstream of Western thought. In Pushkin's words "Russia entered Europe like a ship down a slipway—to the clatter of axes and the thunder of cannon." Peter was a soldier, a politician, a diplomat, and an organizer par excellence. He gained outlets on the Black Sea through the Treaty of Nystadt in 1721, which ceded Estonia, Latvia, Lithuania, and strategic areas of the Gulf of Finland to Russia. By defeating Sweden, Peter was able to realize his dream of a Russian navy that sailed all the seas. Nor did he neglect economic reforms. With the help of state funds, he encouraged mining in the Urals and manufacturing, particularly in textile mills. By 1720 Russia was a major exporter of iron and copper, principally to England. The Treaty of Burin signed with China in 1720 conceded trading rights in Mongolia and Siberia to Russia.

When Peter the Great died in 1725, the period of Russian obscurity was ended. Ivan I had transformed the simple wooden fort of the Kremlin into the massive stone stronghold that is still symbolic of Russia. Peter the Great's transfer of the capital to St Petersburg signalled the transformation of Russia into an imperial power whose affairs were inextricably interwoven with those of the other Western imperial powers. For two hundred years Russia was to have a decidedly European air about it.

♦ Samovar, brass and wood, Russia, marked 1883. Height 49.5 cm, length 33.0 cm, width 30.0 cm. Collection of Dr Vladimir Ignatieff.

FOUNDATIONS OF A NEW ORDER

By the end of the 17th century the picture of direct European trade with East Asia was very different from what it had been at the beginning of the century. In Japan only the Dutch remained; in China the Portuguese, the Dutch, and the English were all established in Guangzhou; in India the English were virtually unopposed, challenged only by minor settlements of the French Compagnie des Indes Orientales in Bengal and southern India. Although the Dutch had effectively inhibited English and Danish interests in Southeast Asia, they had not completely ousted the Spanish and the Portuguese. When Portugal reclaimed its freedom from Spain in 1640, the Philippines went to Spain, but Macao, trade bases in the Lesser Sunda Islands of Indonesia, and Goa were retained by Portugal. Nonetheless, the Dutch had become the major colonial power in the islands of Southeast Asia and were to remain so until the 20th century.

Developments in naval engineering and navigation had made maritime trade more efficient, cheaper, and faster. Europe's supremacy on the high seas increasingly gave the West control of world markets. European firearms had decimated many Palaeolithic cultures in the New World and in West Africa. Europe's military power was regarded with awe by the rest of the world, and in the next century the West's industrial potential would leave the technology of non-Western countries far behind that of Europe.

The port of Goa, engraving, in *Grands voyages*, volume VII, Théodore de Bry, Germany, Frankfurt, 1590/1624. Royal Ontario Museum, 962.79.7.

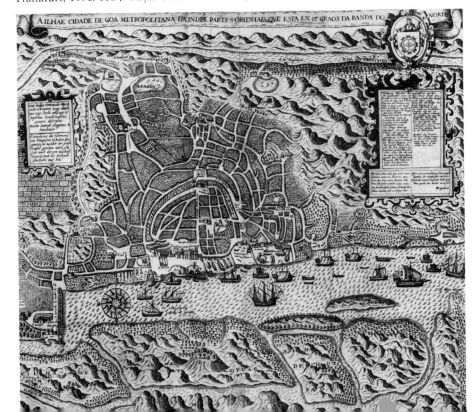

COMMERCE AND EMPIRE BUILDING

THE RISE OF THE BRITISH EMPIRE IN THE NEW WORLD

Early 17th-century colonialism set the stage for European domination of much of the world's population. In the New World, Spain claimed Central America and much of South America, although Portugal retained Brazil. England, France, and the Netherlands all had interests in North America and the Caribbean region, but in the second half of the 17th century the balance of power shifted from France and the Netherlands to England, and increasingly colonial destinies lay in English hands.

The Treaty of Breda in 1667 brought a halt to hostilities between England and the Netherlands that had been prompted by trade disputes. Louis XIV had also declared war on England in 1666, though France took little part in the fighting. According to the terms of the treaty, trading privileges and the colony of Dutch Guiana on the Caribbean coast of South America were restored to the Netherlands, but New York, New Jersey, and Delaware were ceded to England. French claims to territories in Canada and to the watershed of the Mississippi River were recognized.

The London East India Company, whose charter had granted it trade monopolies both in Asia and in the New World, moved quickly to consolidate its advantage. The company capitalized on the plantation system established in the New World by Spain in the early 16th century. Cultivation of sugar cane, which

Slaves from West Africa bound together before boarding ships to the New World, engraving, in *Letters on the Slave-Trade*, Thomas Clarkson, England, London, 1791. 23.1 × 18.8 cm. Thomas Fisher Rare Book Library, University of Toronto.

English ships in Virginia, engraving, in *Grands voyages*, volume I, Théodore de Bry, Germany, Frankfurt, 1590/1624. Royal Ontario Museum, 962.79.1.

146

had been introduced to the Caribbean islands from Madeira and the Azores, is labour-intensive. Diseases brought to the New World by Europeans and punitive wars reduced the Native American populations in the Caribbean to such an extent that within twenty-five years of Columbus's landing in the Bahamas, it was necessary to import labourers. By 1517 slaves from West Africa were being shipped to the New World to work on sugar plantations and in the cultivation of tobacco and cotton, which are also labour-intensive crops.

England's trade with the New World followed the pattern of three-way exchange: ships were loaded with manufactured goods in English ports; the goods were bartered for slaves on the west coast of Africa; and the slaves were carried in the same ships to the West Indies. There the ships took on new cargoes of sugar, molasses, rum, tobacco, and cotton, which were sold for currency in

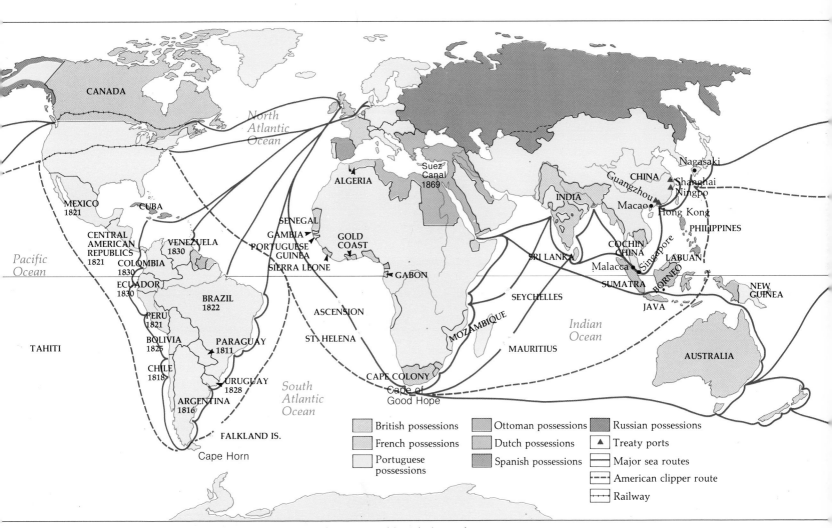

European territorial possessions; former European colonies in the New World, with dates of independence; and major trade routes in the 19th century.

♦ Dress, cotton tabby with cotton embroidery, India, for the English market, 1824–1825. Royal Ontario Museum, 921.37.2. Gift of Mrs George A. Sweny. Shawl, cashmere wool twill with silk embroidery, India (wool from Kashmir, embroidered in Gujarat), for the European market, early 19th century. 261.0 cm × 54.5 cm. Royal Ontario Museum, 977.264.2. Gift of Miss Hilda Simister.

England and on the continent. Raw cotton from the New World supplied English textile mills; rum made from sugar cane became a staple of the British navy; and tobacco was in demand in most European, and eventually in many Asian, countries.

While the trade was very profitable, the chain was weakened by the inability of English factories to produce enough goods to meet the market demands. It is no accident that the primary inventions of the early years of the industrial revolution— John Kay's fly shuttle of 1733, James Hargreaves's spinning jenny of 1764, and Edmund Cartwright's power loom of 1785—were all designed to accelerate production of English textiles, which came to dominate world trade in the 19th century.

Snuff box with watch, case of agate with gold mounts, gold watch, England, c. 1760, James Cox. Height of box 5.2 cm, length 8.2 cm, width 6.2 cm. Royal Ontario Museum, 978.360a−c. Gift of Dr Morton Shulman, Mr Sam Sarick, and Dr J. Moldofsky.

149

THE BRITISH EMPIRE IN ASIA

• *Lieutenant Colonel Edward Montagu* (British Army in India), miniature painting, watercolour on ivory, John Smart, England, dated 1790. 8.2 cm × 5.3 cm. Royal Ontario Museum, 964.100.1a. Bequest of Miss Anna M. Sterns.

In the 18th century the spice trade with Southeast Asia also continued to follow a traditional pattern of three-way exchange — bullion and manufactured goods from England to India, textiles from India to Southeast Asia, and spices from Southeast Asia to Europe. China, however, demanded that at least two-thirds of all payments for the vast quantities of tea, silks, and spices sold to England be in the form of silver bullion. Both the London East India Company and the English parliament became alarmed at the serious drain of the silver reserves. It was more important than ever for the company to maintain a monopoly on Asian trade, so that profits would be as high as possible. Competition from other nations and from independent traders was sufficient to prompt the London East India Company in 1689 to seek the support of the English crown in establishing a "nation of traders in India". This decision to extend the aims of the company from commercial to colonial interests heralded an era of civil administrators and career soldiers who would dominate the history of Western trade in the 18th century, and in the process create a global empire.

The political overtones of the desire of what was still a privately owned company to establish colonies in foreign countries made the English parliament uneasy. The morality of trade monopolies and of interference in the affairs of foreign nations was questioned. For a brief period in the 1690s a second trading company, the English East India Company, was encouraged, but sharing the trade proved a financial disaster. The response of the London East India Company was amalgamation; the new company was named the United East India Company.

Although both France and England had maintained trading stations along the Coromandel Coast of India since the second quarter of the 17th century, they had shown little interest in the politics of the country, except when trade was affected. With the disintegration of the Mughal Empire in the early 18th century, India was fragmented into numerous rival kingdoms. The collapse of the central authority compelled European traders to develop new strategies for keeping their supply lines open. Increasingly, the trading companies relied on force of arms. The East India Company recruited officers and soldiers in England, and frequently augmented garrisons with Indian soldiers called sepoys. While the military force defended and expanded territories, civil administrators maintained the trade operations.

The rivalry between France and Britain which was intensified by the War of the Austrian Succession in the 1740s, crystallized into a power struggle that spread to Asia and the New World. In India neither France nor Britain was sufficiently strong to dominate the other, so that in their struggles the presence of a trading fleet from one country was often enough to tip the balance against the other. In 1741 the Marquis Joseph François Dupleix was appointed to govern the colony of the Compagnie des Indes Orientales in India. His successful management of French trade in Asia proved remarkably profitable for France and also increased French prestige in India. Dupleix, who had ambitions for French supremacy in the region, made the War of the Austrian Succession an excuse to seize the East India Company's fort at Madras. British prestige suffered as a consequence, although Madras was restored by the terms of the treaty that ended the War of the Austrian Succession in 1748.

Over the next several years France and England continued to struggle for supremacy in India, with both countries vying for the support of native rulers. In 1751 Robert Clive, who had entered the East India Company's military service in 1744, set out from Madras to try to improve the company's position by reducing French competition along the Coromandel Coast. His successes of the next few years culminated in a battle at Plassey, where he decisively defeated the Nawab of Bengal and paved the way for British dominion of northeastern India. Clive's appointment in 1758 as acting governor of British territories in Bengal ushered in the era of the British raj in India. By now Dupleix had been recalled to France, and the French had been driven from Bengal. The collapse of the Compagnie des Indes Orientales in 1769 brought an end to French involvement.

By 1772 the East India Company had suffered its own reverses in international markets and was on the verge of bankruptcy. Parliament saw an opportunity to impose some control on the ailing and controversial company. The government arranged a loan of 1.5 million pounds and at the same time passed a regulating act that brought the administration of British India into the hands of a crown-appointed governor general.

The empire builders of the East India Company continued to consolidate Britain's position. The company's army, the largest military force in East Asia, helped to establish trade bases in Burma, Malaysia, and Borneo. By 1805 the British had direct rule over Bengal and Madras and had made vassal states of Mysore and the Mahrattas. Britain now regarded India as an agricultural reservoir and a market for British goods, which were admitted duty free.

Britain, however, faced a territorial threat in the northwest. Since Peter the Great's founding of a Russian navy in the early 18th century, Russia had been searching for a port that would be open all year round. Rebuffed in the Crimea by the combined forces of Turkey, England, and France, and thwarted in the Baltic Sea by Sweden, Russia cast a longing eye at the Indian Ocean.

In the hope of eventually securing a port on the Indian Ocean — which could be reached by a route through Central Asia and Afghanistan and then along the Indus River — Russia supported Afghan tribesmen who opposed the British raj in northern India in the 1830s and 1840s. Diplomatic and military conflicts between Russia and Britain — known as the Great Game — prompted British expansion into the Punjab in 1849; the goal was to extend British influence into Afghanistan and create a buffer zone between British India and Russia. At the end of the second of the full-scale Afghan Wars in 1880, a ruler who was sympathetic to the British claimed the throne of Afghanistan, but the country maintained its independence.

In the mid-19th century growing social and political unrest culminated in the Sepoy Rebellion of 1857, when thousands of sepoys recruited into the British army in Bengal revolted against their officers. The ostensible reason for the mutiny was the proposed issue of the new Enfield rifle, which used greased cartridges that had

The King of Oudh, miniature portrait, watercolour and gouache on ivory, gold frame, northern India, British colonial, c. 1820, 3.9 cm × 2.7 cm (with frame). Royal Ontario Museum, 980.74.2. Acquired with the generous help of the McColl Foundation and seven friends of the European Department.

to be bitten open to release the powder. The grease, which was thickly smeared on the cartridges, contained animal tallow. Early in 1857 a rumour began to circulate through the sepoy forces that the grease contained both pig's fat (the pig was anathema to Muslims), and cow's fat (the cow was sacred to Hindus). The belief took hold among the sepoys that the new device had been designed by the British to defile the Muslim sepoy and make an outcaste of the Hindu.

The rebellion, which was quelled by Britain in 1858, left a wake of bitterness on both sides. Within a century the empire founded by Clive would have gained independence.

Detail of cotton kerchief showing European soldiers in India, printed, painted, and resist-dyed in red, blue, yellow, and violet, India, dated 1737. 94 cm × 92 cm. Royal Ontario Museum, 934.4.65. Harry Wearne Collection. Gift of Mrs Harry Wearne.

REDRESSING THE
BALANCE OF TRADE

In the 1750s conflict between France and England in the New World erupted into war. When General James Wolfe's troops defeated a French army under the command of General Louis Joseph de Montcalm on the Plains of Abraham in Quebec in 1759, the claims of France were extinguished. British supremacy was confirmed in 1763 by the Treaty of Paris, which ceded Canada to England.

South of the St Lawrence, in England's Thirteen Colonies, there was growing resentment of the taxes and duties imposed by the British parliament on goods imported into the colonies. Although the East India Company officially held a monopoly of the trade, it faced competition from private traders and smugglers. The colonists increasingly felt that England's mercantile policy unfairly restricted their own commercial activities. The crisis came when parliament rescinded the taxes on all imports except tea, which was carried from Asia to England and then trans-shipped to North America, where the drink had become as popular as it was in England. The tax on tea was maintained partly as a symbol of the right of the British parliament to tax colonies, and partly to help the financially embarrassed East India Company. Although the East India Company lowered the price of tea, the colonies declined to be placated. They refused shipments or failed to unload them. A letter to the directors of the company in London reflects the uncompromising view of the colonists: "The Americans will not be slaves; neither are they to be trapped under the notion of cheap tea. Death is more desirable to them than slavery—it is impossible to make the Americans swallow the tea." In 1773 a group of indignant colonists slipped aboard three tea ships lying in Boston harbour and threw their cargoes into the water. Two years later the colonies were in armed revolt. In 1783 they gained their independence, and the United States of America came into being.

Independence provided the impetus for many American merchants to develop their own potential for maritime trade. With vast forests to draw on for lumber to build ships, it was not long before fleets of whalers and merchant ships were sailing out of Boston, Salem, New Bedford, New York, Philadelphia, and Baltimore. By the 1790s American merchants had discovered that New England ginseng, west coast furs, and Mexican silver coins were prized in China. Soon the United States was successfully challenging the trade monopoly of the East India Company in Asia.

The New World

Coin, silver, with Chinese chop marks, Mexico, 1902, used in China trade. Diameter 3.9 cm. Collection of Hillel Kaslove.

Western warehouses outside Guangzhou, oil on canvas, China, probably Guangzhou, c. 1850, •
artist unknown. 66 cm × 97 cm. Courtesy the China Trade Museum, Milton, Massachusetts.

China

In the 18th century English traders began to redress the balance of trade with China. The East India Company's operations in India provided large and stable supplies of cotton and opium, both of which were much in demand in China. The cotton was used for clothing and bedding, and the opium satisfied the growing addiction to opium-smoking, which was to become an increasingly vexatious problem for the imperial government of China.

As early as 1729 an imperial edict had decreed that the sale and smoking of opium were prohibited; an edict of 1796 banned the importation and domestic production of opium. The difficulty was that those edicts and subsequent ones could not be properly enforced, since traffic in opium was extremely profitable for English traders from India—who continued to smuggle the drug into China—and for the Chinese merchants who purchased it. In fact, profits from the opium trade went a long way towards supporting Britain's commercial expansion.

An imperial edict of 1756 had decreed that all foreign trade in China should be conducted through one port of entry, and in 1799 the East India Company was permitted to move its factory to Guangzhou. In theory, all foreign trade was strictly regulated by the government, whose aims were was to keep disruptive

154

The opium scales, with their case, and the three opium vials made in China in the 19th century, and the spirit lamp for opium made in the United States in the early 20th century are from the collections of the Museum of the History of Medicine, Academy of Medicine, Toronto. The opium pipe, also made in China in the 19th century, is from the collections of the Royal Ontario Museum, gift of Mrs Johnson and Miss MacLaren. For full details of the objects see page 213.

A group of snuff bottles from the collections of the Royal Ontario Museum, all made in China in the 19th or early 20th century. From left to right: hair crystal (922.20.459); glass, carved polychrome (976.181.3); coral (976.181.7a–b); turquoise matrix (956x18.4); amber (973x85.345). For complete details see pages 200, 213.

effects to a minimum and to ensure that as much wealth as possible flowed into the imperial treasury. Countless stipulations were formulated: foreigners were confined to a small area outside the city walls near the shore of the Pearl River; Western ships were obliged to anchor at Whampoa, an island about twenty kilometres downstream from Guangzhou; merchants were prohibited from dealing in forbidden goods such as opium, from going ashore with side arms or guns, or in the company

156

of foreign women, and from leaving the factory site, except at times and for purposes decreed by Chinese officials. The responsibility for the conduct of foreign trade was vested in an official merchant guild of some thirteen members who were appointed by the emperor and were known as the *hong* merchants. That complicated the situation, since when it was to their advantage to do so, the *hong* merchants themselves sometimes connived at illegal practices.

Although other European powers and the United States also engaged in the opium trade, the Chinese preferred the type produced in Bengal and western India. The mark of the East India company was considered a guarantee of quality. By the early 19th century the value of goods produced in India and traded in Guangzhou by the British was roughly six times that of goods produced in England and exported to China. Moreover, after 1804 very little European silver arrived in China, and large quantities of silver bullion began to move from China to India in payment for goods of the East India Company.

It has been estimated that by the mid-1830s there were more than 40 million opium addicts in China. Although the government tried to alleviate the situation by expelling opium traders and seizing and destroying stocks, the Western merchants refused to desist from the profitable trade. At last the issue came to

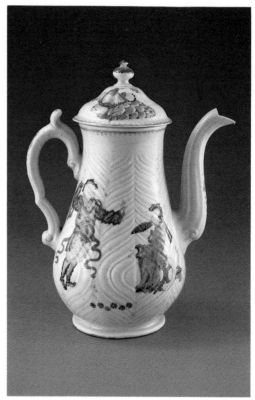

Coffee pot, porcelain (soft paste), overglaze polychrome enamel, England, Derby factory, 1760–1765. Height 23.5 cm, diameter of foot 9.5 cm. Royal Ontario Museum, 954.90.2a–b. Gift of Miss Amice Calverley.

Boxed carved ivory fan, box of lacquer and silk satin, and painted silk satin fan, China, for the European market, late 19th century. Length of ribs of fan 35.5 cm; length of box 39.4 cm. Royal Ontario Museum, 964.245.31, 967. 235a–b.

157

armed conflict between the English trading company and the Chinese imperial government in the First Opium War of 1839. The Chinese were decisively defeated, mainly because of the modern arms of the East India Company. By the terms of the Treaty of Nanjing in 1842 China was required to open up several other ports, including Shanghai; to cede Hong Kong to Britain; and to permit the opium trade to continue. She fared little better in the Second Opium War of 1856, in which French troops also participated. In fact, what has been termed the foreign "occupation" of China stemmed from the Opium Wars.

With new ports open for trade, the volume of Chinese goods shipped to Europe and the United States continued to increase, and so did the competition. More and more, success grew to depend on fast, well-designed ships. Throughout the 18th century the trading ships of the East India Company were well-armed, full-rigged vessels known as East Indiamen. Although the early ones averaged only 470 tons, ships twice as large were built towards the end of the century. But the East Indiamen were slow, plying the seas in leisurely fashion and often heaving to at night. A complete journey, from loading of export cargo in England to clearance of import cargo when the ship returned, took fourteen to eighteen months.

Within sixty years of the Declaration of Independence, the United States had become a maritime power second only to Britain. After Britain terminated the monopoly of the East India Company in the 1830s, the competition between the two countries intensified, particularly in the tea trade. In the 1840s the United States developed the clipper ship for the China trade; it was both faster and more capacious than the East Indiamen. The arrival in London in 1850 of the sleek,

• An English tea setting assembled from the collections of the Royal Ontario Museum. The mahogany table and chairs, the silver tea caddy set, the silver tea kettle, with stand and burner, and the set of porcelain dishes were all made in England between 1755 and 1770. For a complete description of the objects see pages 192-193.

The China tea trade, oil on canvas, Chinese Export School, c. 1800, artist unknown. 123.8 cm × 185.4 cm. Private collection. Courtesy Berry-Hill Galleries, Inc., New York.

Robert Bennet Forbes, an important clipper-ship captain, oil on canvas, China, Guangzhou, c. 1832, attributed to Lamqua studio. 32 cm × 24 cm. Courtesy of the heirs of Allan Forbes on permanent loan to the China Trade Museum, Milton, Massachusetts.

♦ Model of the American clipper *Houqua*, launched in 1844. Height of model 123 cm, length 182 cm. Mystic Seaport Museum, 53.3081, Mystic, Connecticut.

streamlined clipper *Oriental* to claim the high premium paid on the cargo of the first vessel to deliver new teas to the West each season shocked the British mercantile community. Britain, however, soon developed her own clipper ship.

Throughout the twenty-five years of the clipper era, the United States and Britain continued to compete in the Asian tea trade, which was lucrative for both countries. The new ship reduced the time, and consequently the cost, of the journey appreciably. A typical clipper voyage from Boston to Guangzhou and back to England by way of the Cape of Good Hope took nine or ten months—little more than half the time required by some East Indiamen.

In the 1860s steam-powered vessels were making inroads in the maritime traffic. By 1870 the Suez Canal was in operation and steamships began to follow the shorter route through the Mediterranean and the canal. The clipper ship was made redundant, and the era of adventurous sailors in sailing ships came to an end.

JAPAN IN THE
INTERNATIONAL ARENA

For more than two centuries Japan's only direct communication with the outside world was through the Dutch residents on the small island of Dejima in Nagasaki harbour and the Chinese merchants who traded in Japan. By the mid-18th century, however, a group of intellectuals in Nagasaki had begun to study Western thought through books and treatises that they obtained from Dutch traders. The "Nagasaki school", as the group came to be known, realized the inevitability of Japan's emergence from isolation. When Mutsuhito was installed as emperor in 1867, many Japanese sympathetic to modern Western ideas moved decisively to end Japan's isolation and bring down her repressive feudal system. The development of a new and modern state coincided with Mutsuhito's reign, called Meiji. When the Meiji period ended in 1912, Japan was a strong world power.

The first breach had come more than a decade earlier, when Commodore Matthew Perry undertook the delicate task of penetrating Japanese isolation. After one unsuccessful attempt, Perry in 1854 managed to persuade the insecure Tokugawa shogun to accede to his request that Japan open the ports of Shimoda and Kahodate to American trading ships. With the accession of the Meiji emperor, Westernizing of Japan accelerated. The emperor moved the court from Kyoto to Tokyo and placed the government in the hands of officials sympathetic to Westerners and Western views. Countless foreign emissaries were received and before long Westerners and Western styles were a common sight. Japan's leading officials readily assimilated the new ideas and in doing so created a craze for all things Western. The imperial family itself wore European clothes and posed for photographers in the palace gardens. European languages, sciences, arts, foods, and customs became ever more popular.

Many Japanese manufactured and handcrafted goods were introduced to Western markets through international exhibitions held in several European capitals in the last half of the 19th century. A vogue for japonaiserie — reminiscent of the European passion for chinoiserie a century earlier — created a ready market for Japanese goods. Tatami mats and folding fans, gilt Satsuma ceramics, and silk crêpe kimonos became the rage.

◆ *Printemps*, etching, drypoint on Japanese paper, James Tissot, France, 1878. 38.1 cm × 13.5 cm. Art Gallery of Ontario, 66/18. Purchase, 1966. Tissot's painting shows the influence of the Japanese "pillar" print.

Furniture, Japan, late 19th century. Corner chair ◆ and cabinet, carved wood; desk and chair, carved wood, ivory and bone inlay. Margaret Woodbury Strong Museum, Rochester, 74.1844, 75.2263, 74.1718. For complete descriptions see page 223.

• *Dong Yong, herdsman during the Han dynasty, and Zhi Nu, the weaver maiden,* woodcut, printed in colours on paper, Utagawa Kuniyoshi, Japan, c. 1841. Royal Ontario Museum, 926.18.1029. Sir Edmund Walker Estate.

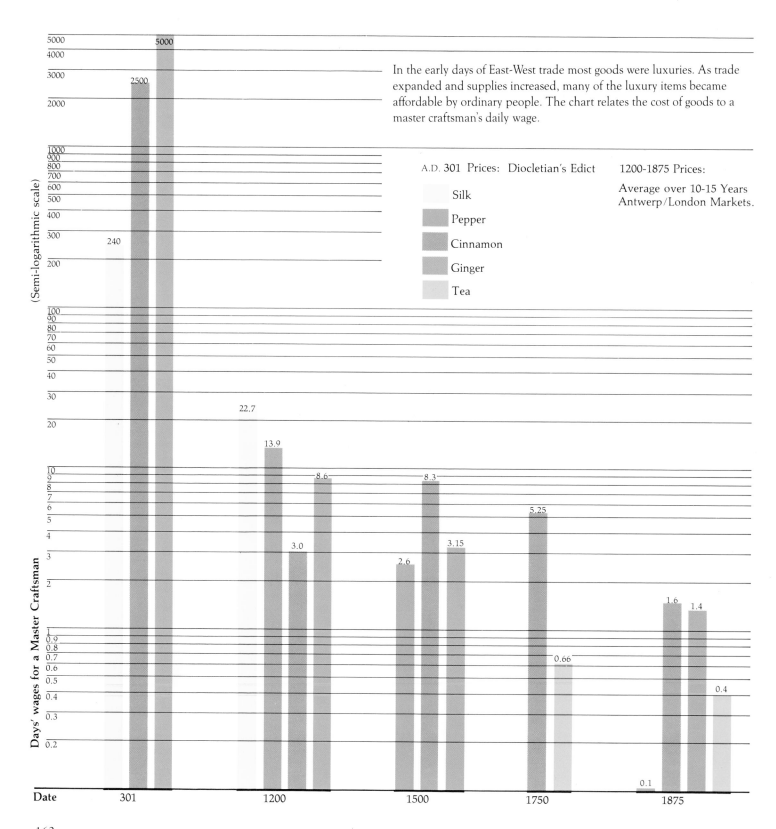

In the early days of East-West trade most goods were luxuries. As trade expanded and supplies increased, many of the luxury items became affordable by ordinary people. The chart relates the cost of goods to a master craftsman's daily wage.

A.D. 301 Prices: Diocletian's Edict

1200-1875 Prices:

Average over 10-15 Years
Antwerp/London Markets.

Silk

Pepper

Cinnamon

Ginger

Tea

(Semi-logarithmic scale)

Days' wages for a Master Craftsman

Date

301   1200   1500   1750   1875

162

From fragrant isles and scented shores...

The penchant of Westerners for spices and aromatics was a strong impetus for exploration of the sea routes to the Eastern lands where the spices grew. Long before the beginning of recorded history, spices played a part in religious ceremonies, in embalming the dead, in flavouring and preserving food, and in producing medicines, dyes, and cosmetics. Inevitably these exotic substances found their way to the West. Greeks and Romans of classical antiquity were lavish users of spices, although the original sources of supply were unknown to them.

Precious aromatics were highly prestigious and sometimes as costly as gold. Frequently they were the currency of homage and diplomacy—witness the offerings of frankincense and myrrh brought by the Magi to the Infant Jesus, along with gold.

Reliquary casket or châsse, gilt copper and champlevé enamel, France, Limoges, c. 1225 to 1250. Height 23 cm. From the Lee of Fareham Collection, on loan to the Royal Ontario Museum from the Massey Foundation. L960.9.20.

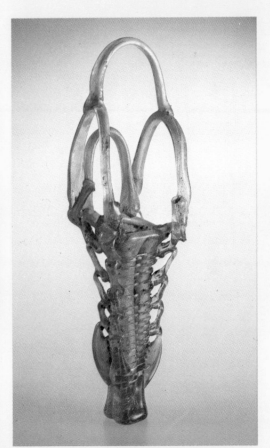

Flask for perfume or aromatics, blown glass with trail decoration, Syro-Palestinian, 5th to early 6th century. Height 26.6 cm. Royal Ontario Museum, 950.157.92. Gift of Miss Helen Norton.

Most spices were indigenous to the tropical regions of the Orient. For centuries Middle Easterners were middlemen in the trade between East and West. All along the routes, both by land and by sea, taxes, duties, and tolls were imposed on the merchandise. By the time the spices reached the West, their prices were exorbitant.

In the interests of maintaining the lucrative monopoly, Middle Eastern merchants spread fantastic stories about the origins of the spices. In the 5th century B.C. the Greek historian Herodotus was convinced that cassia, a type of cinnamon native to China, grew in remote swamps protected by monstrous batlike creatures. By the 1st century A.D. the Roman naturalist Pliny was expounding a more realistic view of the situation. He estimated that by the time certain spices reached Rome their original prices had increased a hundredfold.

Pepper plant.   Handcoloured etching on paper, ♦
in *Medical Botany*, William Woodville, London,
1790/93. Thomas Fisher Rare Book Library,
University of Toronto.

Black pepper is native to India, particularly the Malabar Coast, but it also thrives in Southeast Asia. It was one of the earliest spices known. Pepper was the favourite spice of a renowned Roman gourmand named Apicius; he used it, for example, in his recipe for *locustum elixam cum cuminato* (broiled lobster with cumin sauce). At one time in England peppercorns could be used to pay rents, taxes, tolls, and dowries; they were considered to be so precious that they were counted out one by one.

Cinnamon, another popular spice, was native to the island of Sri Lanka. In the 18th century the Dutch initiated the cultivation of cinnamon, both in Sri Lanka and in Southeast Asia. Cassia, which was held to be somewhat inferior to the Sri Lanka cinnamon, is the basis of most modern ground cinnamon, and only true connoisseurs can distinguish it from the superior type.

♦ Cinnamon plant.   Handcoloured etching on paper,
in *Medical Botany*, William Woodville, London,
1790/93. Thomas Fisher Rare Book Library,
University of Toronto.

The spice called clove comes from the unopened flower buds of an evergreen tree native to the Moluccas. Cloves were prized in ancient times for their flavour and for their scent. In the 17th century the Dutch tried to gain control of the clove trade by eliminating the trees from all but two small islands. They had in the meantime stored fifteen hundred tons of cloves in their warehouses in Batavia in order to profit from the inevitable shortage in Europe. The French managed to smuggle clove seedlings to islands in the Indian Ocean and the New World, but production today is concentrated in Malagasy and Zanzibar.

◆ Clove buds.   Handcoloured etching on paper, in *Medical Botany*, William Woodville, London, 1790/93. Thomas Fisher Rare Book Library, University of Toronto.

Ginger is native to India and Southeast Asia. In fact, Southeast Asian mariners took potted ginger on early sea voyages to ward off scurvy. The spice was introduced to Europe quite early and became very popular. Romans, for example, were willing to buy ginger at fifteen times the price of pepper. Ginger was prized as a food flavouring, but it was also used medicinally. Elizabeth I of England is said to have invented the all-time favourite, the gingerbread man, when she ordered small ginger-flavoured cakes made in the shapes of her courtiers. England transmitted her fondness for ginger to the New World.

Ginger plant.   Handcoloured etching on paper, ◆ in *Medical Botany*, William Woodville, London, 1790/93. Thomas Fisher Rare Book Library, University of Toronto.

165

The sources and properties of spices are well documented for the world of medieval Islam, though little is known about the spice trade in Europe during much of that period. But the First Crusade in the 11th century, whose purpose was to recover the Holy Land from Islam, set in motion events that were to assure Europe's resumption of a role in international trade. From the 11th to the 14th century, ships regularly left Italian ports laden with wool, clothing, and metals for the thousands of crusaders and pilgrims in Syria and Palestine. The vessels returned to Italy with cargoes of spices and jewels. The wealth that Venice and Genoa acquired from the trade established the monetary foundation for the Italian Renaissance.

Turmeric plant. Handcoloured etching on paper, in *Medical Botany*, William Woodville, London, 1790/93. Thomas Fisher Rare Book Library, University of Toronto.

Turmeric, a relative of ginger, has been used for centuries as a food flavouring, and the bright yellow powder it yields was one of the earliest dyes. The same colour as saffron, turmeric was long known as "the poor man's dye", because it was cheaper.

Nutmeg comes from the red pit in the fruit of the nutmeg tree; the outer casing yields mace. The nutmeg tree is native only to the Moluccas, where it was discovered in 1521 by Magellan, although the spice had been known earlier in Europe. Even to this day the specific conditions required for the nutmeg tree to thrive exist only in the Moluccas and Grenada.

♦ Nutmeg. Handcoloured etching on paper, in *Medical Botany*, William Woodville, London, 1790/93. Thomas Fisher Rare Book Library, University of Toronto.

166

At the end of the 13th century Marco Polo's accounts of China rekindled European interest in East Asia, although it was not until late in the 15th century that European explorers and traders set out to find a different route to the spice islands. They were encouraged to do so by the skyrocketing prices of spices and the restrictions imposed by Muslims on overland trade. An account written in England in 1418/19 reveals that half a kilogram of saffron cost as much as a horse, half a kilogram of ginger as much as a sheep, and a kilogram of mace as much as a cow.

At the end of the 15th century the race for the spice trade began in earnest. In 1497 Vasco da Gama, a Portuguese navigator, was the first to journey by sea from Europe to India; he reached Calicut on the Malabar Coast. When he returned to Portugal, he carried this message from the Indian ruler to the Portuguese king.

A gentleman of your household came to my country, whereat I was much pleased. My country is rich in cinnamon, cloves, ginger, pepper, and precious stones. That which I ask in exchange is gold, silver, corals, and scarlet cloth.

Ointment jar, alabaster, Egypt, 600 to 400 B.C. Height 7.9 cm; diameter 10.8 cm. Royal Ontario Museum, 909.80.82a–b.

Major sources of spices.

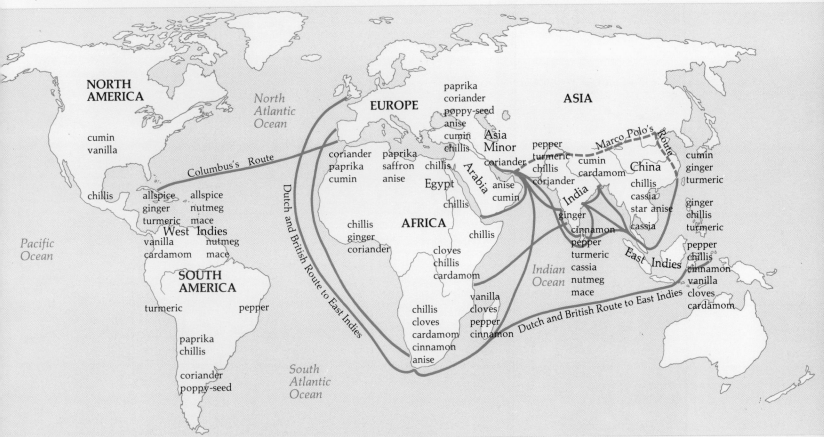

Although Portugal made early gains in the spice trade, by the beginning of the 17th century the Dutch and the British more or less held a monopoly. Both had established East India companies. By mid-century the Dutch controlled the lucrative cinnamon trade from Sri Lanka and the pepper trade from Malabar, Java, and the Celebes. By the end of the century they had added the clove trade from Amboina. In the 18th century, however, the Dutch East India Company, which had become scandalously corrupt and was almost insolvent, was dissolved.

Now London became the centre of the world's spice trade. Before long, though, the Americans with their clipper ships entered the race.

Spice box for ceremony of Havdalah, ivory and silver, probably Indian, 19th century. Height 38.5 cm. Royal Ontario Museum, 974.14.1. Gift of Dr Morton Shulman.

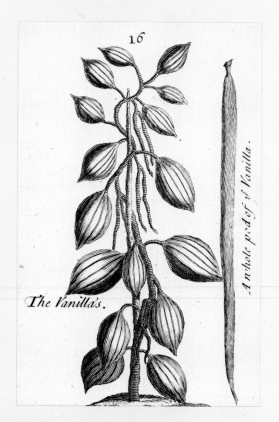

Vanilla was discovered in the New World by Christopher Columbus, along with allspice and chilli peppers. Vanilla pods are the fruit of a Central American orchid vine that was known to the Aztecs, who used vanilla to flavour chocolate. By the 16th century most European countries were importing vanilla. Today the cured pods are percolated with alcohol to produce vanilla extract, which is widely used in cooking. Vanilla is cultivated in Réunion, the Seychelles, Malagasy, Tahiti, and Java.

Vanilla plant with pods. Engraving, in *Complete History of Drugs*, Monsieur Pomet, London, 1748. Thomas Fisher Rare Book Library, University of Toronto.

Ephaedra, under the name *mahuang*, has been used in China to treat respiratory diseases for five millennia. Native to Eurasia, the plant is undistinguished in appearance; it resembles the common horsetail. Renaissance herbalists recognized the efficacy of concoctions of ephaedra, although the active chemical was not identified until this century. The alkaloid drug ephedrine, the oldest and still most popular decongestant, was made from ephaedra, although it is now synthesized. Ephaedra is an excellent example of an ancient herbal remedy that has undergone the tests of modern science and been found effective.

The opium poppy, which since Neolithic times has been cultivated for its seeds, probably originated in the eastern Mediterranean. The derived drug was known to Homer, who in his *Odyssey* described an infusion that was served as a beverage. The opium poppy spread eastwards, reaching China in the 7th century and Japan in the 15th. The smoking of opium began after the 15th century. Opium, the liquid extruded from the seed pod of the poppy, contains alkaloids, including morphine and codeine, which have invaluable medical properties. From morphine comes the drug heroin.

Opium poppy.   Handcoloured etching on paper, in *Medical Botany*, William Woodville, London, 1790/93. Thomas Fisher Rare Book Library, University of Toronto.

◆ Apothecary jars, earthenware, tin glaze, painted blue. England, 18th century. Heights: CD560, 8.8 cm; CD562, 8.8 cm; CD563, 8.6 cm; CD668, 12 cm. Museum of the History of Medicine, Academy of Medicine, Toronto. Dr T. G. H. Drake Collection.

Ephaedra.   Woodcut in *The Herball* or *Generall historie of plants*, J. Gerard, amended by Thomas Johnson, London, 1633. Thomas Fisher Rare Book Library, University of Toronto.

The evergreen tree or bush that produces tea leaves is indigenous to Assam, but it was grown in China in prehistoric times. By the 8th century both China and Japan were cultivating tea commercially.

Tea was first brought to Europe by the Dutch East India Company in the 17th century. Before long it was a vogue, particularly in England and in Russia. The story is that afternoon tea became a ritual in England after Anna, Duchess of Bedford, introduced the custom of serving cakes with five o'clock tea to allay "that sinking feeling". In Russia the samovar was invented so that hot water for tea would be always readily available.

Commerce in tea played a large part in trade between East and West. Until 1834 the British East India Company held a monopoly on the importing of tea into Great Britain and purchased tea exclusively from China, either directly or indirectly. During the disruption of trade with China at the time of the Opium Wars in the 19th century, the British tried growing tea in India. The experiment was a success, and India, along with Sri Lanka, Indonesia, China, and Japan, remains a major source of tea.

Tea leaves.   Handcoloured etching on paper, in *Medical Botany*, William Woodville, London, 1790/93. Thomas Fisher Rare Book Library, University of Toronto.

◆ Tea kettle, stand, and burner, silver, England, London 1761, Thomas Whipham and Charles Wright. Height, of kettle, 23 cm, of stand, 14.5 cm. On loan to the Royal Ontario Museum from Dr Philip G. Downs. L970.6.2a–d.

THE WORLD ENCOMPASSED

Until James Cook's epic voyages of the 1760s and 1770s, the Southern Hemisphere remained largely unknown, although some maps showed a large land mass labelled *Terra Incognita Australis*. The ostensible purpose of Cook's first voyage was to convey a team of Royal Society members to a suitable point in the South Pacific from which to observe the transit of the planet Venus across the face of the sun on 3 June 1769. Cook, however, was under secret orders from the British Admiralty to search for the rumoured "Great Southern Continent". The expedition, moreover, was the first voyage of exploration to sail prepared to assess and record whatever might be encountered in the sphere of natural sciences, since along with astronomical observers (of whom Cook was one), it included naturalists, artists, and a secretary. By the time Cook returned to England in 1771, he had circumnavigated the globe and explored the coasts of New Zealand and eastern Australia.

It was not until his second voyage in 1772, when he circumnavigated the globe at latitude 60° south that Cook demonstrated beyond question that the Southern Hemisphere was largely comprised not of a "Great Southern Continent", but of a

Detail of tobacco pouch, deerskin, decorated with •
European glass trade beads, Canada, Manitoba,
Cree Indian, 1871. Length 52 cm, width 15 cm.
Royal Ontario Museum, HK1609.
A. H. Smith Collection.

Cup and saucer, (for chocolate, a drink native to •
the New World), porcelain, gilt, Germany, Meissen
factory, mid-19th century. Height of cup 6.8 cm,
diameter of saucer 12.7 cm. Royal Ontario
Museum, 950.214.7a–b. Bequest of Elizabeth
Gordon MacDonald.

171

A "cabinet of curiosities" assembled from the collections of the Royal Ontario Museum. The specimens and artifacts are described in detail on pages 201–203.

vast ocean. Cook's third voyage in 1776 dispelled yet another geographical misconception. Vitus Bering's discovery in 1728 of the strait that was named for him had rekindled interest and belief in the elusive Northwest Passage. Cook's probings of the Arctic Ocean revealed only endless ice. In his explorations Cook encountered cultures that were generally unknown in Europe: the flourishing Polynesian civilization of Oceania, the Indians of the Pacific coast of North America, the Melanesian cultures of the Pacific Ocean, and the aboriginal populations of Australia.

Government recognition of the value of scientific observation reflected the shift in focus to the natural sciences, physics, and mathematics that had occurred at Western universities in the 16th century. The curiosities that explorers, traders, and scientists brought back from ever more distant realms sparked the interest of collectors and scholars, whose studies of the objects and specimens led to the classification of natural and cultural phenomena. Much of that work provided the basis of modern scholarship. The nucleus of the first English public museum, the Ashmolean at Oxford University, for example, was the cabinet of curiosities that Elias Ashmole donated to the university in 1667 (some of the curios he himself had collected, but many had been bequeathed to him by his friend John Tradescant). When Ashmole later donated his library to the university, Sir Christopher Wren was commissioned to design a building to house the bequests. And in the field of natural sciences, the taxonomic system developed by Carolus Linnaeus, who taught botany and medicine at the University of Uppsala in the 18th century, remains the model of modern classification of plants and animals. Throughout the 19th century the exploration of little-known regions continued. One notable example is the five-year expedition in the 1830s of the *Beagle*, to which Charles Robert Darwin was appointed official naturalist. The assimilation of data on the thousands of new species of flora and fauna collected on that expedition led to the formulation of Darwin's then revolutionary theory of evolution.

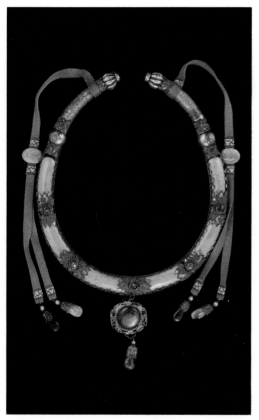

Necklace, coral, gilt silver, kingfisher feather, rose quartz, nephrite, and pearls, Mongolia, late 19th century. Length with tapes 30 cm. Royal Ontario Museum, 975.332.1. Anonymous gift.

THE ENDURING LURE OF THE EXOTIC

• Fragment of a wall painting with Buddhas, colours on clay, Eastern Turkestan, Dandan Uiliq, 3rd to 4th century. Height approximately 30 cm. Collected by the English archaeologist Sir Marc Aurel Stein. Fragment now in National Museum, New Delhi.

By the end of the 19th century the foundations of modern international commerce had been laid, although no one then could have foreseen the marvels of technology that the 20th century would bring. Today we live in a world enmeshed in trade, which seems to leave no aspect of our existence untouched. From caravans of camels plodding through desert sands we have come to aircraft that travel at unbelievable speeds and supertankers whose electronic communications systems sometimes defy comprehension.

And yet the goal of trading nations is still the same—to turn commerce to both political and financial advantage. And the goal of merchants remains unchanged—to create fashions and fads in goods whose sale will bring them profits. And the exotic still lures and enchants us. The ginseng root, for example, which has long been regarded by East Asians as a cure for a variety of ills, including impotence, is esteemed in the West today largely because of its exotic origin. Similarly, blue jeans have become popular throughout the world mainly because they seem to represent the youth, the vigour, and the modernism of the United States.

The exchange of ideas, knowledge, and cultural influences that from the beginning accompanied international commerce continues. John Dryden's poetic summation of world trade remains as valid today as it was when he penned it in the 17th century.

> Instructed ships shall sail to quick commerce,
> By which remotest regions are allied;
> Which makes one city of the universe,
> Where some may gain, and all may be supplied.

> *Annus Mirabilis*, John Dryden.

174

SELECTED READING LIST

Boulnois, Luce. *The Silk Road*. Translated from the French by Dennis Chamberlin. London: Allen and Unwin, 1966.

Boxer, Charles R. *The Great Ship from Amacon: Annals of Macao and the Old Japan Trade 1555–1640*. Lisbon: Centro de Estudos Historicos Ultramarinos, 1963.

Divine, David. *The Opening of the World: The Great Age of Maritime Exploration*. New York: Putnam, 1973.

Fairbank, John, Edwin O. Reischauer, and Albert M. Craig. *A History of East Asian Civilization. East Asia: The Modern Transformation*, volume 2. Boston: Houghton Mifflin, 1964.

Gittinger, Mattibelle. *Master Dyers to the World: Technique and Trade in Early Indian Dyed Cotton Textiles*. Washington, D.C.: Textile Museum, 1982.

Honour, Hugh. *Chinoiserie: The Vision of Cathay*. London: John Murray, 1961.

Humble, Richard. *Marco Polo*. London: Wiedenfield and Nicholson, 1975.

Impey, Oliver. *Chinoiserie: The Impact of Oriental Styles on Western Art and Decoration*. London: Oxford University Press, 1977.

Lach, Donald F. *Asia in the Making of Europe*. 5 vols. Chicago: University of Chicago Press, 1965–1978.

Morris, James. *Pax Britannica Trilogy: Heaven's Command, Pax Britannica, Farewell the Trumpets*. London: Penguin, 1979.

Needham, Joseph. *Science and Civilisation in China*. 9 vols. to date. Cambridge: Cambridge University Press, 1954–1971.

Parry, John Horace. *Trade and Dominion*. New York: Praeger, 1971.

Reischauer, Edwin O., and John K. Fairbank. *A History of East Asian Civilization. East Asia: The Great Tradition*, volume 1. Boston: Houghton Mifflin, 1958.

Schafer, Edward H. *The Golden Peaches of Samarkand*. Berkeley and Los Angeles: University of California Press, 1963.

Schafer, Edward H., and the Editors of Time-Life Books. *Ancient China*. Great Ages of Man: A History of the World's Cultures. New York: Time Incorporated, 1967.

Sherrard, Philip, and the Editors of Time-Life Books. *Byzantium*. Great Ages of Man: A History of the World's Cultures. New York: Time Incorporated, 1966.

Stewart, Desmond, and the Editors of Time-Life Books. *Early Islam*. Great Ages of Man: A History of the World's Cultures. New York: Time Incorporated, 1967.

SILK ROADS · CHINA SHIPS

An Exhibition of East-West Trade

CATALOGUE

INTRODUCTION

Caravans of camels laden with silk or other exotic wares lumbering into the bazaars in Changan, Samarkand, and Antioch . . .

The docks of Lisbon, Amsterdam, and London piled high with aromatic peppers and cloves . . .

Clipper ships loaded with tea skimming over the high seas . . .

These are the traditional romantic images of East-West trade in exotic goods. But the grim underlying reality is that extraordinary hardships and great risks to life and fortune were endured to maintain fragile trade links between widely separated markets.

The exhibition encompasses many dimensions of the trade between Asia and the West. With objects drawn primarily from the collections of the Royal Ontario Museum, it explores commerce as a means of disseminating widely divergent manners, customs, arts, technologies, and religious beliefs.

The presentation is thematic. An overview of the geography, the transportation methods, and the peoples and their wares introduces the exhibition. In the next section, a variety of products, both curiosities and necessities, demonstrate the scope of the trade between East and West from the 2nd century B.C. to the early years of the 20th century. Then comes a section devoted to archaeological explorations along the silk routes, highlighted by the Royal Ontario Museum's excavations at Qaleh-i Yazdigird in Iran. The fourth section explores the results of the trade in the imitations and adaptations of the goods themselves and in the less obvious exchange of ideas. A summary of contemporary international commerce and the influence it exerts on all aspects of our daily lives concludes the exhibition.

Means of Transport

Tomb figure of Bactrian camel
Earthenware, buff; yellow, brown, and green glaze
China, late 7th to 8th century
Height 69.8 cm
Royal Ontario Museum, 918.21.300
George Crofts Collection

Tomb figure of Central Asian groom
Earthenware, buff; brown and green glaze
China, late 7th to 8th century
Height 60.5 cm
Royal Ontario Museum, 918.21.293
George Crofts Collection

Tomb figure of Central Asian groom
Earthenware, buff; yellow, brown, and
green glaze
China, late 7th to 8th century
Height 45.5 cm
Royal Ontario Museum, 921.21.9
George Crofts Collection

Tomb figure of Bactrian camel
Earthenware, buff; yellow, brown, and
green glaze
China, late 7th to 8th century
Height 80 cm
Royal Ontario Museum, 918.22.11
George Crofts Collection
Gift of Mrs H. D. Warren
(See illustration page 1.)

Tomb figure of Central Asian groom
Earthenware, buff; yellow, brown, and green
glaze
China, late 7th to 8th century
Height 67 cm
Royal Ontario Museum, 918.22.8
George Crofts Collection
Gift of Mrs H. D. Warren
(See illustration page 1.)

Tomb figure of Bactrian camel
Earthenware, buff; yellow, brown, and
green glaze
China, late 7th to 8th century
Height 41 cm
Royal Ontario Museum, 981.177
Gift of Peter Meltzer

Model of American clipper Houqua
Launched in 1844; built by Brown and
Bell, New York; owned by A. A. Low
and Brother
Height 123 cm, length 182 cm
Mystic Seaport Museum, 53.3081
Mystic, Connecticut
(See illustration page 159.)

Trading Peoples and Trade Routes

In the 1st century three powerful empires—Rome, Parthian Iran, and China—controlled trade routes. They initiated a transcontinental trade that continued for centuries.

From the 7th to the 12th century, Islamic civilization prevailed across the Middle East and North Africa. The Muslims encouraged commerce and developed sophisticated marketing systems. Although Islam monopolized East-West trade, many foreign merchants moved freely across its lands.

Tomb figure of Han nobleman
Earthenware, grey; traces of white slip and pigment
China, 1st century B.C. to 1st century A.D.
Height 23.5 cm
Royal Ontario Museum, 918.17.71
Gift of Sir Edmund Walker
(See illustration page 11.)

Tombstone with family of weavers
Marble
Phrygia, 2nd to 3rd century; said to be from Kutahya, Turkey
Height 63.5 cm, length 60.0 cm, width 6.5 cm
University of Toronto, U. of T. M.82.323
The Malcove Collection

Tomb figure of Semite merchant
Earthenware, buff; yellow glaze
China, 7th to 8th century
Height 27.5 cm
Royal Ontario Museum, 920.1.78
George Crofts Collection

Tomb figure of West Asian wine merchant
Earthenware, buff; brown, yellow, and green glaze
China, late 7th to 8th century
Height 36.1 cm
Royal Ontario Museum, 918.21.7
George Crofts Collection
(See illustration page 65.)

Muslim merchants continued to act as middlemen in the trade between Europe and the East. Despite conflicts, trade flourished. Beginning in the 11th century, the Crusades—European wars waged to recover the Holy Land from Islam—brought western Europe into direct contact with the Middle East. As a result, European appetites for exotic luxuries from the Orient were stimulated. European merchants, especially the Venetians, developed trade links with the Middle East and the Orient.

Bowl with Turkish or Persian prince
Earthenware (quartz compound); overglaze lustre painted
Iran, late 13th to 14th century
Height 8.6 cm, diameter 19.6 cm
Royal Ontario Museum, 972.339
(See illustration page 79.)

Port of Venice
Woodcut, handcoloured
Michael Wolgemut (1434–1519), Germany, Nuremberg, 1493; in *Weltkronik*, from a leather-bound fragment of the German edition containing 121 of the original 260 leaves
Each leaf 41 cm × 28 cm
Art Gallery of Ontario
Courtesy the American Friends of Canada Committee, Inc.
(See illustration page 64.)

The capture of Constantinople by the Ottoman Turks in 1453 effectively blockaded European access to eastern Mediterranean areas. Portugal and Spain were among the first European nations to seek alternative trading routes to the East. Europe's direct trading links with the East broke the Islamic monopoly of trade with the Orient.

Screen with Portuguese ships and traders
Paper; ink and colours on gold leaf; six-fold, left of a pair
Japan, early 17th century
147.0 cm × 334.3 cm
Cleveland Museum of Art
Purchase, Leonard C. Hanna, Jr, Bequest
(See illustration page 136.)

Plate with Dutch trader
Copper; polychrome enamel
China, 19th century; illustrates 17th-century type
10.2 cm × 10.2 cm
Royal Ontario Museum, 953x86

In the 18th century the British Empire emerged as a dominant world power, with trading interests that spanned the globe. European colonization changed the world, and Europe came to control more and more of the world markets. In the next century the United States and Japan were to become active participants in world trade.

Lieutenant Colonel Edward Montagu
(British army in India)
Miniature painting, watercolour on ivory
John Smart (1741–1811), England, dated 1790
8.2 cm × 5.3 cm
Royal Ontario Museum, 964.100.la
Bequest of Miss Anna M. Sterns
(See illustration page 150.)

Robert Bennet Forbes (1804–1889)
Oil on canvas
China, Guangzhou, c. 1832; attributed to Lamqua studio
32 cm × 24 cm
Courtesy the heirs of Allan Forbes, on permanent loan to the China Trade Museum, Milton, Massachusetts
(See illustration page 159.)

Puan Ke-qua III
Oil on canvas
China, Guangzhou, style of Spoilum, early 19th century
81 cm × 61 cm
Private collection, courtesy Berry-Hill Galleries, Inc., New York
(See illustration page 156.)

Two Thousand Years of Trade

Comparison of the trade networks and merchandise of the 1st century with those of the 19th century reveals the evolution of a complex web of overland routes and shipping lanes that spanned the globe.

ROME, 1st CENTURY

Although Rome had a wide range of marketable commodities, including glass and bronze, that met with favour in the East, Roman demand for Asian goods outstripped exports. As a result, large quantities of gold and silver coins were tied up in trade payments.

Denarius
Silver
Rome, reign of Vespasian (69–79)
Diameter 1.82 cm
Royal Ontario Museum, 950.56.40

Denarius
Silver
Rome, reign of Vespasian (69–79)
Diameter 1.95 cm
Royal Ontario Museum, 950.56.15

Denarius
Silver
Rome, reign of Vespasian (69–79)
Diameter 1.8 cm
Royal Ontario Museum, 964x226.101

Denarius
Silver
Rome, reign of Titus (79–81)
Diameter 1.79 cm
Royal Ontario Museum, 908.55.48

Denarius
Silver
Rome, reign of Domitian (81–96)
Diameter 2 cm
Royal Ontario Museum, 924.3.213
University College Collection

Denarius
Silver
Rome, reign of Nerva (96–98)
Diameter 1.77 cm
Royal Ontario Museum, 964x226.126

Beaker
Glass, light green; mould-blown
Syria, Roman period, second half of
1st century
Height 12.6 cm
Royal Ontario Museum, 950.157.40
Gift of Miss Helen Norton
(See illustration page 25.)

PARTHIA, 1st CENTURY

Horses from Central Asia were coveted by
Chinese nobles; Parthian aristocrats were
equally desirous of Chinese silks. The
exchange of embassies between China and
Parthia helped to establish direct trade
links. Expensive gifts to heads of state
facilitated trade talks. Among the Parthian
gifts sent to the Chinese emperors were
West Asian acrobats and dancers.

Tomb figure of acrobat
Earthenware, grey; traces of white slip
and pigment
China, 1st to 2nd century
Height 10.3 cm
Royal Ontario Museum, 923.1.29
George Crofts Collection

Tomb figure of acrobat
Earthenware, grey; traces of white slip
and pigment
China, 1st to 2nd century
Height 11.9 cm
Royal Ontario Museum, 923.1.30
George Crofts Collection

Tomb figure of dancing dwarf
Earthenware, grey; traces of white slip
and pigment
China, 1st to 2nd century
Height 21.6 cm
Royal Ontario Museum, 923.1.24
George Crofts Collection

Ferghana horse
Bronze
China, 2nd to 1st century B.C.
Height 15.2 cm
Royal Ontario Museum, 930.21.24
Bishop White Collection
(See illustration page 12.)

CHINA, 1st CENTURY

The production of silk became a monopoly of the Chinese state by the 2nd century B.C.; this monopoly helped to enrich the imperial treasury.

China exported both silk thread and finished fabric throughout Asia. The materials were then reexported farther afield; eventually the demand for silk spread. Foreign dependence on silk often gave China political advantage over her neighbours.

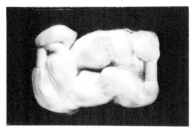

Skein of silk thread
China, early 20th century
Length 25 cm
Royal Ontario Museum, study collection

Tomb model of cash box
Earthenware; green glaze
China, 1st to 2nd century
Height 19.2 cm, length 22.4 cm, width 16.1 cm
Royal Ontario Museum, 924.26.23a–b
George Crofts Collection

EUROPE AND NORTH AMERICA, 19th CENTURY

The great European trading empires exploited the natural resources of their possessions around the world. Some were traded in their raw state; others were used in the manufacture of products that were traded. Mass-produced goods of Western industry found ready and profitable markets in less industrialized regions.

Coin
Silver; with Chinese chop marks
Mexico, 1902; used in China trade
Diameter 3.9 cm
Collection of Hillel Kaslove
(See illustration page 153.)

Gorget
Silver
Canada, Montreal, made for Indian trade, late 18th century, Robert Cruickshank (1767–1809)
Diameter 11 cm
Royal Ontario Museum, 981.1.53.1

Tobacco pouch
Deerskin; decorated with European glass trade beads
Canada, Manitoba, Cree Indian, 1871
Length 52 cm, width 15 cm
Royal Ontario Museum, HK1609
A. H. Smith Collection
(See illustration page 171.)

SOUTH ASIA, 19th CENTURY

By the 19th century trade in southern Asia was largely controlled by European nations. Spices and locally manufactured products continued to supply international markets. Cheap labour increasingly drew the attention of Western imperialists.

Sewing box
Lacquer; painted, gilt; bone fittings
India, mid-19th century
Height 12.7 cm, length 29.2 cm, width 22.9 cm
Royal Ontario Museum, 969.247a–az
Gift of Mrs John E. Langdon

Beads of myrrh on a string
Arabia, 20th century
Length 47 cm
Collection of Dawn B. van Graft-Blackstock, A. O. C. A.

EAST ASIA, 19th CENTURY

The continuing demand for oriental luxury goods and a desire to find new markets for Western manufactured goods focused European attention on the East. Despite attempts by the imperial government to ban foreign merchandise, China was forced to open her ports to Western commercial traffic after her defeat by the British in the Opium Wars of the 1840s and 1850s.

Japan responded differently to European expansion. After 250 years of isolation Japan opened her ports to international trade, thus beginning the transformation from feudal kingdom to modern industrial power.

Folding fan
Paper, with colour; ivory sticks
Japan, for the Western market, c. 1880
Length 39.2 cm
Royal Ontario Museum, 972.116.2
Gift of Miss J. Slingsby

Cup and saucer
Porcelain; underglaze blue, overglaze polychrome enamel, gilt
China, for the American market, late 18th to early 19th century
Height of cup 5.1 cm, diameter 8.3 cm; height of saucer 3.1 cm, diameter 14.0 cm
Royal Ontario Museum, 956.143.12a–b
Gift of the Winfield Foundation

TRADE GOODS

Horses from Ferghana, bolts of silk cloth, porcelain dishes, tea, tobacco, and pepper . . .

Thousands of exotic and costly trade goods were transported between East and West. Most goods began as expensive luxuries restricted to a privileged few. However, regular supply, wider distribution, and habitual use turned some goods, such as tea and pepper, into affordable daily staples and cultural necessities. Others such as silk and porcelain are still perceived as costly luxuries.

Horses

China learned of a breed of "heavenly horse" from a land to the west during the 2nd century B.C. From that time the Chinese court sent trade expeditions to Ferghana in Central Asia to secure these fabled beasts.

Hardier and larger than native Chinese horses, they were eagerly sought for military purposes. Ferghana horses, capable of carrying heavily armed soldiers, revolutionized Chinese battle tactics. Such horses were highly prized status symbols of the Chinese aristocracy. Ceramic models were often interred with their wealthy owners.

Wall tile from a tomb structure
Earthenware, grey; impressed
China, Henan province, 2nd to 1st century B.C.
Height 45.7 cm, length 117.0 cm, width 14.2 cm
Royal Ontario Museum, 931.13.261
Bishop White Collection
(See illustration page 12.)

Wall tile from a tomb structure
Earthenware, grey; impressed
China, Henan province, 2nd to 1st century B.C.
Height 44.7 cm, length 100.0 cm, width 13.0 cm
Royal Ontario Museum, 931.13.127
Bishop White Collection

Gable tile from a tomb structure
Earthenware, grey; impressed
China, Henan province, 2nd to 1st
century B.C.
Height 84 cm, length 90 cm, width 16 cm
Royal Ontario Museum, 931.13.142a
Bishop White Collection

Gable tile from a tomb structure
Earthenware, grey; impressed
China, Henan province, 2nd to 1st
century B.C.
Height 85.0 cm, length 90.0 cm,
width 15.5 cm
Royal Ontario Museum, 931.13.142b
Bishop White Collection

Tomb figure of Ferghana horse
Earthenware, buff; traces of pigment
China, 7th to 8th century
Height 67.5 cm
Royal Ontario Museum, 918.21.369
George Crofts Collection
Gift of John Trumbell Warren Band, Jr
(See illustration page 69.)

Tomb figure of Ferghana horse
Earthenware, buff; brown, green,
and yellow glaze; marked with brand
"Flying Phoenix"
China, late 7th to 8th century
Height 75.5 cm
Royal Ontario Museum, 918.22.6
George Crofts Collection
Gift of Mrs H. D. Warren
(See illustration page 68.)

Tomb figure of Ferghana horse
Earthenware, buff; yellow, brown, and
green glaze
China, late 7th to 8th century
Height 62 cm
Royal Ontario Museum, 918.21.284
George Crofts Collection
(See illustration page 68.)

Tea

The dried leaves and stems of the tea plant, an evergreen shrub, are used to brew a popular beverage. Originally tea grew wild in Assam; Buddhist missionaries introduced its cultivation to other parts of East Asia. By the 7th century tea was grown in China, where the custom of tea drinking became widespread. Western traders learned about tea in China in the 17th century; they soon made it an important item of global trade.

Tea drinking has produced distinctive social customs in each culture that adopted the beverage. Settings for preparing tea are illustrated here for five different countries: Japan, Tibet, Russia, China, and England.

TEA IN JAPAN

Tea drinking was introduced to Japan from China by Buddhist missionaries in the 8th century. The beverage was used both as a stimulant to help monks stay awake during meditation and as a medicine.

Initially its secular use was restricted to the Japanese court, which in imitation of the traditions of Chinese literati made tea an excuse for extravagant parties at which the merits of different teas were discussed, poems celebrating tea were written, and games about the names of teas were devised. Buddhist monks, however, also introduced the beverage to their congregations, and the custom of tea drinking became the focus of informal gatherings among the lower classes.

In the 14th century, a period of social upheaval, this humble tradition was melded with the more elaborate practices of the aristocracy to produce a tea ceremony, *cha-no-yu*, unique to Japan. The setting for the tea ceremony was designed to appeal to all senses. The *tokonoma*, or niche, with its painting or calligraphy scroll and flower arrangement, created a focus for the eye of the guest. Incense imparted a subtle ambience. The bowl in which tea

was prepared appealed to the hand; its slightly astringent contents stimulated the palate.

Incense box (kogo)
Lacquer; gilt
Japan, mid-19th century
Height 5.2 cm, length 8.0 cm
Henry M. Gustin Collection
On loan to the Royal Ontario Museum
from the Ontario Heritage Foundation
L975.24.11

Flower vase
Stoneware, grey; green glaze (celadon)
China, 12th to 13th century
Height 26.3 cm, diameter 11.4 cm
Royal Ontario Museum, 940.12.20
Gift of Mrs A. Leslie

Hanging scroll
Ink on paper; calligraphy entitled *Shu-fu*
(Pine Wind)
Japan, 20th century
Height 124.3 cm, width 48.6 cm
Teruko Shin Collection

Teabowl (chawan)
Earthenware; black glaze (*Raku* ware)
Japan, 18th century, Dohachi
Height 9.3 cm, diameter 10.2 cm
Royal Ontario Museum, 944.16.4
Gift of Lieutenant William C. C. Van
Horne

Teabowl (chawan)
Stoneware; polychrome enamel
decoration, gilt (*Satsuma* ware)
Japan, late 19th century
Height 7.7 cm, diameter 12.1 cm
Royal Ontario Museum, 941.15.12
Gift of Mrs J. S. Burnside

Tea caddy (chaire)
Stoneware; brown glaze; lacquer lid;
silk compound satin bag
Japan, 16th to 17th century
Height 10.6 cm
Royal Ontario Museum, 935.7.2, 935.7.4,
935.7.62

Fresh-water jar (mizusashi)
Porcelain; underglaze blue
China, 17th century
Height 19 cm, diameter 19 cm
Royal Ontario Museum, 923.17.45
George Crofts Collection

Teabowl (chawan)
Earthenware; red-brown glaze
(*Raku* ware)
Japan, 19th century
Height 8.3 cm, diameter 12.7 cm
Royal Ontario Museum, 944.16.9
Gift of Lieutenant William C. C. Van
Horne

Through carefully observed ritual, a
teamaster prepared tea for guests. Each
utensil was essential and played a prescribed
function. In the diversity of these utensils
and in the setting itself, the teamaster
sought to create a suggestion of harmony
appropriate to the specific occasion, the
time of year, and the interests of the guests.

Kettle (kama)
Cast iron with bronze lid
Japan, 19th century
Height 17.7 cm, diameter 23.0 cm
Royal Ontario Museum, 910.178.17a–b

Container for tea utensils (hishaku-tate)
Stoneware; white slip
China, 18th to 19th century
Height 18.0 cm, diameter 10.2 cm
Royal Ontario Museum, 960.238.326
James Menzies Collection

Waste-water jar (kensui)
Stoneware; white slip, clear glaze on
exterior, brown glaze on interior
(*ci-zhou* ware)
China, 11th to 12th century
Height 8.4 cm, diameter 14.0 cm
Royal Ontario Museum, 960.238.13
James Menzies Collection

Futaoki or lid rest
Porcelain; overglaze polychrome enamel
Japan, Ishikawa, late 18th to early 19th
century
Height 4.6 cm, diameter 5.8 cm
Musée des Beaux-Arts de Montréal
Gift of Joseph-Arthur Simard

TEA IN TIBET

Tea, which was imported in brick form
from China, was an important element in
Tibetan society. The beverage was a dietary
staple, and the tea bricks were commonly
used as currency.

Tea was traditionally drunk with every
meal. Pieces of a tea brick were broken off
and cooked in water, to which salt and
butter had been added. The mixture was
simmered for half an hour to produce a
bouillon-like liquid. It was served in cups,
but only half the serving was drunk. Barley
flour was mixed with the remainder to make a
nourishing dumpling called *tsampa*.

Four tea bowls
Copper
Tibet, early 20th century
Height 3.9 cm, diameter 9.5 cm
Royal Ontario Museum, 981.117.3.1–4
Gift of Mrs S. E. Paget

Flint case
Steel and leather
Tibet, late 19th century
Length 5.8 cm, width 10.2 cm
Royal Ontario Museum, 981.117.2
Gift of Mrs S. E. Paget

Ewer
Copper and brass
Tibet, late 19th century
Height 33.2 cm, width 18.2 cm
Royal Ontario Museum, 936.51.5

Tea brick
China, 19th century
Height 23.6 cm, width 18.5 cm
Royal Ontario Museum, study collection

TEA IN RUSSIA

Tea drinking was introduced to Russia in the 18th century and soon became popular. Any social occasion provided an excuse for serving tea. In most homes a samovar held a ready supply of hot water, which was added to loose tea leaves placed in a glass. Russian tea was commonly served with sugar.

Samovar
Brass and wood
Russia, marked 1883
Height 49.5 cm, length 33.0 cm,
width 30.0 cm
Collection of Dr Vladimir Ignatieff
(See illustration page 142.)

Tea caddy
Glass with silver lid
Russia, late 19th century
Height 11.2 cm, diameter 8.0 cm
Collection of Dr and Mrs George Ignatieff

Tea glass and holder
Glass and silver filigree
Russia, late 19th century
Height 11.1 cm, diameter 7.9 cm
Collection of Dr and Mrs George Ignatieff

Teaspoon
Silver
Russia, late 19th century
Length 14.3 cm
Collection of Dr and Mrs George Ignatieff

TEA IN CHINA

According to Chinese legend, the wife of an impoverished scholar once had nothing to cook for her husband's meal. She cut some twigs from a bush in their garden and made a soup. The brew transformed the scholar's life, for he later made his fortune selling the leaves of the plant from which the soup was made. The bush, of course, was a tea plant.

For centuries green tea has been the variety most commonly used in China. It was usually brewed in covered cups and drunk clear, but it was also steeped in pots. Tea drinking was enjoyed privately or in groups on a wide variety of occasions.

Teapot
Pewter
China, 19th century
Height 10.5 cm, length 13.0 cm
Royal Ontario Museum, 978.87a–b
Gift of Mr Herman Levy

Pair of teacups
Stoneware, tan; brown, red, and white
enamel (*Yi-xing* ware)
China, late 19th century
Height 6.4 cm, diameter 7.8 cm
Royal Ontario Museum, 909.74.5–6

Vase
Bronze
China, 19th century; archaistic form
Height 28.8 cm, diameter 16.0 cm
Royal Ontario Museum, 976x20.16

Table
Lacquer, red; carved
China, 19th century
Height 23 cm, length 54 cm, width 24 cm
Royal Ontario Museum, 911.21.11
Gift of Mrs H. D. Warren

Couch (kang)
Wood
China, 19th century
Height 90.2 cm, length 179.0 cm, width
82.2 cm
Royal Ontario Museum, 955.16.1
Anonymous gift

TEA IN ENGLAND

Cha, the "China drink", was introduced to
Europe by the Dutch in 1628. Green tea
was the first tea used in England, but it
was soon supplanted by black tea. Initially
the high cost of tea limited its consumption
to the wealthy. Early tea utensils made of
silver or of imported Chinese porcelain
reflect this fact.

By the end of the 17th century the
demand for tea had increased to such an
extent that imports climbed to an average
of ten tons a year. Large supplies lowered
prices, and during the 18th century tea
challenged beer and ale as the most
popular beverage in England.

The following items are illustrated in the
English tea setting on page 158.

Table
Mahogany
England, in the manner of Thomas
Chippendale, c. 1760
Height 76.3 cm, length 92.5 cm,
width 51.4 cm
Royal Ontario Museum, 975.196.14
Gift of the W. Garfield Weston
Charitable Foundation

Pair of chairs
Mahogany; from a set of eight
England, c. 1760
Height of each chair 105 cm; height of seat
45 cm
Royal Ontario Museum, 971.146.8a–b
Gift of the W. Garfield Weston Charitable
Foundation

Tea caddy set with pair of lidded tea canisters and lidded sugar canister
Silver; shagreen case
England, London, 1755; canisters
by Samuel Taylor
Height of case 21.9 cm, length 33.5 cm,
width 15.0 cm; height of each tea canister
15.2 cm, length 7.8 cm, width 6.4 cm;
height of sugar canister 14.6 cm,
diameter 8.2 cm
Royal Ontario Museum, 972.60.64a–g

Tea kettle, stand, and burner
Silver
England, London, Thomas Whipham and
Charles Wright, 1761
Height of kettle 23.0 cm; height of stand
14.5 cm
On loan to the Royal Ontario Museum
from Dr Philip G. Downs. L970.6.2a–d
(See illustration page 170.)

Teapot
Porcelain (soft paste); underglaze blue,
overglaze polychrome enamel, gilt
England, Worcester factory, c. 1770
Height 17.0 cm, diameter 12.5 cm
Royal Ontario Museum, 978.334.2a–b
Gift of Mrs Donald Early

Butter dish, cover, and stand
Porcelain (soft paste); underglaze blue,
overglaze polychrome enamel, gilt
England, Worcester factory, c. 1770
Height of dish 4.5 cm, diameter 10.6 cm;
diameter of stand 15.8 cm
Royal Ontario Museum, 978.334.4a–c
Gift of Mrs Donald Early

Two plates
Porcelain (soft paste); underglaze blue,
overglaze polychrome enamel, gilt
England, Worcester factory, c. 1770
Diameter of each 19.2 cm
Royal Ontario Museum, 978.334.5d,
978.334.8c
Gifts of Mrs Donald Early

Tea caddy and cover
Porcelain (soft paste); underglaze blue,
overglaze polychrome enamel, gilt
England, Worcester factory, c. 1770
Height 13.1 cm, diameter 7.0 cm
Royal Ontario Museum, 978.334.9a–b
Gift of Mrs Donald Early

Sugar bowl and cover
Porcelain (soft paste); underglaze blue,
overglaze polychrome enamel, gilt
England, Worcester factory, c. 1770
Height 6.7 cm, diameter 10.6 cm
Royal Ontario Museum, 978.334.12a–b
Gift of Mrs Donald Early

Spoon tray
Porcelain (soft paste); underglaze blue,
overglaze polychrome enamel, gilt
England, Worcester factory, c. 1770
Length 15.5 cm
Royal Ontario Museum, 978.334.15
Gift of Mrs Donald Early

Slop bowl
Porcelain (soft paste); underglaze blue,
overglaze polychrome enamel, gilt
England, Worcester factory, c. 1770
Height 7.6 cm, diameter 17.0 cm
Royal Ontario Museum, 978.334.14
Gift of Mrs Donald Early

Milk jug and cover
Porcelain (soft paste); underglaze blue,
overglaze polychrome enamel, gilt
England, Worcester factory, c. 1770
Height 10.4 cm; diameter of cover 5.5 cm
Royal Ontario Museum, 978.334.17a–b
Gift of Mrs Donald Early

Two teacups with saucers
Porcelain (soft paste); underglaze blue,
overglaze polychrome enamel, gilt
England, Worcester factory, c. 1770
Height of each cup 4.8 cm, diameter
8.2 cm; diameter of each saucer 12.9 cm
Royal Ontario Museum, 978.334.19f,j;
978.334.21d-e
Gifts of Mrs Donald Early

Chinese Ceramics

Early preeminence in ceramic production is reflected in China's long and diversified trade in stoneware and porcelain. For more than two thousand years both utilitarian objects and fine wares have been exported. Foreign artisans often copied Chinese wares, but were seldom able to match their quality. Chinese potters exhibited considerable skill in catering for foreign markets.

STONEWARES

Glazed stonewares were produced throughout China. These non-porous, durable ceramics were sought-after imports throughout much of East Asia from very early times.

Teabowl
Stoneware; brown glaze (*Jian* ware)
China, 11th to 12th century; type exported to Japan
Height 6.8 cm, diameter 10.2 cm
Royal Ontario Museum, 972.117.66
Gift of Mrs William W. C. Van Horne

Plate
Stoneware, grey; green glaze (celadon)
China, 14th century; type exported to the Middle East
Height 7.0 cm, diameter 33.6 cm
Royal Ontario Museum, 963x76.3

Saucer
Stoneware; white glaze
China, 9th century; type exported to the Middle East
Height 4.6 cm, diameter 15.8 cm
Royal Ontario Museum, 925.26.238
Bishop White Collection

Bowl and cover
Stoneware, grey; green glaze (celadon)
China, 12th to 13th century; type exported to the Philippines and Southeast Asia
Height 10.0 cm, diameter 12.7 cm
Royal Ontario Museum, 934.17.35a–b
Bishop White Collection

PORCELAIN

Porcelain was first manufactured in China during the 8th century and soon became a highly prized trade item. China remained the supplier of porcelains to Europe until the 18th century, when suitable clays and methods of manufacture were discovered in Germany. Even after this discovery Chinese porcelains remained luxury commodities.

Plate
Porcelain; overglaze red and green enamel (*Swatow* ware)
China, 16th to 17th century; type exported to Southeast Asia
Height 9.5 cm, diameter 37.0 cm
Royal Ontario Museum, 959.191

Vase
Porcelain; underglaze blue
China, late 17th to early 18th century; type exported to Europe
Height 40 cm
Royal Ontario Museum, 911.5.5

Bowl
Porcelain; pale blue-green glaze (*ying qing* ware)
China, 11th to 12th century; type exported to the Middle East
Height 5.5 cm, diameter 19.7 cm
Royal Ontario Museum, 927.19.84
Bishop White Collection

Sugar caster
Porcelain; underglaze blue; silver mounts (Dutch, dated 1853)
China, early 18th century; type exported to Europe
Height 16.5 cm, diameter 9.0 cm
Royal Ontario Museum, 949.242
(See illustration page 130.)

Jar and cover
Porcelain; underglaze blue
China, early 15th century; type exported to the Middle East
Height 34.3 cm, diameter 31.8 cm
Royal Ontario Museum, 925.25.15a–b
George Crofts Collection

Vase
Porcelain; underglaze blue, overglaze polychrome enamel
China, late 17th to early 18th century; type exported to Europe
Height 44.3 cm
Royal Ontario Museum, 909.8.11

Silk

Sericulture, the cultivation of silkworms for the production of raw silk, was an invention of the Chinese more than four thousand years ago. The process remained a jealously guarded state secret until the 4th century, when knowledge of it spread through East and Central Asia. In the 6th century silkworms were smuggled into Byzantium by some monks who knew the secret of sericulture. Although the manufacture of silk became widespread, China remained a major exporter of silk fabrics until the late 19th century.

Textile fragment
Silk damask; dark green
China, for the Egyptian market, 13th to 14th century
18.0 cm × 17.1 cm
Royal Ontario Museum, 979.196
Anonymous gift

Cope face
Silk compound satin, red, blue, and yellow with gilt strip
China, Macao, for the Spanish or Portuguese market, late 16th to early 17th century; furnishing fabric
139 cm × 300 cm
Royal Ontario Museum, 973.422
(See illustration page 19.)

Length of dress silk
Silk tabby, yellow; painted and silvered
China, for the English or French market, mid-18th century
107.5 cm × 74.5 cm
Royal Ontario Museum, 980.205a
Gift of the Fashion Group Incorporated of Toronto

Cotton

Cotton is derived from the seed hairs of the cotton plant, which has been cultivated in India for more than four thousand years. India became the major supplier of raw cotton and cotton fabrics for Asia and eventually for Europe. From very early times cotton fabrics were widely traded through the lands bordering the Indian Ocean. After the Islamic conquest of the Middle East, North Africa, and Central Asia in the 7th and 8th centuries, Muslim merchants controlled the cotton trade. They were responsible for the dissemination throughout the Islamic world of the technology of cotton growing.

The Portuguese replaced the Muslim middlemen in the Indian Ocean trade in the 16th century and expanded the market for cotton fabrics to Europe. The increase in the volume of cotton imports in the 17th century when the Dutch and the English controlled the sea trade provided the impetus for Europe's industrial production of printed fabrics.

In the 18th and 19th centuries the demand for raw cotton for European mills, and for cotton fabrics throughout the world, increased dramatically. Cotton-trading networks became more and more complex. The cotton used by Indonesian batik painters, for example, may well have been grown in America, milled in Britain, and transported by Dutch merchants.

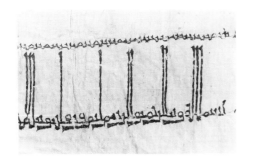

Textile fragment
Cotton tabby, white; inscription
embroidered in blue silk
Iraq, 9th to 10th century
48 cm × 60 cm
Royal Ontario Museum, 978.76.85
The Michel Abemayor Collection
Gift of Albert and Federico Friedberg in
memory of Dr Veronika Gervers

Textile fragment
Cotton tabby, warp *ikat* design in blue
and tan; inscription embroidered in
white cotton
Yemen, 10th century
50 cm × 78 cm
Royal Ontario Museum, 978.76.303
The Michel Abemayor Collection
Gift of Albert and Federico Friedberg in
memory of Dr Veronika Gervers

Textile fragment
Cotton tabby, white; block-printed and
resist-dyed in red and brown
India, for the Egyptian market, 15th to
16th century
68 cm × 31 cm
Royal Ontario Museum, 978.76.117
The Michel Abemayor Collection
Gift of Albert and Federico Friedberg in
memory of Dr Veronika Gervers

Coverlet
Cotton tabby, white; embroidered in
yellow tussah silk
India, Bengal, for the Portuguese market,
early 17th century
320 cm × 251 cm
Royal Ontario Museum, 972.117.8
Gift of Mrs William W. C. Van Horne
(See illustration page 121.)

Shoulder cloth
Cotton tabby, pale yellow; wax resist-dyed
designs in blue, red, green, and black
Java, north coast, 19th century
294 cm × 83 cm
Royal Ontario Museum, 983.56.2
Gift of the Textile Endowment Fund
Committee

Wool

Wool spun from the fleece of sheep is valued for its warmth: the separate fibres trap body heat and provide excellent insulation. Although wool was produced in many parts of the world, European woollens were prized as trade goods.

Most wool originated in England and Spain and was exported to other European centres for processing. By the 13th century, Flanders was the centre for the manufacture of woollens of high quality, which were widely traded throughout Europe, Africa, and the Middle East.

England came to dominate wool production in the 15th century by refusing to export raw wool and encouraging Flemish weavers to settle in England. By the 19th century, the English woollen industry supplied fabrics to much of the world.

Coat (capote)
Wool twill (fulled), white; striped in red, green, yellow, and black
Canada, Alberta, Blackfoot Indian, early 20th century; Hudson's Bay Company trade blanket made in England
Length 127 cm
Royal Ontario Museum, 960.270.123

Coat
Hemp tabby, white; supplemental weft in red wool
Taiwan, Atayal tribe, late 19th century; red weft unravelled from British trade cloth
Length 78.7 cm
Royal Ontario Museum, 915.3.32
Knox College Collection

Hood
Wool tabby, red
China, late 19th century; British trade cloth
Length 64 cm
Royal Ontario Museum, 915.3.145
Knox College Collection

Precious Goods

The limited volume of goods that could be transported overland by camel caravan encouraged traffic in items of high value on which maximum profits would be assured. As a result, transcontinental trade helped to promote extravagant tastes. Precious stones, jade, ivory, and other exotic raw materials from all over the world were dispersed to distant markets, where local craftsmen transformed them into expensive consumer goods.

Necklet
Amethyst and gold
England, mid-19th century
Length 38 cm
Royal Ontario Museum, 969.81.2a

Necklace
White sapphires, pearls, and emeralds set in gold
India, 19th century
Length of pendant 14.5 cm
Royal Ontario Museum, 969.290.1

Necklace
Ruby and seed pearls
England, 1830s
Length 34 cm
Royal Ontario Museum, 972.36

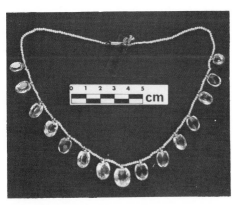

Necklace
Pearls and citrines
India, for the English market, c. 1885
Length 39 cm
Royal Ontario Museum, 969.106.6

Necklace
Coral, gilt silver, kingfisher feather, rose quartz, nephrite, and pearls
Mongolia, late 19th century
Length with tapes 30 cm
Royal Ontario Museum, 975.332.1
Anonymous gift
(See illustration page 173.)

Turban clasp (kalgi)
Diamonds, rubies, and emeralds set in gold, with polychrome enamel
India, Lucknow or Benares, 18th century
Height 9.0 cm, width 16.6 cm
Royal Ontario Museum, 969.271.9

Chain
Enamelled gold with pearls, rubies, and emeralds
Northern Europe, 17th century
Length 46.5 cm
Royal Ontario Museum, 970.242.107
Gift of Mr and Mrs Egerton Brown

Cup
Rhinoceros horn
China, 18th century
Height 9.0 cm, length 19.8 cm,
width 9.2 cm
Royal Ontario Museum, 957x83.3

Table screen
Ivory
China, 19th century
Height 27.5 cm, width 33.0 cm
Royal Ontario Museum, 923.24.154
George Crofts Collection

Necklace
Coral and silver
Palestinian, 19th century
Length without ties 44 cm
Royal Ontario Museum, 910.208.42

Snuff bottle
Turquoise matrix
China, 19th century
Height 6.5 cm
Royal Ontario Museum, 956x18.4
(See illustration page 155.)

Snuff bottle
Amber
China, early 20th century
Height 5.3 cm
Royal Ontario Museum, 973x85.345
(See illustration page 155.)

Snuff bottle
Coral
China, 19th century
Height 5.2 cm
Royal Ontario Museum, 976.181.7a–b
Anonymous gift
(See illustration page 155.)

Snuff bottle
Hair crystal
China, 19th century
Height 9.3 cm
Royal Ontario Museum, 922.20.459
George Crofts Collection
(See illustration page 155.)

Dish
Jadeite
China, 19th century
Height 3.3 cm, length 12.7 cm
Royal Ontario Museum, 908.31.3

Dish
Nephrite
India, Mughal style,
19th century; Arabic inscription
Height 1.6 cm, length 21.6 cm,
width 13.3 cm
Royal Ontario Museum, 972.180.1
Gift of Mr and Mrs Henry M. Gustin

Fragment of plaque
Ivory
France, late 17th century
Height 5.7 cm, width 12.0 cm
Royal Ontario Museum, 921.8.10

Tea caddy set: pair of lidded tea canisters and lidded sugar canister
Silver; case of tortoise shell with silver mounts
England, London, 1759; canisters by Samuel Taylor
Height of case 16.3 cm, length 24.5 cm, width 15.0 cm
Royal Ontario Museum, 970.225.4a–h
Bequest of Helen S. and Henry M. V. Weller

Watch
Silver with brass *verge fusée* movement; outer case of brass covered in tortoise shell with silver inlay (*piqué* work)
England, London, c. 1680, James Markwick (active 1666–1698)
Height 5.5 cm, length 5.0 cm, width 2.5 cm
Royal Ontario Museum, 981.21.1a–b
Friends of the Museum

Collected Curiosities

Some trade goods from the East were coveted because they were curiosities and hard to obtain. Possession of these exotic and expensive rarities conferred status and prestige on their owners. Merchants often catered for the desires of wealthy collectors by seeking out rare items in distant marketplaces.

THE WEST COLLECTS

Beginning in the Middle Ages, European princes of the church and state became eager to acquire curiosities of foreign manufacture and exotic natural specimens. These items were often ostentatiously displayed in rich mounts of gold and silver set with precious stones. The tradition of collecting exotic objets d'art as status symbols continues.

Cup
Nautilus shell with gilt-silver mounts
Germany, Augsburg, c. 1600–1630; Daniel Müller or Daniel Michael
Height 33.7 cm
Royal Ontario Museum, 922.19.11
(See illustration page 107.)

Altar ornament
Quartz crystal with gilt-silver mount
Italy, late 16th to 17th century
Height 16.5 cm
Royal Ontario Museum, 927.10.4
(See illustration page 107.)

Cup
Coconut shell with gilt-copper ("latten") mounts
The Netherlands, Flanders, or England, 1612
Height 20.2 cm, diameter at base 11.5 cm
Royal Ontario Museum, 925.23.19
(See illustration page 107.)

Vase
Porcelain; green glaze; gilt-bronze mounts (French c. 1850); one of a pair
China, mid-19th century
Height 44.7 cm
Royal Ontario Museum, 941.6.114a
Gift of Mrs J. S. Burnside

The curio cabinets of European amateur collectors of the 16th and 17th centuries housed an array of natural specimens, ethnographic artifacts, and historical works of art. Such cabinets might be housed in pieces of furniture or they might fill entire rooms. The spirit of an 18th-century curio cabinet is recreated here with objects from the wide-ranging collections of the Royal Ontario Museum. The first group is illustrated on page 172.

Canopic jar
Alabaster
Egypt, 6th century B.C.; fake 19th-century inscription
Height 50 cm
Royal Ontario Museum, B3640A; B3639B

201

Egg fossil of dinosaur
(Protoceratops andrewsi)
Mongolia, Upper Cretaceous period
Height 5.2 cm, length 10.2 cm, width 7.6 cm
Royal Ontario Museum, 12775

Tooth fossil of mastodon
(Mammut americanum)
Ontario, Upper Pleistocene period
Height 12.7 cm, length 15.3 cm, width 7.6 cm
Royal Ontario Museum, 4184

Tooth fossil of mammoth
(Mammuthus primigenius)
Ontario, Pleistocene period
Height 7.7 cm, length 33.0 cm, width 25.4 cm
Royal Ontario Museum, 1159

Ammonoid *(Promicroceras planicostum)*
England, Jurassic period
Length 28 cm, width 21 cm
Royal Ontario Museum, 2101L

Two scallop specimens *(Chlamys nobilis)*
Japan
Length of each 7.0 cm, width 6.5 cm
Royal Ontario Museum, 35265
Shafer Collection

Two scallop specimens *(Chlamys swifti)*
North Pacific
Length of each 8 cm, width 7 cm
Royal Ontario Museum, 41889
Shafer Collection

Auger *(Terebra subulata)*
Indo-Pacific
Length 9.5 cm
Royal Ontario Museum, 41881

Marlinespike *(Terebra marulata)*
Indo-Pacific
Length 14 cm, width 4 cm
Royal Ontario Museum, 35319

Conch *(Strombus gigas)*
Florida
Length 24 cm
Royal Ontario Museum, 41877

Turban *(Turbo marmoratus)*
Pacific
Length 14 cm, width 14 cm
Royal Ontario Museum, 41882

Volute *(Fulgoraria cancellata)*
Japan
Length 16 cm
Royal Ontario Museum, 41879

Abalone *(Haliotis* sp.)
Pacific
Length 16 cm, width 13 cm
Royal Ontario Museum, 41892

Nautilus *(Nautilus pompilius)*
Philippines
Length 17 cm, width 13 cm
Royal Ontario Museum, 41893

Set of horns of water antelope
(Kobus vardoni)
Africa
Length 45.7 cm, width 26.0 cm
Royal Ontario Museum, 79139

Right tusk of walrus *(Odobenus rosmarus)*
Baffin Island
Length 32 cm, width 5 cm
Royal Ontario Museum, 33.8.23.18

Left hind foot of elephant
(Elephas maximus)
Sri Lanka
Height 26.0 cm, diameter 28.5 cm
Royal Ontario Museum, 75156

Bird of paradise *(Paradisae novaeguinae)*
New Guinea
Length 59 cm
Royal Ontario Museum, 50122

Decorated ostrich egg
Africa, Khoisan Bushman, 20th century
Height 14.5 cm
Royal Ontario Museum, 970.224.46

Basket
Spruce root
Canada, British Columbia, Haida Indian,
19th century
Height 18.2 cm, greatest width 19.0 cm
Royal Ontario Museum, 23127

Shield
Hide, reed, and wood
Uganda, Banyoro tribe, late 19th to early
20th century
Height 26 cm, length 93 cm, width 50 cm
Royal Ontario Museum, 948.1.495
Lord Kitchener Collection

Neck ornament
Shell
New Guinea, Melanesia, 20th century
Length of pendant 17.8 cm, width 17.5 cm
Royal Ontario Museum, 969.330.28

Dagger
Bone, clay, shell, grass, ivory, feather, and hair
New Guinea, Middle Sepik, 20th century
Length 38.2 cm
Royal Ontario Museum, 969.330.94

Dwarf crocodile *(Osteolaemus tetraspis)*
West Africa
Height 20 cm, length 109 cm, width 32 cm
Royal Ontario Museum, H360

Skin of python *(Python molurus)*
India
Length 287 cm, width 23 cm
Royal Ontario Museum, H415

Sword of sawfish (*Pristis pectinatus*)
Atlantic
Length 64.0 cm, width 10.5 cm
Royal Ontario Museum
Gift of the Dufferin Public School
Trenton, Ontario

Jaws of shark (*Carcharhinidae*)
Locality unknown
Height 8 cm, length 29 cm, width 15 cm
Royal Ontario Museum

Amethyst geode
Brazil
Height 16.0 cm, length 26.0 cm,
width 20.0 cm
Length of fragments 10.5 cm, 8.0 cm,
10.0 cm
Royal Ontario Museum

Ruby ore
India
Height 2.6 cm, length 6.8 cm, width 4.5 cm
Royal Ontario Museum

Pyrite
Peru
Height 2.5 cm, length 7.0 cm, width 5.5 cm
Royal Ontario Museum

Fragment from a sarcophagus
Marble
Ostia, Roman, 2nd century
Height 14.0 cm, width 16.5 cm
Royal Ontario Museum, 924.16.20

Lamp
Earthenware; mould-made with
sepia slip
North Africa, Roman, 2nd or early
3rd century
Height 4.5 cm, length 12.2 cm,
width 8.5 cm
Royal Ontario Museum, 975.248.18

Plate
Porcelain; underglaze blue; silver mounts
(Dutch, c. 1850)
China, early 18th century
Diameter 28.8 cm
Royal Ontario Museum, 980.99.123
Anonymous gift

**Tooth fossil, left canine, of sabre-
toothed tiger** (*Smilodon neogaeus*)
Peru, Upper Pleistocene period
Height 2.6 cm, length 22.8 cm, width 5.0 cm
Royal Ontario Museum, 2119

Two trilobite specimens
(*Dalmanitina insignis*)
Czechoslovakia, Ordovician period
Lengths 8.0 cm and 9.0 cm,
widths 5.5 cm and 6.0 cm
Royal Ontario Museum, 1025T

Crinoid (*Encrinus carnalli*)
Germany, Triassic period
Length 11 cm, width 7 cm
Royal Ontario Museum, 2499

Seven scallop specimens (*Pecten senatorius*)
Indo-Pacific
Length, average, 6 cm, width 5 cm
Royal Ontario Museum, 41890
Shafer Collection

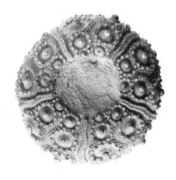

Echinoid (*Plegiocidaris coronata*)
Germany, Jurassic period
Length 4.0 cm, width 1.5 cm
Royal Ontario Museum, 37270

Clam (*Glycimeris* sp.)
Indo-Pacific
Length 7 cm, width 6 cm
Royal Ontario Museum, 41895
Shafer Collection

Two murex specimens (*Chicoreus brunneus*)
Indo-Pacific
Lengths 7 cm and 5 cm, widths 5 cm
and 3 cm
Royal Ontario Museum, 41888

Three coral specimens
(*Zonophyllum parvitabulatum*)
Germany, Devonian period
Length of each 6 cm, width 3 cm
Royal Ontario Museum, 1502D

Two cowrie specimens (*Cypraea arabica*)
Fiji
Lengths 6 cm and 4 cm, widths 4 cm
and 3 cm
Royal Ontario Museum, 41884

Top shell (*Trochus conus*)
Japan
Length 6 cm, width 5 cm
Royal Ontario Museum, 41886

Volute (*Aulica imperialis*)
Indo-Pacific
Length 8 cm, width 5 cm
Royal Ontario Museum, 41878

Murex (*Hexaplex erythrostomus*)
Gulf of California
Length 12 cm, width 8 cm
Royal Ontario Museum, 41887

Cowrie (*Cypraea talpa*)
Indo-Pacific
Length 6.5 cm, width 3.5 cm
Royal Ontario Museum, 41883

Two cowrie specimens (*Cypraea tigris*)
Fiji
Length of each 8.5 cm, width 5.5 cm
Royal Ontario Museum, 41885

Murex (*Murex* sp.)
Locality unknown
Length 22 cm, width 18 cm
Royal Ontario Museum, 41894

Two cone specimens (*Conus marmoreus*)
Indo-Pacific
Lengths 11 cm and 7 cm, widths 6 cm
and 4 cm
Royal Ontario Museum, 41880

Three clam specimens (*Tellina punicea*)
Atlantic
Lengths range from 1 cm to 5 cm
Royal Ontario Museum, 41891

Giant clam (*Tridacna squamosa*)
Fiji
Length 11 cm, width 8 cm
Royal Ontario Museum, 41896

Skeleton of dodo (*Didus ineptus*)
Mauritius
Height 76 cm, length 91 cm, width 46 cm
Royal Ontario Museum, 1214

Three tinamou eggs (*Eudromia elegans*)
One tinamou egg (*Nothoprocta cinerascens*)
Argentina
Length of each 3.8 cm
Royal Ontario Museum

String of beads
Ivory-nut-palm seeds
Japan?, 19th century
Length 50.7 cm; diameter of each bead
3.0 cm
Royal Ontario Museum, 955.110a–p
Gift of Miss Nora Lewis

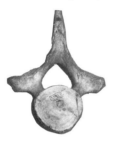

Vertebra of white whale
(*Delphinapterus leucas*)
Baffin Island
Height 25.4 cm, length 35.6 cm,
width 33.0 cm
Royal Ontario Museum, R848

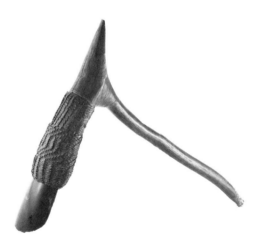

Headrest
Wood
Possibly East Africa, late 19th century
Height 12.8 cm, length 9.5 cm, width 9.3 cm
Royal Ontario Museum, 960.69.101
Harris Collection

Blue and yellow macaw (*Ara ararauna*)
South America
Length 80 cm
Royal Ontario Museum, 36.6.16.1

Adze
Stone (head), wood, and reed or split root
New Guinea, early 20th century
Length overall 54.0 cm; length of head
39.6 cm
Royal Ontario Museum, HB775

Horn
Conch shell
New Guinea, 20th century
Length 30.5 cm, width 12.7 cm
Royal Ontario Museum, 969.330.27

Throwing knife
Metal, cord, cloth, and fibre
Central Africa, Uelle, late 19th to early
20th century
Length 37.5 cm, width 36.0 cm
Royal Ontario Museum, HA2466

Pair of moccasins
Skin; moosehair embroidery
Canada, Huron? Indian, 19th century
Height of each 8.9 cm, length 25.4 cm,
width 12.8 cm
Royal Ontario Museum, 980.32

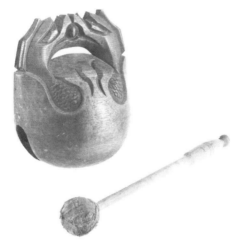

Gong and stick
Wood
Japan, 20th century
Height of gong 13.0 cm, length 15.3 cm,
width 10.2 cm; length of stick 30.5 cm
Royal Ontario Museum, 971.280.12a–b

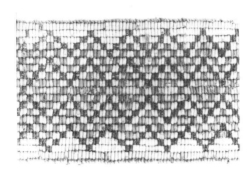

Band
Quill and sinew
Canada, Northwest Territories, Northern
Athapaskan Indian, late 19th to early
20th century
Length 28 cm, width 4 cm
Royal Ontario Museum, 956.101.3

Hercules and the Cretan Bull
Bronze, hollow cast
The Netherlands or France, 18th century;
after a model by Ferdinando Tacca, inspired
by prototype by Giovanni Bologna
Height 58 cm
Royal Ontario Museum, 939.4.1

Quartz crystal
United States, Arkansas
Height 5.0 cm, length 7.4 cm, width 6.5 cm
Royal Ontario Museum

Jadeite
Burma
Height 3.8 cm, length 7.1 cm, width 5.0 cm
Royal Ontario Museum

Knife
Copper
Peru, Chimu, c. 1200
Length 16.9 cm, width 9.4 cm
Royal Ontario Museum, 962.90.19

THE EAST COLLECTS

Entertainers, courtesans, household servants, mercenaries and slaves also moved along the trade routes. Throughout the world and through the ages, human beings have represented a profitable aspect of international trade. Ownership of slaves and servants assured economic advantage and frequently conferred status.

From the 2nd century on, Chinese emperors and nobles delighted in collecting West and Central Asian dancers, jugglers, and acrobats for their courts. By the 7th century it was customary for Chinese nobles to be buried with ceramic figures to indicate their social status.

Tomb figure of man
Earthenware, red; traces of slip and pigment
China, mid-8th century
Height 38.2 cm
Royal Ontario Museum, 920.1.65
George Crofts Collection

Tomb figure of woman
Earthenware, red; traces of slip and pigment
China, mid-8th century
Height 39 cm
Royal Ontario Museum, 920.1.66
George Crofts Collection

Tomb figure of mounted musician
Earthenware, buff; yellow glaze, traces of pigment
China, 7th century
Height 23.0 cm, length 21.2 cm
Royal Ontario Museum, 920.1.135
George Crofts Collection

Tomb figure of mounted female dwarf
Earthenware, buff; traces of slip and pigment
China, 7th to 8th century
Height 28.2 cm, length 23.1 cm
Royal Ontario Museum, 918.21.266
George Crofts Collection

Tomb figure of mounted musician
Earthenware, buff; yellow glaze, traces
of pigment
China, 7th century
Height 23.6 cm, length 20.1 cm
Royal Ontario Museum, 920.1.136
George Crofts Collection

Tomb figure of mounted musician
Earthenware, buff; yellow glaze, traces
of pigment
China, 7th century
Height 23.2 cm, length 21.1 cm
Royal Ontario Museum, 920.1.139
George Crofts Collection

**Tomb figure of mounted hunter
or acrobat**
Earthenware, buff; traces of slip and pigment
China, 7th to 8th century
Height 29.2 cm, length 25.2 cm
Royal Ontario Museum, 921.21.110
George Crofts Collection

Tomb figure of mounted foreigner
Earthenware, buff; brown, green, and
yellow glaze
China, late 7th to 8th century
Height 40.3 cm, length 30.7 cm
Royal Ontario Museum, 918.21.329
George Crofts Collection
(See illustration page 46.)

Tomb figure of mounted musician
Earthenware, buff; yellow glaze, traces
of pigment
China, 7th century
Height 23.6 cm, length 19.9 cm
Royal Ontario Museum, 920.1.138
George Crofts Collection

Tomb figure of mounted musician
Earthenware, buff; yellow glaze, traces
of pigment
China, 7th century
Height 23.7 cm, length 20.2 cm
Royal Ontario Museum, 920.1.140
George Crofts Collection

Tomb figure of greyhound
Earthenware, buff; yellow and brown glaze
China, late 7th to 8th century
Height 16.4 cm
Royal Ontario Museum, 920.5.165
George Crofts Collection

Tomb figure of Southeast Asian dancer
Earthenware, pink; traces of pigment
China, 7th to 8th century
Height 29.4 cm
Royal Ontario Museum, 920.1.76
George Crofts Collection

Tomb figure of foreign guard
Earthenware, buff; green glaze, traces
of pigment
China, 7th century
Height 56.5 cm
Royal Ontario Museum, 918.21.370
George Crofts Collection

Tomb figure of foreign guard
Earthenware, buff; green glaze, traces
of pigment
China, 7th century
Height 58.7 cm
Royal Ontario Museum, 918.21.371
George Crofts Collection
(See illustration page 67.)

Tomb figure of Southeast Asian dancer
Earthenware, buff; traces of slip and pigment
China, 7th to 8th century
Height 27.3 cm
Royal Ontario Museum, 920.1.77
George Crofts Collection

Tomb figure of Southeast Asian dancer
Earthenware, buff; pale green glaze
China, 7th to 8th century
Height 24.2 cm
Royal Ontario Museum, 920.1.179
George Crofts Collection

Tomb figure of civil official
Earthenware, buff; brown, green, and
yellow glaze
China, late 7th to 8th century
Height 110 cm
Royal Ontario Museum, 918.22.12
George Crofts Collection
Gift of Mrs H. D. Warren
(See illustration page 47.)

Tomb figure of civil official
Earthenware, buff; brown, green, and
yellow glaze
China, late 7th to 8th century
Height 110 cm
Royal Ontario Museum, 918.22.13
George Crofts Collection
Gift of Mrs H. D. Warren
(See illustration page 47.)

Spices and Medicines

The seeds, leaves, bark, resins, and roots
of many plants native to tropical Asia
have been traded throughout the world
from earliest times, accruing fabulous
profits to merchants in spices, medicines,
aromatics, and drugs.

**Medical Botany containing systematic
and general descriptions, with plates
of all the medicinal plants, indigenous
and exotic, comprehended in the catalogues of the Materia Medica, as
published by the Royal Colleges of
Physicians of London and Edinburgh:
accompanied with a circumstantial
detail of their medicinal effects, and of
the diseases in which they have been
most successfully employed**
William Woodville, M.D.
London, James Phillips, 1790/93,
3 volumes
Each leaf 23.5 cm × 18.7 cm
Thomas Fisher Rare Book Library
University of Toronto
Jason A. Hanna Collection in the History of
Medical and Related Sciences
(See illustrations pages 164–166.)

Jar and lid ("ginger jar")
Porcelain; underglaze blue
China, late 17th to early 18th century
Height 25.4 cm, diameter 24.2 cm
Royal Ontario Museum, 923.17.44a–b
George Crofts Collection

Nutmeg grater
Silver
Canada, early 19th century
Height 14 cm
Royal Ontario Museum, 952.23
The John and Eustella Langdon Collection
of Canadian Silver

Spice box for ceremony of Havdalah
Ivory and silver
Probably India, 19th century
Height 38.5 cm
Royal Ontario Museum, 974.14.1
Gift of Dr Morton Shulman
(See illustration page 168.)

Apothecary jar
Marked: P:EX:DUOB (pills of two things,
probably colocynthis and scammony used
as a purgative?)
Earthenware; tin glaze, painted blue
England, 18th century
Height 8.8 cm
Museum of the History of Medicine, CD560
Academy of Medicine, Toronto
Dr T. G. H. Drake Collection
(See illustration page 169.)

Apothecary jar
Marked: P:SAPON (saponaceae or soap pill,
compound with opium used as a sedative)
Earthenware; tin glaze, painted blue
England, 18th century
Height 8.8 cm
Museum of the History of Medicine, CD562
Academy of Medicine, Toronto
Dr T. G. H. Drake Collection
(See illustration page 169.)

Apothecary jar
Marked: P:DIAMBRAE (diaromaton powder,
compound of cinnamon, cardamom, ginger,
and pepper used to heat and strengthen
the brain and to cause mirth)
Earthenware; tin glaze, painted blue
England, 18th century
Height 12 cm
Museum of the History of Medicine, CD668
Academy of Medicine, Toronto
Dr T. G. H. Drake Collection
(See illustration page 169.)

Apothecary jar
Marked: P:MERCUR:LAX (Honey of
Mercury used as a purgative)
Earthenware; tin glaze, painted blue
England, 18th century
Height 8.6 cm
Museum of the History of Medicine, CD563
Academy of Medicine, Toronto
Dr T. G. H. Drake Collection
(See illustration page 169.)

**Nutmeg, ephaedra, areca nut, and
plantago, herbs from a traditional
Chinese pharmacopoeia**
Stored in matchboxes
Collected in Taiwan, 19th century
Height of matchboxes 2 cm, length 6 cm,
width 4 cm
Royal Ontario Museum, study collection

Tobacco and Opium

Habit-forming drugs and stimulants derived
from various plants have yielded the highest
profits to international traders. Their use
and cultivation have been spread across the
world through international commerce.

Water pipe
Pewter
China, 19th century
Height 39.5 cm
Royal Ontario Museum, 973x85.44

Pipe
Stoneware, white
England, 17th century
Length 14.5 cm
Royal Ontario Museum, 927.28.179a

Snuff box with watch
Agate, orange and white; gold mounts;
gold watch
England, c. 1760, James Cox
(active c. 1760–1788)
Height 5.2 cm, length 8.2 cm, width 6.2 cm
Royal Ontario Museum, 978.360a–c
Gift of Dr Morton Shulman, Mr Sam Sarick,
and Dr J. Moldofsky
(See illustration page 149.)

Snuff box
Wood; carved
Africa, Angola, late 19th to early 20th century
Height 8.3 cm, diameter 7.0 cm
Royal Ontario Museum, 937.25.3

Rasp for snuff
Steel; case of carved walnut
Probably France, late 17th century
Length 22.0 cm, width 8.8 cm
Royal Ontario Museum, 930.15.20

Snuff bottle
Glass, layered polychrome; carved
China, 19th century
Height 8.6 cm
Royal Ontario Museum, 976.181.3
Anonymous gift
(See illustration page 155.)

Snuff accessories (spoon, palette, and funnel)
Ivory
China, 19th century
Diameter of palette 3.2 cm; height of funnel 4.4 cm, diameter 2.7 cm; length of spoon 28.3 cm
Royal Ontario Museum, 914.43.14a–c

Western warehouses (hongs) outside Guangzhou
Oil on canvas
China, probably Guangzhou, artist unknown, c. 1850
66 cm × 97 cm
Courtesy the China Trade Museum, Milton, Massachusetts
(See illustration page 154.)

Opium pipe
Tortoise shell and pewter
China, 19th century
Length 57.3 cm
Royal Ontario Museum, 934.71.3
Gift of Mrs Johnson and Miss MacLaren
(See illustration page 155.)

Opium scales
Bone with brass; case of bamboo
China, 19th century
Length of balance beam 35.6 cm; length of case 38.5 cm
Museum of the History of Medicine, x940.5.7
Academy of Medicine, Toronto
(See illustration page 155.)

Spirit lamp for opium
Steel; silver plated
United States, marked Menden Company, early 20th century
Height 8.0 cm, diameter 6.2 cm
Museum of the History of Medicine, x969.315
Academy of Medicine, Toronto
(See illustration page 155.)

Vial for opium
Horn with silver
China, 19th century
Height 6.5 cm
Museum of the History of Medicine, x969.10.4a–b
Academy of Medicine, Toronto
(See illustration page 155.)

Vial for opium
Horn
China, 19th century
Height 6.1 cm
Museum of the History of Medicine, x969.10.5a–b
Academy of Medicine, Toronto
(See illustration page 155.)

Vial for opium
Horn
China, 19th century
Height 4.7 cm
Museum of the History of Medicine, x969.10.6a–b
Academy of Medicine, Toronto
(See illustration page 155.)

A PERSIAN CASTLE ON THE SILK ROADS

Archaeology contributes to our knowledge of international trade through the recovery of artifacts and information in context. The Royal Ontario Museum's excavations at the site of Qaleh-i Yazdigird in the Zagros Mountains of western Iran was another step in the continuing study begun in the late 19th century of the trade routes along the Silk Roads.

Excavations revealed a fortified palace with elaborately decorated rooms. In all likelihood Qaleh-i Yazdigird was built and maintained by a self-styled robber baron in defiance of Parthian authority in the 2nd century. Support for the lavish lifestyle undoubtedly came from fees exacted from the caravans that passed beneath the defensive walls.

Site model
Scale model of Qaleh-i Yazdigird tableland
1.2 m x 2.4 m
Royal Ontario Museum
(See illustration page 38.)

Reproduction casts of plaster decorations from Qaleh-i Yazdigird
Iran, Parthian, 2nd century
Royal Ontario Museum

Engaged column capital with talismanic figures
Pair of intertwined beasts flanked by stylized tree
Height 38 cm, width 44 cm, depth 19 cm
(See illustration page 41.)

Frieze with animal procession
Addorsed griffins, with deer; coffered design beneath
Height 14 cm, width 50 cm, depth 11 cm
(See illustration page 42.)

Engaged column capital with Aphrodite
Nude female holding tails of dolphins
Height 47 cm, width 61 cm, depth 17 cm
(See illustration page 41.)

Engaged column with theatrical figures
Four repeat figures in separate registers on three facets
Height 108 cm, width 42 cm, depth 22 cm
(See illustration page 43.)

Engaged half-column with ritual hunt scene
Nude male and animals in separate registers
Height 48 cm, width 26 cm, depth 15 cm

Frieze with Dionysus
Reclining figure with grapes; Cupids sporting with feline; coffered design beneath
Height 33 cm, width 119 cm, depth 17 cm
(See illustration page 42.)

Panel with mythical beast
Griffin protome
Height 39 cm, width 61 cm, depth 7 cm
(See illustration page 42.)

Jewellery pendant
Gold; repoussé
Iran, Parthian, 1st to 2nd century
Height 1.7 cm
Royal Ontario Museum, 971.394.7

Drachm
Silver
Iran, Parthian, "Unknown King", c. 140
Diameter 1.9 cm
Royal Ontario Museum,
Qaleh-i Yazdigird expedition
(See illustration page 44.)

RESULTS OF TRADE

Trade in luxury goods was accompanied by a reciprocal flow of ideas. In this section the exchange of fashions, styles, and tastes promoted by trade goods is demonstrated in Western imitations of Eastern goods, in goods that show the impact of Western arts on East Asia, and in goods that combine Eastern and Western influences.

Trade also facilitated the transmission of religious beliefs, first through the activities of the traders themselves, and later by missionaries and travellers. Technical ideas and inventions, too, moved freely along the trade routes.

Exchange by Imitation

Imported trade goods such as Chinese porcelain introduced local craftsmen to new art styles and new technology. Unaware of kaolin, the basic ingredient of the porcelain, however, Persian and European potters found ingenious ways of imitating Chinese import wares to supply demands for objects that resembled the Chinese wares but were less expensive. The underglaze painted blue decoration imitated Chinese originals.

Plate
Porcelain; underglaze blue
China, late 16th to 17th century
Height 9.9 cm, diameter 49.3 cm
Royal Ontario Museum, 908.14.3
(See illustration page 129.)

Plate
Earthenware (quartz compound); underglaze blue
Iran, 17th century
Height 6.6 cm, diameter 40.3 cm
Royal Ontario Museum, 909.25.2

Plate
Earthenware; tin glaze, painted blue
The Netherlands, late 17th century
Height 7 cm, diameter 34 cm
Royal Ontario Museum, 933.13.8
Gift of Mr Bernard Allen

Exchange by Adaptation

Market demands and expectations influenced production of goods for local use and for export in the 17th and 18th centuries. The *flowering tree* was one of the characteristic motifs of the European China taste of that period. European trade companies ordered large coverlets decorated with the flowering-tree design from Indian cotton painters. English embroiderers in turn created their own versions of the celebrated theme.

Coverlet
Cotton tabby, white; mordant-painted and resist-dyed in red, blue, violet, green, and black
India, early 18th century
270 cm × 221 cm
Royal Ontario Museum, 961.7.6
(See illustration page 134.)

Curtain or wall hanging
Linen satin, white; embroidery in polychrome wool
England, early 18th century
207 cm × 184 cm
Royal Ontario Museum, 971.227c
(See illustration page 123.)

West Imitates East

The increased demand in Western markets for oriental luxury goods throughout the 17th and 18th centuries inspired a new decorative style called chinoiserie. Whether in the pavilions built by European nobles and aristocrats or in the less ambitious, but equally sensuous boudoirs of fashionable ladies of taste, the chinoiserie decoration projected an aura of intimacy.

Length of furnishing fabric
Silk tabby, white; polychrome painting
France, mid-18th century
218.0 cm × 57.5 cm
Royal Ontario Museum, 978.295.2

IMITATION
The shiny, durable finish of oriental lacquers was greatly admired in Europe. Both true lacquer — derived from the sap of an Asian tree botanically related to the American poison oak — and a variety of varnishes were employed by Westerners to imitate the appearance of oriental lacquer wares.

Cabinet
Lacquer, red; carved; hardstone inlay
China, 18th century
Height 41.5 cm, length 34.4 cm, width 25.5 cm
Royal Ontario Museum, 955.97.2
Bequest of Major James E. Hahn

Cabinet
Pine with red varnish and gilt; marquetry of assorted woods over drawers
Cabinet Tyrolean; varnishing possibly Italian, c. 1730
Height 57.7 cm, length 70.5 cm, width 34.0 cm
Royal Ontario Museum, 929.14.1

Where technical abilities of the West matched those of the East, copies of Asian imports were produced. Unglazed stoneware ceramics from China were imitated at many kilns in Europe.

Once the secret of kaolin clay was known in Europe, many ceramic factories produced copies of plain white wares with moulded decoration in imitation of Chinese wares. The fine Chinese *blanc de Chine* wares were always highly admired for their translucent delicacy.

Cup, lid, and saucer
Porcelain
France, St Cloud, c. 1730
Height of cup 7.2 cm, diameter 7.2 cm; diameter of lid 7.7 cm; diameter of saucer 12.4 cm
Royal Ontario Museum, 950.78a–c

Teapot
Stoneware, brown (*Yi-xing* ware)
China, late 19th century
Height 14.0 cm, length 18.3 cm, diameter 11.4 cm
Royal Ontario Museum, 923.18.18a–b
George Crofts Collection

Cup (rhinoceros-horn shape)
Porcelain (*de-hua* ware)
China, 18th century
Height 9.0 cm, length 14.9 cm, width 10.8 cm
Royal Ontario Museum, 914.38.11

Teapot
Stoneware, red
England, c. 1760
Height 11.3 cm, diameter at base 7.0 cm
Royal Ontario Museum, 948.146

Tester cup
Porcelain
Germany, Meissen factory, c. 1710; attributed to J. F. Böttger
Height 6.4 cm, diameter 6.4 cm
Royal Ontario Museum, 955.182

ADAPTATION

Growing populations and a wealthier middle class increased the demand for goods in the fashionable China taste. Merchants responded by ordering Asian trade goods made to Western specifications; they also encouraged local craftsmen to imitate, adapt, and invent their own versions of the imports.

The result was a plethora of authentic and imitative, original and "improved", designs. Specific goods were identified by their supposed countries of origin. All porcelain, for example, became "china", and wool pile fabrics were known as "turkey".

Plate
Earthenware; tin glaze, painted blue
England, Bristol, mid-18th century
Height 5.2 cm, diameter 34.0 cm
Royal Ontario Museum, 931.10.5
Bequest of Mary Louise Clarke

Teabowl and saucer
Porcelain (soft paste); underglaze blue
England, Lowestoft, c. 1780
Height of cup 4.0 cm, diameter 7.6 cm;
diameter of saucer 11.6 cm
Royal Ontario Museum, 954.90.99a–b
Gift of Miss Amice Calverley

Bowl
Porcelain; underglaze blue
China, late 17th
to early 18th century
Height 8.4 cm, diameter 20.7 cm
Royal Ontario Museum, 911.8.51
Gift of Mrs H. D. Warren

Tankard
Earthenware; tin glaze, painted blue
England, probably Leeds, dated 1780
Height 14.5 cm, diameter 10.2 cm
Royal Ontario Museum, 962.213.2

Plate
Earthenware; white slip, blue transfer-printed decoration
England, Swansea, c. 1800
Diameter 21 cm
Royal Ontario Museum, 954.90.114
Gift of Miss Amice Calverley

Rug
Knotted wool pile, polychrome
Turkey, late 17th century
214.5 cm × 173.0 cm
Royal Ontario Museum, 979.280
Gift of Mrs John Alexander Wilson in
memory of Dr Veronika Gervers
(See illustration page 113.)

Chair
Oak; upholstery of polychrome knotted
wool pile
England, Norwich, late 17th century
Height 104 cm, width 53 cm; height of seat
44 cm
Royal Ontario Museum, 969.323.la
Anonymous gift

FANTASIES

The China taste was characterized by imitations of exotic Asian trade goods, as well as by "improvements" on oriental imagery, which European decorators felt were better suited to Western tastes. A range of specific motifs—bird on branch, pavilion in garden, moustachioed Chinese figures, and rockeries—became the hallmarks of the style. The motifs, with appropriate materials and colour schemes that evoked oriental goods—blue and white porcelain, polychrome embroidery on light-coloured silk grounds, and shiny dark lacquer with lighter ornament—were freely used and adapted by European decorators. Many of these hybrid designs were sent eastwards to be copied in turn and re-exported. Printed pattern books and manuals popularized oriental styles and encouraged domestic adaptations in all manner of decorative media.

Longcase clock
Case of green japanned oak with gilt
England, mid-18th century; clockwork
signed by John Ogden of Sunderland
(1725–1759)
Height 233.7 cm, width 48.2 cm,
depth 24.1 cm
Royal Ontario Museum, 911.7.1
Gift of the T. Eaton Company Limited

Teapot
Stoneware, red
England, c. 1740
Height 8.2 cm, diameter 7.6 cm
Royal Ontario Museum, 934.7.1

Child's coverlet
Linen twill, white; embroidery in polychrome wool
England, dated 1728
130.8 cm × 139.0 cm
Royal Ontario Museum, 970.128
Anonymous gift in memory of Gerard Brett
(See illustration page 124.)

Porringer (cup)
Silver
England, London, 1688-1689; maker's mark TA
Height 11.1 cm, diameter 13.7 cm
Royal Ontario Museum, 950.82.4
Gift of Mrs F. N. G. Starr
(See illustration page 124.)

Uncut waistcoat fronts
Silk satin, white; embroidery in polychrome silk
France, late 18th century
69 cm × 56 cm
Royal Ontario Museum, 934.4.425
Harry Wearne Collection
Gift of Mrs Harry Wearne
(See illustration page 126.)

Coffee pot
Earthenware; painted blue ("Pearlware")
England, possibly Leeds, 1780–1790
Height 26.6 cm
Royal Ontario Museum, 934.7.22a–b

Plate
Porcelain (bone china); overglaze
polychrome enamel
England, probably Miles Mason, c. 1805
Diameter 21.9 cm
Royal Ontario Museum, 936.8.2
(See illustration page 115.)

Goblet
"Hyalith" glass, black; gilt
Germany, c. 1830
Height 15.7 cm, diameter of base 6.7 cm
Royal Ontario Museum, 970.253.24
Bequest of Leo David Drucker

Plate
Earthenware; tin glaze, overglaze poly-
chrome enamel
France, Strasbourg type, c. 1770
Diameter 21.8 cm
Royal Ontario Museum, 980.99.117a
Anonymous gift

Two covered dishes from a dinner set
Earthenware; white slip, blue transfer-
printed decoration; pattern "Chinoiserie
High Bridge"
England, Davenport, 1810–1815
Height 12.7 cm, length 28.0 cm, width
22.0 cm
Royal Ontario Museum, 945.25.6a–d
Anonymous gift

China case
Mahogany
England, c. 1840; after a design published
by Thomas Chippendale in 1753
Height 269.0 cm, length 161.3 cm, width
43.7 cm
Royal Ontario Museum, 923.20.1
Gift of the T. Eaton Company Limited
(See illustration page 128.)

Butter dish and lid
Porcelain (bone china); underglaze blue,
overglaze red enamel, gilt ("Brocaded"
Imari style)
England, Derby factory, 1810–1820
Height of dish 5.2 cm, diameter 11.8 cm;
diameter of attached saucer 18.0 cm;
diameter of lid 12.3 cm
Royal Ontario Museum, 975.331.17a–b
Gift of Dr Walter Tovell

221

West Meets East: Made to Order

Concern for ready profits, with minimal risk to capital investment, led merchants to request specific forms and types of goods. Thus the processes of imitation and adaptation were influenced and complicated by a wide range of made-to-order objects, which craftsmen willingly produced to meet market demands and expectations created in part by the traders themselves. Requests for specific patterns and models and special orders frequently required craftsmen to modify traditional methods of production.

Cabinet with drawers and drop front
Lacquer, black; gilt, mother-of-pearl inlay
Japan, for the European market, late 16th to 17th century
Height 53 cm, length 75 cm, width 40 cm
Royal Ontario Museum, 967.33.1
Gift of Mr and Mrs Frank H. Ferris, Jr
(See illustration page 120.)

Punch bowl
Porcelain; overglaze polychrome enamel, gilt
China, c. 1760
Height 16.0 cm, diameter 38.5 cm
Royal Ontario Museum, 950.87.1

Plate with coat of arms of an Italian cardinal
Copper; polychrome enamel
China, for the Italian? market, 18th century
Diameter 22.6 cm
Royal Ontario Museum, 924.10.15
(See illustration page 120.)

Tankard
Porcelain; underglaze blue
Japan, for the European market, 17th century
Height 25.1 cm
Royal Ontario Museum, 910.59.1

Hot-water plate
Porcelain; overglaze sepia enamel, gilt
China, for the European market, 19th century
Diameter 24.2 cm
Royal Ontario Museum, 956.143.48
Gift of the Winfield Foundation

Punch bowl with Gordon coat of arms
Porcelain; overglaze polychrome enamel
China, for the European market, late 18th century
Height 12.0 cm, diameter 28.6 cm
Royal Ontario Museum, 956.143.16
Gift of the Winfield Foundation

Plate with arms of Lee of Stoke quartering Ashley of Astley
Porcelain; grisaille, overglaze polychrome enamel, gilt
China, for the English market, early 18th century
Diameter 35.5 cm
Royal Ontario Museum, 949.159.1

Central fragment of coverlet
Cotton tabby, white; chainstitch embroidery in red, green, and yellow silk
India, Gujarat, for the English market late 17th century
250.5 cm × 178.5 cm
Royal Ontario Museum, 978.339
(See illustration page 122.)

Yardage for waistcoat
Cotton tabby, white; mordant-painted and
resist-dyed in red, blue, green, black, and
yellow
India, for the European market, mid-18th
century
86 cm × 63 cm
Royal Ontario Museum, 963.179.1
(See illustration page 132.)

Dress
Cotton tabby, white; embroidery in
white cotton
India, for the English market, 1824–1825
Royal Ontario Museum, 921.37.2
Gift of Mrs George A. Sweny
(See illustration page 148.)

Shawl
Cashmere wool twill, red; embroidery in
polychrome silk
India (wool from Kashmir, embroidered in
Gujarat), for the European market, early
19th century
261.0 cm × 54.5 cm
Royal Ontario Museum, 977.264.2
Gift of Miss Hilda Simister
(See illustration page 148.)

Platter
Porcelain; underglaze blue
China, mid-19th century; imitating blue
willow transfer ware
Height 6.2 cm, length 37.0 cm, width
29.2cm
Royal Ontario Museum, 954.90.116
Gift of Miss Amice Calverley

East Imitates West

JAPANESE INTERIOR 1875–1915
After the Meiji emperor opened Japan to
international trade in 1858, the Japanese
people came into contact with Westerners
and Western ideas. For the next half-
century fashionable Japanese made a vogue
of Western dress, manners, and diversions.

Having discovered that ornately carved
furniture was popular in Europe, the
Japanese created their own unique version
of this ornate style. It was as different as
could be from the traditional austere style
of Japanese interior, in which a matted
floor served as dining, sleeping, and seating
space. Meiji carpenters produced an
imitation of Western furniture, both for
domestic use and for export. This unusual
furniture is a testament to the enthusiasm
with which 19th-century Japan accepted
Western creations.

The harbour of Nagasaki
Oil on canvas
Albert Berg (1825–1884), Germany,
c.1860
60.7 cm × 98.5 cm
Royal Ontario Museum, 977.63
Gift of Tip Top Remaco, Limited, to
commemorate the curatorship of
Dr Hsio-Yen Shih

Cabinet
Wood; carved
Japan, late 19th century
Height 172 cm, length 89 cm, width 50 cm
Margaret Woodbury Strong Museum,
75.2263, Rochester
(See illustration page 161.)

Contents of cabinet

Pair of vases
Glass, yellow; engraved
China, mark of Qien-lung (1736–1796)
Height 17.8 cm
Royal Ontario Museum, 961.228.19a–b

Pair of mythical animals
Jade, pale green with amber veining
China, 18th century
Height 10.8 cm, length 18.4 cm
Royal Ontario Museum, 911.8.114

"Jade" tree
Coral and assorted hardstone; lacquered metal container
China, 19th century
Height 30.4 cm
Royal Ontario Museum, NB349

Pair of teacups, stands, and lids
Copper; polychrome enamel
China, Guangzhou, 19th century
Height of each cup 10.8 cm, diameter 10.2 cm
Royal Ontario Museum, 973x85.32a–b

Corner chair
Wood, carved
Japan, late 19th century
Height 77.7 cm, length 75.0 cm, width 69.0 cm
Margaret Woodbury Strong Museum, 74.1844, Rochester
(See illustration page 161.)

Desk and chair
Wood, carved; ivory and bone inlay
Japan, late 19th century
Height of desk 137 cm, length 112 cm, width 73 cm; height of chair 94 cm, width 51 cm
Margaret Woodbury Strong Museum, 74.1718, Rochester
(See illustration page 161.)

Jar and cover
Porcelain; underglaze blue, overglaze red enamel, gilt (*Imari* ware)
Japan, 19th century
Height 78.0 cm, diameter 41.5 cm
Royal Ontario Museum, 923.44.1a–b
(See illustration page 137.)

CHINA

Trade goods entered China from the west, the south, and the east. Some, such as glass, had a widespread impact. Others, such as European clocks and automata, were largely confined to the imperial court.

CHINA AND WEST ASIA

The cosmopolitan tastes of Tang China were nurtured by luxury goods brought by Buddhist monks from India, Middle Eastern merchants, and Southeast Asian traders. Gold and silver vessels from Sasanian Iran inspired Chinese craftsmen to copy them in fine metals as well as in ceramics.

Ewer with rooster's head
Earthenware (quartz compound); underglaze blue
Iran, Kashan, early 13th century
Height 28 cm
Royal Ontario Museum, 936.29.2

Wine Ewer with rooster's head
Earthenware, buff; yellow, brown, and green glaze
China, late 7th to 8th century
Height 34.3 cm
Royal Ontario Museum, 910.40.2
Gift of Sir Edmund Walker
(See illustration page 70.)

Deer-head rhyton (drinking cup)
Earthenware, buff
Southern Italy, Apulian, c. 330–300 B.C.
Length 23.7 cm
Royal Ontario Museum, 919.5.56
Gift of Dr Sigmund Samuel

Ox-head rhyton (drinking cup)
Earthenware, buff; light green glaze
China, 7th to 8th century
Height 8.8 cm
Royal Ontario Museum, 927.19.7
Bishop White Collection
(See illustration page 71.)

Amphora (vase)
Stoneware, white
China, 7th century
Height 53.5 cm, diameter 28.4 cm
Royal Ontario Museum, 914.7.106

Pilgrim bottle
Earthenware, buff; moulded; green glaze
China, 7th to 8th century
Height 12.7 cm, width 11.5 cm
Royal Ontario Museum, 920.20.2
George Crofts Collection
(See illustration page 73.)

Bracelet
Glass, uncoloured; moulded
China, 7th to 8th century
Length 7.5 cm, width 8.1 cm
Royal Ontario Museum, 921.21.355b
George Crofts Collection

Bowl
Copper; polychrome cloisonné enamel
China, 16th to 17th century
Height 9.0 cm, diameter 20.9 cm
Royal Ontario Museum, 920.22.1

CHINA AND EUROPE
European Jesuits, who arrived at the Chinese imperial court in the 16th century, introduced Western scientific knowledge and baroque painting styles.

Informal portrait of first-rank official in the Qing court
Oil on paper
China, 18th century; head and shoulder replacement possibly early 19th century
145.0 cm × 115.5 cm
Royal Ontario Museum, 921.32.74
Gift of Mrs H. D. Warren
(See illustration page 138.)

Vase
Porcelain; overglaze polychrome enamel
China, early 19th century
Height 30.8 cm, diameter 17.8 cm
Royal Ontario Museum, 911.8.162
Gift of Mrs H. D. Warren
(See illustration page iii, title page)

Eastern and Western Influences on the Middle East

YEMENI INTERIOR 1875–1900

Yemeni cotton textiles were prized throughout the Islamic world in the 9th and 10th centuries, but the country's most famous export, coffee, did not become a major trade item until the 16th century. Traffic in coffee was largely controlled by foreign traders, but when Westerners transplanted coffee to Africa and the New World in the 18th century the Yemeni economy declined.

Early in the 19th century Yemen became a dependency of the Ottoman Turks. Although the country had little industry, her favoured position on the Red Sea shipping lanes made a wide range of exotic goods available to well-to-do Yemeni households. Yemeni interiors might be furnished with a mixture of goods from Europe, North America, the Middle East, and East Asia. Multipurpose high beds kept residents away from the damp floor and bedding out of reach of termites. Decorative niches and shelves held lamps and precious heirlooms. Storage was provided by trunks and cupboards, which were often built into the walls and closed with curtains or wooden doors.

Mat
Cotton tabby, white; printed, painted, and resist-dyed in red and blue; quilted
India, 19th century
133.5 cm × 89.0 cm
Royal Ontario Museum, 927.40.2

Pillow cover
Silk velvet, red and blue, voided on white satin ground
Turkey, Bursa, 19th century
135 cm × 64 cm
Royal Ontario Museum, 941x28.7

Pillow cover
Silk velvet, red and blue, voided on white satin ground
Turkey, Bursa, 19th century
118.5 cm × 60.0 cm
Royal Ontario Museum, 941x28.4

Wall curtain
Warp-patterned wool tabby, polychrome
Northwestern Iran, 19th century
205 cm × 167 cm
Royal Ontario Museum, 982.86.1
Gift of Miss A. Elizabeth Brown

Rug
Knotted wool pile, polychrome
Caucasus, 19th century
198 cm × 131 cm
Royal Ontario Museum, 910x145.13

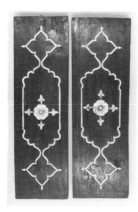

Doors for wall cabinet
Wood; ivory inlay
India, Punjab, 19th century
Height of each 77.2 cm, length 26.0 cm,
width 4.0 cm
Royal Ontario Museum, 927.53.48 – 49

Decanter
Glass, uncoloured; pressed, mould-blown
United States, possibly Boston & Sand-
wich Glass Company, Massachusetts,
c. 1850
Height 28.0 cm, diameter 9.7 cm
Royal Ontario Museum, 945.7.5
Gift of Miss Jean Robertson

Ewer
Glass, uncoloured; moulded; painted poly-
chrome enamel; stopper of silvered brass
Germany, 19th century
Height 22.5 cm, diameter 7.5 cm
Royal Ontario Museum, 921.21.559a–b
George Crofts Collection

Ewer
Earthenware; green glaze, gilt
Iran, 19th century
Height 45 cm
Royal Ontario Museum, 908x25.70

Cup
Glass, uncoloured; pressed
United States, c. 1880
Height 6.8 cm, diameter 6.3 cm
Royal Ontario Museum, 980.99.65
Anonymous gift

Plate
Porcelain; underglaze blue, overglaze red
enamel, gilt (Chinese *Imari* ware)
China, 18th century
Height 4.0 cm, diameter 32.2 cm
Royal Ontario Museum, 911.4.49

Jar
Porcelain; underglaze blue
China, 19th century
Height 13.0 cm, diameter 13.7 cm
Royal Ontario Museum, 969.199.1
Gift of Dr Hsio-Yen Shih

Saucer
Porcelain; underglaze blue
China, 19th century
Height 3.0 cm, diameter 15.3 cm
Royal Ontario Museum, 940.12.32
Gift of Miss A. Leslie

Plate
Porcelain; underglaze blue
China, 19th century
Height 5.7 cm, diameter 27.5 cm
Royal Ontario Museum, 977.228

Candlestick
Zinc alloy, silver inlay (*Bidri* ware)
India, 19th century
Height 24.0 cm, diameter 12.7 cm
Royal Ontario Museum, 910.217.3

Bowl
Porcelain; underglaze blue inside, brown
glaze outside
China, 19th century
Height 6.2 cm, diameter 22.4 cm
Royal Ontario Museum, 909.74.7
Gift of Sir Edmund Walker

Pipe base
Zinc alloy, silver and gold inlay (*Bidri* ware)
India, 19th century
Height 22.0 cm, diameter 22.5 cm
Royal Ontario Museum, 910.217.4

Tray
Zinc alloy, silver inlay (*Bidri* ware)
India, 19th century
Length 32.7 cm, width 25.6 cm
Royal Ontario Museum, 974.336
Gift of Mrs H. B. Marcoolyn

Koran chest
Brass; interior lining of wood
Turkey, 19th century
Height 28 cm, length 45 cm, width 45 cm
Royal Ontario Museum, 983x9.1

PERSIA IMITATES THE EAST

East Asian trade goods, particularly Chinese porcelain, influenced Middle Eastern tastes from the 9th century on. The Mongol invasion of Iran and Iraq in the 13th century brought closer contacts with China. Chinese craftsmen who were moved to the new capital of Tabriz left an enduring influence on Persian arts.

Throughout the 14th and 15th centuries, Central Asian conquerors dominated Persia, but in the 16th century a native dynasty, the Safavids, gained control of the Persian throne. Under Safavid rule, Persia prospered and a cosmopolitan court flourished first at Tabriz, and later at Isfahan. Far-reaching trade contacts stimulated a taste for the exotic. Safavid imitations of Chinese styles—in the manner of European chinoiseries—were applied to a wide range of objects.

Plate
Porcelain; underglaze blue
China, early 18th century
Diameter 45.1 cm
Royal Ontario Museum, 911.4.66
Gift of Mrs H. D. Warren

Plate
Earthenware (quartz compound);
underglaze blue
Iran, 16th century
Diameter 45.7 cm
Royal Ontario Museum, 909.25.4
(See illustration page 141.)

Album page with chinoiserie border
Ink and gold on paper
Iran, 17th century; calligraphy signed by Amir Sayyid
35.8 cm × 23.6 cm;
Royal Ontario Museum, 980.115.5

Drawing of drinking dervishes
Ink and slight colour on paper
Iran, early 17th century
19.3 cm × 13.4 cm;
Royal Ontario Museum, 937.40
Gift of the Members' Volunteer Committee

Plate
Earthenware (quartz compound);
underglaze blue
Iran, 17th century
Diameter 34.4 cm
Royal Ontario Museum, 908.22.1

Vase
Earthenware (quartz compound);
underglaze blue and black
Iran, 17th century
Height 14.5 cm, diameter 18.5 cm
Royal Ontario Museum, 940.90.1
Gift of Mr G. D. Hornblower

229

PERSIA INFLUENCED BY EAST AND WEST

Both Eastern and Western influences found favour at the court of the Persian Safavids in Isfahan during the 16th and 17th centuries. The exotic ladies depicted on this fabric wear European costumes. The pose is classical Graeco-Roman in origin, the garden setting is Persian, and the trailing clouds are East Asian.

Length of furnishing fabric
Silk velvet, polychrome, cut and voided on compound cloth-of-gold field, bouclé d'argent
Iran, late 16th to 17th century
222.0 cm × 74.3 cm
Royal Ontario Museum, 960.257
Gift of Mrs John David Eaton
(See illustration page 141 and cover.)

Transfer of Technology

The direction of movement of technological influences is often difficult to trace. Some inventions, whose sources are obscured by time and distance, later returned to their countries of origin as trade goods. One example is the European clock sent to East Asia as a marvel from the West. Modern research has shown that the principle of clockwork was, in fact, a Chinese invention of about the 6th century, which made its way westwards with traders and was applied to time-keeping mechanisms in 12th-century Europe.

Lantern clock
Brass case
Japan, 19th century
Height 39.3 cm, length 14.7 cm, width 14.7 cm
Royal Ontario Museum, 955.112
Gift of Mr Ralph Jones

PORCELAIN

Chinese potters developed porcelain-making technology in the 9th century. Porcelain is made of secondary clay. The clay is called kaolin, and contains felspar derived from decayed granite. Kaolin is mixed with petuntse, another secondary clay containing felspar and silica. At kiln temperatures of about 1450° centigrade the two clays vitrify. Although porcelain chips easily, its translucency and thinness give it great appeal.

Fragment of bowl
Porcelain; moulded
China, 18th century
Length 10.2 cm, width 15.0 cm.
Royal Ontario Museum, study collection

Large quantities of Chinese porcelain, and stoneware were exported widely in East Asia and the Middle East, and eventually to Europe.

Some of the early porcelains appear so much like stoneware that it is difficult to tell them apart. Stonewares, however, are made of different clays and have their own characteristics. The clay contains large amounts of silica, which fuses at kiln temperatures of about 1200° centigrade and forms durable, watertight vessels.

Fragment of bowl
Porcelain; pale blue glaze (*ying qing* ware)
China, 11th century; recovered near Zabid,
Yemen Arab Republic, by Royal Ontario
Museum Expedition, 1982
Length 5.7 cm, width 4.5 cm
Royal Ontario Museum, study collection

Fragment of saucer
Porcellaneous stoneware, white
China, mid-9th century; recovered at
Samarra, Iraq, by Samarra expedition,
1911
Length 5.2 cm, width 5.0 cm
Royal Ontario Museum, 923.34.4

Fragment of bowl
Stoneware, grey; green glaze (celadon)
China, 10th century; recovered near Zabid,
Yemen Arab Republic, by Royal Ontario
Museum expedition, 1982
Length 3.7 cm, width 9.0 cm
Royal Ontario Museum, study collection

Fragment of plate
Porcelain?; green glaze (celadon)
China, 13th to 14th century; recovered
near Zabid, Yemen Arab Republic, by
Royal Ontario Museum expedition, 1982
Length 3.4 cm, width 3.2 cm
Royal Ontario Museum, study collection

In response to market demands for fine
Chinese ceramics, Middle Eastern potters
invented a compound of clay and ground
quartz, which produced passable imitations of the fine white wares imported
from China

Fragment of vase
Earthenware (quartz compound);
overglaze lustre painted
Iran, 13th to 14th century; recovered at
Ghubeyra, Iran, by University of London
expedition, 1972
Height 8.7 cm, width 10.0 cm
Royal Ontario Museum, 973. 16.74

The significance of Chinese ceramics stems
from their fineness; potters outside China
went to great lengths to duplicate the
originals or to produce passable imitations.

Fragment of small bowl
Porcelain; underglaze blue
China, 15th to 16th century; recovered
near Zabid, Yemen Arab Republic, by
Royal Ontario Museum expedition, 1982
Height 3.5 cm, width 5.0 cm
Royal Ontario Museum, study collection

Fragment of bowl
Earthenware (quartz compound);
underglaze blue
Egypt, 15th century; recovered at Fustat
(Old Cairo), Egypt
Length 12.7 cm, width 12.5 cm
Royal Ontario Museum, 909.42.4

Fragment of bowl
Earthenware, red; white slip,
underglaze blue
Yemen, 15th century; recovered near
Zabid, Yemen Arab Republic, by Royal
Ontario Museum expedition, 1982
Length 8 cm, width 7 cm
Royal Ontario Museum, study collection

Fragment of tile
Earthenware, buff; tin glaze,
painted blue-violet
The Netherlands, late 17th century
Length 10.0 cm, width 5.5 cm
Royal Ontario Museum, study collection

Although kaolin remained a secret until
the 18th century, European potters in the
16th and 17th centuries produced what is
known as "soft-paste" porcelain. It was
made of an artificial compound of ground
glass, which required only a fairly low
firing temperature of 1150° centigrade.

Fragment of saucer
Porcelain (soft paste), overglaze
polychrome enamel, gilt
England, Worcester factory, late
18th century
Height 3.7 cm, width 12.0 cm
Royal Ontario Museum, study collection

The experiments of European potters in
their attempts to improve the shaping of
the soft-paste porcelain eventually led to
the unlocking of the secret in the late 17th
century, when European sources of kaolin
were discovered. The experiments culminated in 1709 at the court of Augustus the
Strong, king of Poland and elector of
Saxony, when the alchemist Johann Böttger
combined felspathic petuntse and kaolin-
ite clay.

A factory was established at Meissen and
an attempt was made to keep the new
formula a secret. Meissen potters, however,
were soon lured to other European centres.
At first the Meissen factory had difficulty
controlling the underglaze painting in
blue. The greatest success came with the
use of overglaze enamels.

Fragment of saucer
Porcelain; overglaze polychrome enamel,
gilt
Germany, Meissen factory, c. 1820
Height 3 cm, width 13 cm
Royal Ontario Museum, study collection

In England, Josiah Spode added bone ash
to the hard porcelain formula and produced what is known as "bone china".
Bone china does not chip as easily as hard
porcelain. It has an ivory-white tone rather
than the natural bluish tinge of true
porcelain.

Fragment of cup
Porcelain (bone china); overglaze
polychrome enamel, gilt
England, Minton factory, 19th century
Height 7.0 cm, width 6.8 cm
Royal Ontario Museum, study collection

COLOUR-FAST DYEING

Master dyers of India developed both mordant-painting and resist-dyeing processes to create brightly coloured cotton fabrics that became a vogue throughout the world. Both processes make fabrics colour-fast.

Reds and violets came from madder plants. Hue was determined by the type and the strength of the mordant, a metallic oxide that causes the dye to form an insoluble coating on cotton fibres. Indigo, another natural dye obtained from plants, produces a blue colour through oxidation when a dyed fabric is exposed to air. Areas of a fabric that are not to be dyed blue must be resisted, that is, covered with paste or wax. The resist process is repeated for each blue hue.

Indian cotton chintzes, such as the valance in this case, created a sensation in Europe after their introduction in the 17th century. The commercial success of the cotton imports was such a threat to the silk and wool textile industries in France and England that the governments were forced to impose bans on the importation of Indian chintzes.

The desire to profit from this lucrative new vogue led European entrepreneurs to found a printed-textile industry. The observations on the craft of the Indian dyers recorded by Western travellers were very useful.

Fragment of curtain
Cotton tabby, white; woodblock-printed in red, violet, black, green, and yellow, painted blue
France, Jouy, Oberkampf factory, c. 1775
165 cm × 97 cm
Royal Ontario Museum, 934.4.172a
Harry Wearne Collection
Gift of Mrs Harry Wearne
(See illustration page 127.)

Valance
Cotton tabby, white; mordant-painted and resist-dyed in red, blue, yellow, green, violet, and black
India, for the French market, mid-18th century
47 cm × 197 cm
Elinor Merrell Collection

GUNPOWDER

In recent times scholars have demonstrated that without question gunpowder was invented in China. A 9th-century Chinese text describes its preparation, but warns the unsuspecting not to manufacture the explosive compound.

Gunpowder was used in Chinese weapons, as well as in rockets and fireworks, in the 10th century. Europeans learned about fireworks in the 13th or the 14th century, either from Middle Eastern merchants or directly from traders who reached China along the Russian trade routes.

Before long Westerners were producing cannons. By the late 14th century they had developed their first primitive handguns. In 1510 Portuguese traders introduced Western firearms to China, and in the 1540s to Japan.

Cannon
Bronze barrel; iron core
China, early 15th century
Length 22 cm
Royal Ontario Museum, 921.1.15
(See illustration page vii.)

Flintlock sporting gun
Steel barrel, lock, and mounts; barrel blued and decorated with scrollwork; gold inlay
Spain, Madrid, dated 1744, Gabriel Algora
Length overall 138 cm
Royal Ontario Museum, 910.42.47
(See illustration page viii.)

Flintlock gun
Steel barrel and lock with silver bands and inlay; wooden stock with ivory and brass inlay
Turkey, 18th century
Length overall 75 cm
Royal Ontario Museum, 908.20.6
(See illustration page ix.)

"India Pattern" musket
Steel barrel and lock; brass mounts, wooden stock
England, early 19th century
Length overall 140 cm
Royal Ontario Museum, 948.78.17
Bequest of Dr N. C. Wallace
(See illustration page viii.)

Matchlock gun
Steel barrel and lock with gold, silver, and copper inlay; wooden stock
Japan, 19th century
Length overall 110 cm
Royal Ontario Museum, 933.7.61
Gift of Mrs Johnson and Miss MacLaren

233

Transmission of Art Styles

East and West have exchanged aesthetic ideas, styles, motifs, and techniques continually for more than three millennia. Despite enthusiastic trade in goods of exquisite craftsmanship and fine quality, most items have in the end been viewed as curios. Throughout this exchange it seems apparent that artists have been willing to adopt motifs and techniques from foreign traditions with only minimal understanding of other aesthetic values. A few outstanding exceptions to the norm provide insights into some of the ramifications of international commerce.

INFLUENCES FROM THE EAST

For more than sixty years art historians have argued that medieval artists in the West must have been exposed to Chinese paintings or prints once direct trade with the East Asia was resumed during the *Pax Mongolica* of the 12th and 13th centuries. While it is difficult to document this connection in the absence of a single Chinese painting or a record of the existence of one in Europe, certain features of European painting seemingly reflect familiarity with oriental aesthetic principles.

Moses striking the rock
Woodcut; white laid paper
Michael Wolgemut (1434–1519), Germany, 1491; in the *Schatzebehalter*
25.0 cm × 17.5 cm (impression)
Art Gallery of Ontario, 76/236
Gift of Mr and Mrs Ralph Presgrave, 1976

Noah's ark on Mount Ararat, a camel train outside a city in foreground
Brown ink, brown, grey, and yellow washes; cream paper
Lambert Doomer (1622/23–1700), The Netherlands, 17th century
26.7 cm × 41.0 cm
Art Gallery of Ontario, 79/98
Purchase, 1978

IMPACT OF JAPANESE AESTHETICS IN THE WEST

Between 1865 and 1900 Japanese art made a significant impact on Western painting, particularly through artists living and working in France, who collected Japanese prints and profited from the lessons in composition, design, and tonal relationships that these works could teach.

Although considered a minor art form in Japan, Japanese woodcuts had filtered into Europe from the beginning of the 19th century. The Paris Universal Exposition of 1867 introduced Japanese prints to the general public and helped to promote the fashion for *japonaiserie* and the experiments of many artists working in Paris.

Afterglow of late summer
Woodcut; printed in colour on paper; from series "Eight Scenes of the Four Seasons"
Torii Kiyonaga (1752–1815), Japan, 1779
25.6 cm × 18.1 cm
Royal Ontario Museum, 926.18.282
Sir Edmund Walker Estate

Les baigneuses
Oil on canvas
Pierre Puvis de Chavannes (1824–1898),
France, c. 1890
58 cm × 38 cm
Art Gallery of Ontario, 74/30
Purchase, Peter Larkin Endowment Fund,
1974

Printemps
Etching; drypoint on Japanese paper
James Tissot (1836–1902), France, 1878
38.1 cm × 13.5 cm (impression)
Art Gallery of Ontario, 66/18
Purchase, 1966
(See illustration page 160.)

**Viewing maple leaves at Kaianji, a
temple in Shinagawa**
Woodcut; printed in colour on paper
Utagawa Hiroshige (1797–1858), Japan,
1853; from series "Famous Views of Edo"
34.1 cm × 21.9 cm
Royal Ontario Museum, 926.18.797
Sir Edmund Walker Estate

Rue, le soir, sous la pluie
Lithograph in five colours on Japanese
paper
Pierre Bonnard (1867–1947), France, 1895;
plate 11 in *Quelques aspects de la vie de
Paris*, C.R.M. 66
25.6 cm × 35.3 cm
Art Gallery of Ontario, 77/38
Gift of Touche Ross, 1977

Hoteiya drapery store
Woodcut; printed in colour on paper
Utagawa Toyokuni (1769–1825), Japan,
1800
37.2 cm × 74.1 cm
Royal Ontario Museum, 926.18.485
Sir Edmund Walker Estate

IMPACT OF WESTERN AESTHETICS IN JAPAN

After 1640 Japan closed itself off from the
West; the only remaining foreign presence
was a small Dutch trading station that was
allowed to receive one Dutch ship each
year. The inhabitants were kept virtual
prisoners on Dejima Island in Nagasaki
harbour. Despite their isolation, they remained a source of Western ideas for the
Japanese.

In the 19th century a circle of artists
and intellectuals from Nagasaki devoted
themselves to Western learning. Painters
studied oil techniques, scientific perspective, three dimensionality, chiaroscuro,
and other effects used to imitate reality.

Scene of a Yoshiwara teahouse
Woodcut; handcoloured on paper
Okamura Masanobu (1686–1764/68),
Japan, c. 1740
29.9 cm × 41.7 cm
Royal Ontario Museum, 926.18.57
Sir Edmund Walker Estate

**Dong Yong, herdsman during the
Han dynasty and Zhi Nu, the weaver
maiden**
Woodcut; printed in colours on paper
Utagawa Kuniyoshi (1797–1861), Japan, c.
1844; from series "24 Chinese Paragons of
Filial Piety"
21.3 cm × 34.8 cm
Royal Ontario Museum, 926.18.1029
Sir Edmund Walker Estate
(See illustration page 161.)

Transmission of Religion

Buddhism, Islam and Christianity all moved eastwards to East and Southeast Asia along the trade routes—both the overland and the sea routes.

BUDDHISM
The religion of the Buddha spread quickly through India and along the Silk Roads and the sea lanes to the rest of Asia. Icons, scriptures, and the ideal of the monastic life were transmitted by monks and other believers. With the religion went iconography and art styles that were copied and adapted in the new realms of Buddhism.

Seated Buddha
Schist, black
Northern Pakistan, Gandharan school
1st to 2nd century
Height 61 cm
Royal Ontario Museum, 930.19.3
(See illustration page 53.)

Buddhist altar group
Gilt bronze
China, 8th century
Height overall 31.4 cm
Royal Ontario Museum, 958.81a–c
(See illustration page 59.)

Maitreya, Buddha of the future
Lacquered wood and gold leaf
Japan, 13th century
Height 1.08 m
Royal Ontario Museum, 939.17.30
Bequest of Reuben Wells Leonard
(See illustration page 59.)

Standing Buddha
Bronze
Southern India, Nagappattinam, 9th century
Height overall 40.8 cm
Royal Ontario Museum, 957.152.2
(See illustration page 60.)

Buddhist stele
Marble, white
China, dated to 678
Height 49.2 cm, length 36.8 cm
Royal Ontario Museum, 952.204
Anonymous gift

Maitreya
Gilt bronze
Nepal, 18th to 19th century
Height 51.9 cm
Royal Ontario Museum, 918.39.3
George Crofts Collection
(See illustration page 60.)

Buddha
Bronze
Java, 9th century
Height 30.5 cm
Royal Ontario Museum, 972.82
(See illustration page 60.)

ISLAM
The religion of the Prophet Muhammad spread very quickly, both eastwards and westwards. Within a century of the prophet's death in 632, force of arms had taken Islam to the Indus Valley in the East and through North Africa to Spain in the West. For the next ten centuries the sea lanes and the overland routes were dominated by Muslim traders who carried Islam and its influences to Central Asia, East Asia, and Southeast Asia.

Prayer mat
Cotton tabby, white; printed, painted, and resist-dyed in red, blue, violet, and green
India, 19th century
131 cm × 80 cm
Royal Ontario Museum, 934.4.77
Harry Wearne Collection.
Gift of Mrs Harry Wearne

Goblet
Glass, uncoloured; blown; polychrome enamel, gilt
Syria, late 14th century; said to be from a mosque in China
Height 28 cm
Royal Ontario Museum, 924.26.3

Bottle
Glass, uncoloured; blown; polychrome
enamel, gilt
Syria, late 14th century; said to be from a
mosque in China
Height 27.2 cm
Royal Ontario Museum, 924.26.1

Bottle
Glass, uncoloured; blown; polychrome
enamel, gilt
Syria, late 14th century; said to be from a
mosque in China
Height 32.2 cm
Royal Ontario Museum, 924.26.2
(See illustration page 76.)

Coat
Compound weft-faced silk twill, red
Sumatra, 19th century; made from a
Turkish tomb pall
Length 52.5 cm
Royal Ontario Museum, 982.28.1

CHRISTIANITY

Christianity, which arose in the eastern
Mediterranean, was adopted by the
Roman legions, who disseminated it
throughout the Roman world. By the 4th
century Christianity was the dominant
religion of Europe.

   Disagreement with the pope in Rome
over the nature of the divinity of Christ
and the role of the Virgin Mary led to the
expulsion of Nestorius, patriarch of
Constantinople, and his followers, in the
5th century. Nestorians moved eastwards
from Syria to Central Asia and then to
China, where a congregation flourished in
the Tang capital in the 8th century.

   In the 9th century Nestorians, along
with Persian Manichaeans and
Zoroastrians, were persecuted and driven
out of China, but many of the border
peoples, including Uighur Turks and
Mongols, converted to the Nestorian creed.
Their presence in Central Asia facilitated
contact between Europe and East Asia
during the period of the *Pax Mongolica* in
the 12th and 13th centuries.

Cross-shaped stamp
Bronze
China, Nestorian Christian, 11th to 14th
century
Length 7.1 cm
Royal Ontario Museum, 960.243.2
James Menzies Collection
(See illustration page 86.)

Cross-shaped stamp
Bronze
China, Nestorian Christian, 11th to 14th
century
Length 5.7 cm
Royal Ontario Museum, 960.243.5
James Menzies Collection
(See illustration page 86.)

Cross-shaped stamp
Bronze
China, Nestorian Christian, 11th to 14th
century
Length 5 cm
Royal Ontario Museum, 960.243.17
James Menzies Collection
(See illustration page 86.)

In the 16th century when Portuguese and
Spanish voyages of exploration were at
their height, the Christian faith and Christian influences were carried to East Asia,
first by the Jesuits and then by other
Roman Catholic orders.

Madonna
Ivory
India, Goa, 18th century
Height 19 cm
Royal Ontario Museum, 981.68.20
Gift of Mr and Mrs A. Murray Vaughan

Jar with "IHS" monogram
Porcelain; overglaze polychrome enamel
China, c. 1860
Height 12.4 cm
Royal Ontario Museum, 910.65.41a–b

World Views Shaped by Trade

International trade established links between widely separated civilizations. The tales of traders and other travellers helped to verify the geography of the world and the location of its various peoples.

From ancient times oral accounts, rare manuscripts, and the trade goods themselves helped to shape popular imagination. The expansion of Western trade in the 13th and 14th centuries brought with it the travel narrative. The development of printing and improved techniques for reproducing illustrations permitted widespread circulation of these accounts, which stimulated interest wherever they went. The voyages of discovery that began in the late 15th century provided opportunities for careful observation and accurate description, which advanced scientific and geographic knowledge.

DESCRIPTIONS OF PEOPLE

Er-ya yin-tu
Illustrated dictionary, woodblock-printed
China, 1801; first published 1081
Each leaf 34.3 cm × 25.0 cm
East Asian Library
University of Toronto

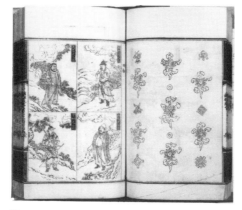

Er-ya tu yin ju
Illustrated dictionary, woodblock-printed
China, 1897 edition
Each leaf 14.6 cm × 9.8 cm
East Asian Library
University of Toronto

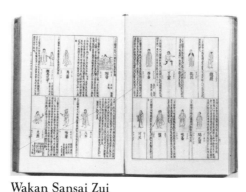

Wakan Sansai Zui
Japanese translation of Chinese encyclopedia, *San-zai tu-hue*, edited by Ryoan Terashima
Lithograph reproduction of woodblock-printed edition
Japan, 1929; first published 1715
Each leaf 18.3 cm × 12.5 cm
East Asian Library
University of Toronto

Voyages faits principalement en Asie dans les XII, XIII, XIV, et XV siecles, par Benjamin de Tudele, Jean du Plan-Carpin, N. Ascelin, Guillaume de Rubruquis, Marc Paul Venitien, Haiton, Jean de Mandeville, et Ambroise Contarini: Accompagnés de l'histoire des Sarasins et des Tartares, et précédez d'une introduction concernant les voyages et les nouvelles découvertes des principaux voyageurs
Pierre de Bergeron (d. 1637)
Printed book with engravings
The Netherlands, The Hague, J. Neaulme, 1735, 2 volumes in 1
Each leaf 30.2 cm × 23.0 cm
Thomas Fisher Rare Book Library
University of Toronto
(See illustration page 86.)

A Description of the Empire of China and Chinese Tartary together with the kingdoms of Korea, and Tibet: containing the geography and history (natural as well as civil) of those countries
Jean Baptiste Du Halde (1674–1743)
Printed book with engravings;
English translation
London, 1738/41
Each leaf 40.0 cm × 25.4 cm
Thomas Fisher Rare Book Library
University of Toronto
(See illustration p. 138.)

Box
Copper; polychrome enamel
China, 18th to 19th century
Height 1.4 cm, diameter 3.3 cm
Royal Ontario Museum, 918.21.17
George Crofts Collection

Table screen
Copper; polychrome enamel
China, 19th century
Height 33.5 cm, width 22.5 cm
Royal Ontario Museum, 923.17.254
George Crofts Collection

**The reception of the diplomatique
and his suite, at the court of Pekin**
Etching, handcoloured on wove paper
James Gillray (1757–1815), England, 1792
31.8 cm × 40.0 cm (impression)
Art Gallery of Ontario, 80/42
Gift of the Trier-Fodor Foundation, 1980

Length of furnishing fabric
Linen and cotton tabby, white; blue
copperplate print
England, Middlesex, Bromley Hall factory,
c. 1765
128.2 cm × 67.2 cm
Royal Ontario Museum, 971.6.1
(See illustration page 116.)

Pair of Turkish figures
Porcelain; overglaze polychrome enamel
Germany, Meissen factory, late 19th-
century versions of models of c. 1750
Height 16.2 cm
Royal Ontario Museum, 948.116.2a–b
Bequest of Helen Boomer

EXPLORATION BY LAND
Overland trade changed very little
after goods began to be transported
by camel caravan from one marketplace to
the next. Despite the obstacles posed by
climate, terrain, politics, wars, famines,
extortion, bribes, taxes, and bandits, merchants continued to be irrepressible in
their search for markets and commodities.

Tomb figure of Bactrian camel
Earthenware, buff; straw-coloured glaze,
traces of pigment
China, 7th century
Height 38.2 cm
Royal Ontario Museum, 918.21.297
George Crofts Collection
(See illustration page 66.)

Schematic road maps, something like modern route maps for public transportation
systems, helped to meet the practical requirements of ancient travellers. Although
distances were often foreshortened, towns
and markets were clearly labelled. Merchants travelling along the roads could
gauge what lay ahead.

**Histoire des grands chemins de
l'empire romain**
Nicolas Bergier
Printed book with engravings,
Belgium, Brussels, 1736
Each leaf 24.4 cm × 19.3 cm
Thomas Fisher Rare Book Library,
University of Toronto
(See illustration page 93.)

EXPLORATION BY SEA
Early geographers and astronomers under-
stood more about the nature of the earth
and its role in the universe than they did
about the precise outlines of the lands and
the seas. Their theories were of little
practical help to mariners who ventured
into unknown waters. But challenges encountered on those journeys into the unknown prompted innovations in ship design and navigational instruments.
Observations made on voyages of discovery brought practical knowledge, which
made more accurate maps possible.

**De regnis septentrion. Monstra
marina & terrestria, quae passim in
partibus aquilonis inveniuntur**
Sea monsters
Engraving, album title page,
Sebastian Münster (1489–1552), 1550
31.0 cm × 49.5 cm
Royal Ontario Museum, 958.209.7
(See illustration page 97.)

Tetradrachm
Billon
Rome, reign of Commodus (180–192),
dated 189; reverse with Roman merchant-
man alongside the lighthouse at Alexandria
Diameter 2.5 cm
Royal Ontario Museum, 910.159.644(1)
(See illustration page 30.)

Plate with sailing vessel
Earthenware (quartz compound);
underglaze red, blue, green, and black
Turkey, Isnik, mid-17th century
Diameter 30 cm
Royal Ontario Museum, 941.21.5
Gift of Miss Amice Calverley

Model of a junk
Silver
China, 19th century
Height 27.3 cm, length 22.5 cm
Mystic Seaport Museum, 76.46
Mystic, Connecticut

240

Because navigational instruments were still
very primitive in the 16th century, explorers often owed their success to earlier
experience of sailing—and sometimes to
sheer luck. Familiarity with the stars was
the first essential for a navigator. Difficulty
arose when his ship left known waters and
he was faced with differences in the relative positions of the stars. In the Southern
Hemisphere the sun was too high in the
sky to permit useful readings, and the
polestar, the preferred reference point of
Arab navigators, was either invisible or too
close to the horizon. It was the Portuguese
who discovered that the Southern Cross
provided an adequate substitute for the
polestar.

Constellation Navis
Ink and colour on paper
al-Sufi, Iran, Isfahan, late 17th century; in
Suwar al-Kawakib al-Thabitah (Treatise on
the Fixed Stars)
15.5 cm × 23.6 cm
Royal Ontario Museum, 971.292.13
(See illustration page 3.)

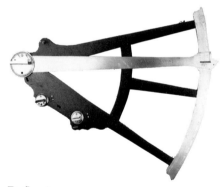

Reflecting octant
Wood and brass
England, 1761
Height 49.5 cm
On loan to the Royal Ontario Museum
from Mr Arend Hoekstra. L974.6

MAPS AND MAPMAKING
The voyages of discovery and the expansion of sea trade that began in the late
15th century vastly extended the limits of
the known world. World maps began to
reflect the new knowledge.

Tabula nova totius orbis
World map based on Claudius Ptolemy's
work
Engraving
Michael Servetus (1511–1553), Austria,
Vienna, 1541
45.7 cm × 28.5 cm
Royal Ontario Museum, 961.146.2
(See illustration page 94.)

Typus cosmographicus universalis
World map
Engraving, handcoloured
Ascribed to Sebastian Münster
(1511–1553), 1532
55.0 cm × 38.5 cm
Royal Ontario Museum, 956.186.2
(See illustration page 91.)

**America sive novus orbis respectu
europaeorum interior globi terrestris
pars**
Map with portraits of the explorers
Columbus, Vespucci, Magellan, and
Pizarro
Engraving, handcoloured
Théodore de Bry (1528–1598), Germany,
Frankfurt, 1596
32.5 cm × 39.0 cm
Royal Ontario Museum, 956.186.6
(See illustration page 108.)

**Planisphaerium terrestra sive terrarum
orbis**
Double hemisphere map
Engraving
Carel Allard, The Netherlands,
Amsterdam, 1706
59.9 cm × 51.8 cm
Royal Ontario Museum, 960.223.2
(See illustration page 95.)